MODBURY THROUGH TIME – A HISTORY OF THE DEVONSHIRE TOWN AND ITS PEOPLE.

This book is dedicated to my daughter Kelly Charlesworth, a more recent resident of the town, and her fiancé Si James, who has lived in Modbury all of his life. Also, to all the residents of Modbury, past and present.

INTRODUCTION.

Modbury, the quaint Devonshire town which sits at the bottom of an undulating valley and surrounded by rolling hills, is very much a characteristic picture postcard Devon market town. Known for its steep streets, quaint old houses, 'olde worlde' inns and of course perched on the crest of the hill; the ancient church of St. George with its lofty spire. Not forgetting the beautiful views that can be observed across the striking South Hams countryside.

Each May the town holds an annual fair which dates back several hundred years. There were also at one time weekly fairs, and as well as livestock, yarn, corn, butter, eggs, other farm produce was also sold. Modbury is also famous for two battles during the English Civil War; the first in December 1642 when the mounted Parliamentarians led by Sir William Ruthven moved under cover of darkness from Plymouth via Ivybridge to invade. An early morning charge saw the retreat of a mostly untrained Royalist force that had gathered in the town, where Sir Ralph Hopton, the King's senior commander in the West Country was holding council at Court House, the home of the Champernowne's. The building was set on fire and badly damaged. Hopton made his escape, but many notable Devon Royalists were captured. The Champernowne family who lived there had been in residence from the time of Edward II to the close of the 17th century. The second battle of Modbury occurred two months later in February 1643, when the Royalists forces, expecting an attack by the Parliamentarian forces, assembled an army of around eight thousand men at nearby Kingsbridge and fortified the town. An army of Royalists numbering around two thousand were holding the bridge at Aveton Gifford. Outnumbered by around approximately four to one, and running low on ammunition, the Royalists gradually retreated towards Modbury. After heavy fighting in the town, the Royalists were compelled to retreat and escape down a sunken lane, today known as 'Runaway Lane.' This victory by the Parliamentarians was largely instrumental in the lifting of the Siege of Plymouth and the driving of the encompassing Royalist forces into Cornwall.

The Church of St. George dates back over several hundred years and is a Grade I listed church. It contains significant historical architectural features of interest from the 13th century onwards, with memorials to the Champernowne and Prideaux families. After a fire in 1621 caused by a lightning strike, it was rebuilt to its present-day form. Some parts of the building though are said to pre-date the Doomsday Book. During the English Civil War, Parliamentarian forces and horses were billeted in the building. If you visit the church today you will notice damage to the effigy of Sir John Champernowne (1457-1503) which was damaged during their stay.

Many of the farms in the area date back many centuries. One such farm, Little Modbury, dates back to the 12th century. The town had in the past just a few streets; Church Street, Brownston Street, Broad Street, Poundwell Street, New Street, Galpin Street and Dark Lane.

'Modbury through time – a history of the Devonshire town and its people' is the fifth in a series of books covering the accounts of events chronicled in newspapers from the early 1700's up until the 20th century in Devon. My previous books on the same subject set in Devon are: Dark tales of Victorian Plymouth 1850-1899; Grim and Gruesome Plymouth, 1860-1959; Plymouth Tales of a Forgotten Past; and Dark Tales of Devon's Past. In this book I shall take the reader through over two hundred years of life in Modbury. Meet the inhabitants and hear their stories of daily life, births, deaths and marriages, murder, mayhem, incidents and accidents. We all like to hear good news; but controversy and catastrophe in the past, just as today, appear macabrely appealing to the readership of newspapers, and therefore these events were more likely to be reported. Many of these stories I have been able to add extra information to, especially names, dates and addresses, by cross referencing with Ancestry.co.uk and the Commonwealth War Graves Commission – both invaluable sources of information for any historian, as well as a number of other online resources.

During the timescale this book covers, the world saw something incredible taking place; the Industrial Revolution which began in Britain and became a pivotal point in world history. Up until the time of its commencement, production of goods had taken place within the home or in small workshops by craftsmen and women using hand tools and simple rudimentary machines. It was during this age of rapid industrialisation that cities began to quickly increase in size; countryside dwellers being forced to find work in the cities, machinery having taken over much of the work of the farmhands. With the age of industrialisation came the invention of the metal printing presses that could churn out hundreds of newspapers an hour. No longer was it a case of waiting for the town crier to pass by, ringing his bell and calling out the latest news. Newspapers were the social media of the day.

Thanks to the British Newspaper Archives and the British Library, who are gradually making copies of all available newspapers as far back as the 1700's, searchable by the public through their online archive facility in conjunction with Findmypast. Also using Ancestry and a number of other online resources, you can now join me in a journey through a very interesting time in British history.

Rather than going further into the history of Modbury in this introduction, let the people of the town's past tell you their own story.

Acknowledgements:

Cover picture image from a private collection, courtesy of Graham Ferguson.

Also, thanks go to Pam Wilson (New Zealand), Graham Ferguson, Samuel Harrison and Susanna Miles, Malcolm Henderson and Marina Walsh (UK) for allowing me to use postcards and images from their personal collection in this book.

1738-1799

A DUTCH SHIPWRECK.

In April 1738, fifty soldiers belonging to the Honourable Colonel Montagu's Regiment of Foot made their way to Modbury in order to assist the civil officers in their duty of searching every house in the neighbourhood and on towards Bigbury Bay, in search of requisitioned goods from a Dutch ship which had recently been shipwrecked there. On Tuesday the 21st of March 1738 the Dutch vessel 'Annalein Hellener' which had left Bordeaux in France bound for Flensburg in Denmark with a cargo of around one-hundred and forty tons of wine, brandy, coffee and other goods onboard, was blown off course in a violent storm and became stranded on Thurlestone sands. Offers of assistance came from a number of several local gentleman who arranged for a number of men to help bring ashore to safety the ship's cargo and equipment. Unfortunately, having heard about the stranded vessel, a large mob of at least several hundred people arrived and began attacking the sides of the vessel with hatchets, cleavers and axes. They made holes in the deck and destroyed the stern post making it impossible to re-float the ship. They then began to loot the cargo and attack the ship's captain and crew. The customs men from Dartmouth who had been sent to record and store the cargo were overwhelmed and could do nothing to stop the pillaging by the heavy-handed mob. Many of those who tried to stop the looting were attacked and injured.

THE UNFORTUNATE MARY LIGHT.

In February 1756, Mary Light aged twenty-one, was brought before the Exeter Assizes charged with having murdered her newly born illegitimate daughter. Mary at that time was a servant to a farmer named Kerswell, near to Modbury.

Giving her evidence, Mary stated that a fellow servant in the same household had courted her for some time, and giving in to his pressure she became pregnant by him. Her mother had challenged her as to her condition noticing her growing stomach, but she had denied being with child. When she eventually told her seducer that she was indeed pregnant, he swiftly abandoned her and his services to farmer Kerswell. Having no one to turn to, Mary continued to hide her condition until the inevitable day of her going in to labour arrived. At night, lying in bed in a room she shared with two other girls, in great agony she gave birth whilst the others continued to sleep. Exhausted, she gathered up her new-born daughter, and wrapping the child in a rug placed her in a corner of the room and left her there. Mary returned to her bed and tried to get some sleep.

At daybreak and at her usual appointed hour, Mary got up and began to carry out her household tasks. Later that morning the mistress of the house had reason to enter the servant's bedroom and noticed in a corner the bundle Mary had placed there during the night. Inquisitive, she opened it up and was horrified to discover the body of a dead child. A surgeon from Modbury was immediately sent for, and after an examination of the child and of the three servant girls, he revealed Mary to be the mother of the child. The coroner was also informed, and Mary, no doubt exhausted, upset, and terrified of her fate, was kept under guard until in a fit enough condition to be removed to prison. The inquest into the child's death returned a verdict of 'wilful murder.'

I'm unable to find any record of what sentence Mary received, if any. Many cases in the Victorian era and in earlier times, the result of young single women having been seduced who then hid the bodies of their illegitimate child to 'hide their shame.' There was often a degree of sympathy with mothers in such a predicament, and those charged with infanticide were frequently found guilty of the lesser offence of 'concealment of birth' or reprieved if convicted.

EARLY ADVERTISING.

This advert recommending 'Dicey & Okell's Dr. Bateman's drops' written by William Distin of North Huish, was regularly published in newspaper across the country from 1759 through till the mid 1760's.

This is to certify to the public, particularly those afflicted with rheumatism, pains of the limbs etc, that I William Distin, in the parish of North Huish in the County of Devon, am ready to make oath of the following particulars, viz. my wife some years since being ill in child bed, having violent rheumatic pains and very feverish, also her milk going away, was surprisingly relieved by of one bottle of 'Dicey & Okell's' Dr. Bateman's Drops, which was bought off Mr. John Tozer, shopkeeper of Modbury. Also, my son, a lad of seven-years-old and confined to his bed unable to turn with the rheumatism, was perfectly cured with only bottle the same famous drops. I myself for many years have been in a low-spirited melancholy way; had scarce any appetite and continual pain in my stomach, of which all complaints I was relieved by taking two bottles the same true Dr. Bateman's Drops. Finding it such an excellent medicine I have recommended it to Mr. J. Gill, a gentleman farmer, in the parish of Ermington, he being very short of breath and pains in his limbs etc. He was not expected to live, but a few valuable drops soon perfected him - Also many of the neighbours have used the same drops with the like good success, even the dangerous cases, when they have been given over part recovery.

It has ever since been my family medicine in colds and feverish disorders etc. This I affirm, that I never knew any ill of it, but on the contrary, it was always considerable service. I desire this may be published in the Bristol Journal and other new papers.

Witnessed by my own hand on this day, 10th February 1759. Wm. Distin.

[*Dr Bateman's Pectoral Drops; also known as 'Batemans Original Pectoral Drops', and 'Bateman's and Stoughton's drops' was a popular patent medicine for disorders of the chest or lungs during the 18th, 19th, and early 20th centuries in Britain and North America. It was later marketed as a remedy for rheumatic and chronic complaints.*]

POOR STAG.

On the 15th of September 1766, the hounds belonging to the Modbury Hunt had what was said to be the finest stag race that had ever been known in the neighbourhood in the memory of anyone living. The terrified animal was chased across the moors and through the forests of Dartmoor, as well as across several rivers. It continued to run and run until it eventually reached the sea, where the poor animal took the water, still followed by the dogs and huntsmen. It swam for nearly a mile before landing at Bigbury, where he was again pursued for many more miles. At length, the chase lasted for eight hours and the exhausted stag was finally caught after a sixty-mile chase.

OUCH!

On the 22nd of December 1767, Robert Edwards, a journeyman hatter, was found lying at the side of a road just outside of Modbury, bleeding heavily after having cut off every part of his genitals with a knife and then thrown them into a hedge. When questioned by doctors as to what had induced him to carry out such a strange act, he refused to give an answer. The strangeness of the act though was later cleared up when he finally admitted that whilst staying in Totnes workhouse, he had got one of the sisters who looked after him pregnant. Discovering what he had done and feeling full of remorse and guilt, as according to the scripture that 'his member had offended,' he decided to cut his genitals off and cast them away. Thankfully due to the skilful surgeon whose care he was under, Edwards was said to 'likely to do well,' whatever that meant.

RUNAWAY HORSES.

On Tuesday the 12th of January 1773, Arthur Holdsworth Esq; Governor of Dartmouth, along with Mr. George Prideaux, attorney at law of Kingsbridge, having just got into a post-chaise at Aveton Gifford, the driver was fastening the door when suddenly the horses without any apparent cause took off in a violent manner. The chaise struck the corner of a house, whereby one of the wheels was knocked off and both gentlemen thrown out. Mr. Holdsworth was much bruised and suffered cuts to his face. Mr. Prideaux was killed on the spot. The horses continued running until the chaise broke to pieces.

CRUSHED BY A WAGGON.

One Friday in January 1775, Robert Hurrell was driving a waggon loaded with of corn near to Ivybridge whilst making his way to Modbury. Coming across an elderly man and a woman who were standing in the road talking, he asked them to each step back to the opposite sides of the road so that his waggon pass. In doing so the old man somehow tripped and got tangled in the waggon and was thrown to the ground - the wheels going over his chest and also breaking his arm. He died instantly.

THAT POOR WOMAN!

A letter from Modbury dated 24th March 1775...

"This week was interred in the parish Church of Thurlestone, a woman who had been married about four years. After the two first years were expired, she thought herself with child, and when the nine months were elapsed and not having any labour pains, but instead excruciating pain in her bowels, she sent for a surgeon and midwife, who after the use of medicine and long attendance declared that the woman was not with child. The poor creature in consequence became the laughter and ridicule of her husband and neighbours. However, after twelve months of suffering, the bones of the child began to work out at her navel; upon which the faculty were again applied to, who told her that they could do nothing for her without her permitting them to cut her open; which she refused, and chose to die without being more tortured."

[*The poor woman the writer refers to was Hannah Worden, who was buried on the 16th of March 1775.*]

ERMINGTON FAIR.

A Letter from Modbury dated 2nd July 1776.

"At Ermington Fair last week, a farmer of Aveton Gifford sent one of his day-labourers with a vicious bull and two bullocks to sell. A man who was already in treaty for these cattle, being fearful that the bull was vicious, went and stroked him down the back and head with his hand and then walked two or three yards away from him. The bull, not liking this familiarity, shook his head at the man, who thereupon offered to strike him with a large stick. Seeing this, the bull charged at the man, tossed him in the air and the wretched soul landed in a gutter where the bull kept at him, endeavouring to get his horn in and to toss him again. At last, he got one of his horns into the knee of the man's breeches and laid the thigh open to the bone from the knee up to the Pope's-eye (What is very remarkable, no blood came.) By this time the whole fair was in uproar. With great numbers coming to the man's assistance, the bull made off out of the fair, and on his way met with a stout young fellow who was driving two cows. These the bull joined, and the cows going over a hedge into a field, the bull followed. The young fellow was then trying to bring the cows back when the bull came to the hedge and beset the man, who luckily caught him by the tail, and with a stick which he had in his hand, belaboured the bull till he was quite exhausted, whereupon the man put him into the Manor Pound.

After the bull had rested there a short time his madness came on again, and when any one ventured to approach the walls, the creature immediately ran at them. At last, to prevent further mischief, the bull was shot. Notwithstanding great care, the man that was tossed died in great agonies yesterday."

A LADY'S EMBARRASMENT.

In September 1783, a farmer's daughter was leading a pony and cart loaded with goods when she had to stop to make an adjustment to the reins attaching the animal to the cart. The animal either having been frightened by something within its line of sight, or not liking what the young woman was doing, kicked out and upset the cart which was heavily front loaded. The poor woman who was standing at the side of the cart was thrown to the ground by her skirts becoming entangled in the wheel and was left trapped until a labourer was able to free her from her embarrassment.

REVEREND TRIGGS.

The Reverend Arthur Triggs was born in Kingston near Modbury in 1787, the son of James Triggs a serge-weaver and his wife Mary. Arthur was described as being an eccentric and quarrelsome genius who went on to build Trinity Chapel in York Street, Plymouth. He started his working life as a farm labourer, then as a mason, and after failing in business as a draper he took to preaching. On Whit-Monday 1821, he made his first appearance in Plymouth. His dress and strong Devonshire dialect excited great curiosity. He was dressed in a green coat with yellow buttons, a coloured handkerchief protruding from his pocket, and wearing a yellow waistcoat.

THE VISIONARY ENTHUSIAST.

On the evening of the 6th of December 1789, forty-two-year-old Caleb Elliott was found in a hayloft near Modbury in the agonies of death and speechless. With great difficulty he was carried to a house in the town where he immediately expired. The poor man had for some months past wandered about the local countryside in a wild and enthusiastic manner and had often preached in Modbury and at Plymouth, declaring he was sent by God to save mankind. About three weeks prior to his death, Caleb told his listeners, who described him as being a 'visionary enthusiast,' that he had been called upon by God to simply live on *righteous food* by fasting for forty days and nights to expiate the sins of the world. He then walked away. For sixteen days he survived without anything passing his lips, until he was eventually found in the barn in such a shocking skeletal state that his acquaintances barely recognised him; so worn away was his skin. At the inquest into his death, a verdict of 'died for want of the necessities of life' was agreed. Caleb Elliott was buried at West Allington where he originally hailed from.

A FRENCH SHIP WRECK AT BIGBURY.

On the 3rd of November 1798 it was reported that a ship, a French privateer with sixteen guns, had been wrecked in a gale at Bigbury Bay. The crew of the ship told rescuers that they were Swedish, but it was soon discovered that they were in fact enemies, and a party of horses and men were sent from Modbury to escort them back to the town. Of the ships complement of one hundred and forty persons, seven had drowned and two were missing.

A VISIT TO MODBURY.

In 1799 a gentleman who paid a visit to Modbury, writing to a friend described it as having nothing curious nor remarkable about it. He said it held a tolerable market on Thursdays, which was generally well supplied with provisions, and held two fairs yearly; on the feasts of St. George and St. James. He said the church which stood on an elevated position and with a tall spire, had a communion plate which was said to be very valuable. Modbury, he said had been well-known since before Henry III's reign, for brewing 'nappy ale,' about which Henry of Auranches, a poet of the day wrote the following; "Of this strong drink, much like a Stygian Lake (most term it ale) I know not what to make; Folk drink it thick, and pass it out full thin, much dregs therefore must needs therein."

1800-1849

CORN RIOTS.

A Letter from Modbury dated the 25th of April 1801 stated the following: "There have been more riots here, in which our worthy friends, H. Legassicke Esq., and the Rev. Mr. Stackhouse have been threatened with being hung. A mob consisting of near seven-hundred people came to their houses with a halter in one hand, and written on paper in the other for signature, limiting the price of corn, butter, and potatoes. One fellow had the impudence to come into Mr. Legassicke's kitchen and take a candle and grease the cord of the halter to make the knot alert round his neck. But on finding this the gentleman and some friends he had with him were prepared with fire-arms, and saying that a messenger had been dispatched for a troop of cavalry. The banditti then drew off without doing any mischief.

Last Tuesday eight armed villains with their faces blacked, entered the farmhouse of one Richard Honey, a respectable farmer near Lord Borringdon's at Saltram at about nine at night; and with violent imprecations, beat and knocked down the farmer and all his domestics. A boy fortunately escaped out of the window and gave the alarm to the neighbourhood which made the thieves decamp without their booty. Honey is very dangerously ill and his recovery is doubtful. If nothing is done, this part of Devonshire will be rendered disagreeable to reside in."

A MODBURY RHYME.

A rhyme, which was thought to have originated in Modbury in 1806, and written by Philip Light, a churchwarden at St George's Church, displayed the once pride of their bells and contempt of those of their neighbours. Modbury's bells having six peals, whereas Ermington only had five. "Hark to Modbury bells how they do quiver! Better than Ermington bells down by the river."

A FABRICATED DEATH.

In November 1807, the 'Bath Chronicle and Weekly Gazette' printed an apology stating that a report they had made in their previous publication in regards to the accidental death of Richard Perring Esq., of Modbury, had been an 'invidious fabrication.' Richard was said to have been riding home from Membland when his horse took fright and threw him to the ground. His shoulder broken

and his skull fractured. He was carried home where it was alleged, he died four days later in great agony. [*This story of Richard Perring's demise was also printed in numerous other newspapers across the country.*] Richard may well have been thrown from his horse – that can't be proved nor disproved today, but he went on to live a long and happy life, dying in 1839 aged seventy-two.

MISSING SERVANT.

Dated March the 27th 1809, Mr. Amos Lakeman of West Lee in the parish of Modbury placed an advertisement for the apprehension of Nicholas Cove aged eighteen, described as having a brown complexion, large face, thick lips, down looking and near sighted, rather deaf, knee-knapped, and about five feet six inches in height. When he absconded, Nicholas was said to have been wearing an everlasting jacket and breeches, worsted stockings, and carried with him other articles of clothing. Mr. Lakeman was offering a half guinea reward for his apprehension, but stated that whoever harboured or employed Nicholas Cove after him having posted the public notice, would be prosecuted according to the law.

DROPPED DOWN DEAD NEAR HIS HOUSE.

On the 21st of October 1818, after enjoying a day's partridge shooting, George E. Langworthy aged fifty-seven, a surgeon and apothecary, was within yards of his front door when he dropped to the ground and expired.

CHARGED WITH HAVING FALSE CERTIFICATES.

In the early part of 1819, a gentleman arrived at the office of Messrs. Rashleigh and Coode, in St. Austell, Cornwall, and demanded three pounds and twelve shillings for the interment of dead bodies found on the shore at Zennor near to Land's End. He produced eleven death certificates, signed as he asserted by a magistrate in that neighbourhood. Suspicions being raised and an investigation carried out, it was discovered that the certificates were forgeries and there had been no bodies washed up on the shore. The gentleman eventually admitted to this and said his name was Floyd, and that he came from Modbury in Devonshire. He was committed to take his trial at the next assizes.

WIFE FOR SALE.

A gentleman named Brooks from near Ivybridge, placed a notice stating that he was disposing of his wife by public sale at the Plymouth Cattle Market in December 1822. He said that not only was his wife young and handsome, but that she would ride into the town on her own horse that morning of her own free will and with his consent, and that he would be acting as auctioneer.

The notice attracted the public's attention and the number of spectators for the novelty event was huge. The husband and wife appeared together in the market place at the appointed time. The wife accompanied by the ostler of the 'Lord Exmouth Inn' Plymouth. Brooks then began the bidding. Five shillings was the first offer, then ten, then fifteen. The ostler who accompanied his wife then bid three pounds. It was at this point, to the disappointment of the husband and his wife, that two constables took possession of the 'goods' and the auctioneer, and took them directly to the Guildhall where the chief magistrate was then sitting. The two of them were placed before the mayor. The husband when asked why he had committed such an illegal act as to attempt the sale of his wife, he very innocently said that they were both willing participants, and he didn't think there was any harm in it as they had not lived together for some considerable time. They had been married for about two and a half years but after only three weeks of marriage his wife had given birth to a child. Up until its sudden arrival he knew nothing of her condition. The child soon after died and he got it a coffin and paid the expenses for the funeral without ever reproaching his wife as to her conduct. She soon after deserted him notwithstanding his kindness, and went to live with another man by whom she had another child. He added that he had recently been informed she was again pregnant.

When asked who had advised or told him that he could sell his wife, Brooks said many people in the countryside had told him he could do it; and in consequence of his wife coming to him and saying that a person had said they would give him twenty-pounds to take her clean off his hands, he had advertised her for sale at Modbury on three separate market days for seventeen pounds, and had come to Plymouth that morning by her appointment to get the business finished.

The wife stated that she and her husband could not agree to get on together, and that in consequence she knew of a person who would take her away for the bargain price of twenty-pounds; three-pounds in hand and another seventeen-pounds at Christmas. She said she wished to be separated from her husband and had been told by different people that the thing could be done by public sale in a market place on market day. Being asked the name of the person who was to buy her, she said it was Kane and that he lived near Plymstock. She further added that he had disappointed her by not coming forward to bid at the market as he had promised to do so, and that in consequence she had employed the ostler of the inn where she had put her horse, to bid for her if the price did not exceed twenty pounds. She added that she had left her own horse on account of it having a sore back, and had borrowed one in lieu of it off a person near Ivybridge, with whom she stated herself to be in habit of intimacy.

After a good deal of consultation, it was decided that the parties should be bound over to answer the charge at the ensuing sessions. Unfortunately, I can't find any further record of what happened to Mr. and Mrs. Brooks. Hopefully they were both allowed to go their separate ways and have a happy life.

GALLOPING STREET.

It could be a miss-spelling, or the Devon accent, especially in an age when many people were illiterate, but the 1822/23 edition of Pigot's Directory called Galpin Street 'Galloping Street.' Two newspaper articles printed in 1829 and another in 1830 also called it by the same name. Possibly at one time it was called Galloping Street and the name shortened and changed over time?

A DISGRACED VICAR.

Revered. P. Perring, Rector of North Huish near Modbury, was in November 1823 charged before the Consistorial Court in Exeter, with having fornicated with a lady named Maria Isabella Blackburn, over a number of months between July 1820 and March 1821 whilst based in Bath. The solicitor acting on behalf of Revered Perring stated that the only evidence of criminal intercourse during this period was that of the woman herself, whose character he said rendered her totally unworthy of credit; also, some letters presumed to be written by Perring.

During the time period mentioned, Perring and his servant had lodged at a house in Bath; possibly Mrs. Blackburn's, though both a woman who slept in the same room as Mrs. Blackburn, and Mr. Perring's servant, denied that any intimacies had taken place, or at least that the couple had not cohabited. Another objection put forward by Reverend Perring's solicitor was that Maria Isabella Blackburn was not her real name and in fact her surname was Badham. He next objected that all the places where intercourse was alleged to have taken place were not submitted in the libel, as they ought to have been. In conclusion, he said that although his client might have imprudently allowed himself to be entrapped by an artful woman, he hoped it would be noted that the scandalous behaviour alleged had not taken place within the parish of which the defendant had the spiritual supervision. Reverend Perring was suspended from his ecclesiastical jurisdictions for three years, including a deprivation of income during that time, and condemned to paying the costs of the case having been brought before the Consistorial Court.

DEATHS OF WILLIAM AND ANNA STACKHOUSE.

On the 11th of August 1824, fifteen-year-old William Stackhouse, the only son of the Revered William Stackhouse, vicar of St. George's Church, died. In January 1831, Anna, the seventeen-year-old daughter of the Reverend Stackhouse also sadly passed away. Both are buried in St. George's Churchyard.

THE STOLEN POCKET-BOOK.

Richard Simpson was indicted for pick-pocketing Nicholas Browse on the 4th May 1825 at Modbury Fair. He took from him a pocket-book containing a bill of exchange for thirty-one pounds, two five-pound notes, and six one-pound note. Mr. Browse, a farmer, had gone into the kitchen of the White Hart Hotel for the purpose of paying for some cattle which he had just purchased. Taking out his pocket-book, the contents of which seemingly excited the itchy palms of Simpson and a companion of his who both happened to be in the kitchen at the time. Browse completed his business and headed out to the stable to collect his horse. Just as he was about to mount the animal, he was pushed to the ground by Simpson and his associate, and his pocket-book taken from him. Fortunately, the whole incident was witnessed by a slater unseen by Simpson and his cohort, who was working on the roof of the stable at the time. Two objections were successfully made against the indictment by Simpson's counsel, who stated that firstly, that the indictment was not made under the Act with which made the Bank of England notes, and secondly that the promissory note of exchange was drawn under an improper stamp and therefore of no value. Simpson's conviction was therefore confined to the stealing of the pocket-book worth two 'pence. Thankfully the Bench saw sense and he was sentenced to seven years transportation.

VERY CLEVER ESCAPE BY A PRISONER.

Twenty-six-year-old James Parsons, a native of Modbury and at that time a prisoner at the Devon County gaol in Exeter on a charge of horse-stealing, contrived in the most artful manner to make an escape. On the evening of the 29th of September 1827, whilst ensuring all the prisoners were safely locked up for the night, the turnkey looking into Parsons's cell saw what he assumed to be James Parsons sitting on the side of his bed. The following morning however it was discovered that the cell was empty of human life and what he had actually seen was a sweeping brush positioned in an upright position on the bed, and at the top of it placed a pillow which Parsons had previously filled with earth for this purpose. This was topped off with a cap that Parsons had been in the habit of wearing. Thrown loosely around the brush and under the pillow were the other outer garments that he usually wore.

To the casual observer it would appear, as it did the turnkey, that the prisoner himself was seated on the bed. Parsons had in-fact very cleverly planned the whole thing. He had spent the previous day wandering round wrapped in his blankets, hiding the fact he was not wearing any outer garments underneath. Just before locking up time, he concealed himself in an outbuilding where he worked on making his blankets into a rope. He filled his stockings with stones and other heavy materials, which he then fixed to the end of the rope, and waited for the right moment to make his move. When he felt the time was right, he threw the stocking which was tied to the end of the rope over a wall and on to the roof of a one of the privies. From there he was able to let himself down into a garden from where he made his exit over a low wall covered with thatch and onto the road which ran behind the prison. James was eventually captured at his home in Modbury where he had returned to after making his daring escape.

CONTRABAND IN A DOG KENNEL.

At an un-named mansion [*likely Flete*] not far from Modbury, four kegs of contraband spirits were found hidden in a dog kennel by the owner's son in October 1827. The son, having returned from a ride on his horse and having occasion to go into the dog kennel, observed a heap of straw which attracted his attention. Removing a portion of it with his whip, he was surprised to find four wooden kegs which he found to contain spirits. The keeper who tended to the dogs was questioned but vehemently declared his ignorance as how they had found their

way in to the kennel. The occupants and staff of the house were also questioned, but like the kennel-keeper they all declared to not having any knowledge of how the contraband had found its way on to the property and into the kennel. The case of attemptedowner of the mansion was informed of the find and immediately sent for the officer commanding the Preventive Service, and gave the kegs into his custody.

FARM TO LET.

Barton Farm at Shilston was being let for a term of seven years in March 1828. The lease ran from Lady Day [*25th March, traditionally a day on which year-long contracts between landowners and tenant farmers would begin and end in England. Farming families who were changing farms would travel from the old farm to the new one on Lady Day.*] The property was said to be eight miles from Ivybridge, ten from Totnes and twelve from Plymouth. It comprised of nine acres of orchard, twenty-nine of meadow, fifty acres of pasture, and seventy acres of arable land, and had a lime rock and kiln. It only needed to be seen to be approved. Tenders were to be sent to Mr. Servington Savery, solicitor of Modbury.

[*Servington Savery was a descendant of Thomas Savery who was born in to a wealthy family at Shilston around 1650 and famous for being an inventor of steam pumps, alongside the more well-known names such as James Watt and George Stephenson. He harnessed the power of steam, creating the first practical steam machine forty years before James Watt. Thomas devoted his mind to engineering and invention, and in 1696 he patented a machine for polishing glass and marble, and another for 'rowing of ships with greater ease.'*]

DR. SOUTHMEAD LANGWORTHY.

Southmead was born in Modbury in November 1828, the sixth and youngest son of Dr. William Southmead Langworthy and his wife Mary. In March 1852, Southmead passed the examination of Science and Practice of Medicine and was awarded his certification to practice as a surgeon at Apothecaries Hall in London. It was also said that he was a fan of hunting; one of the original members of the Modbury Harriers, and had been very active in their implementation.

Southmead married Caroline Andrews in 1866. Caroline had been a near neighbour in Modbury, although their marriage took place at Sarsden, Oxfordshire. Her father Henry Andrews, had formerly been a land surveyor in Modbury and later moved to Sarsden to become the land agent for the Earl of Ducie. Southmead returned to Modbury where he carried out his medical practice. After specialising in mental health, in 1870 he took over the role of the head of Plympton House, a private mental asylum, a role previously held by his late brother Richard. Southmead died at the relatively young age of forty-six on the 17th of June 1875, and is buried in St. George's Churchyard along with many of his relatives.

[*You will come across a good many of the Langworthy family in this book, many with the same names*!]

ANOTHER DARING ESCAPE!

James Parsons made yet another daring and ingenious escape from prison - this time from Bodmin Asylum, at seven o'clock on the evening of Wednesday the 21st of January 1829. Nine months previously he had been yet again been arrested for horse stealing and sent to the asylum under the Secretary of State's warrant and the King's Royal sign-manual. For several months James had conducted himself with great propriety and had pretty much obtained the confidence of everyone. A box in which to keep his belongings had been given to him for his good conduct, and he was promised that on New Year Day he was to receive a suit of new clothes.

On New Year's Eve, he attired himself in the clothes and boots of another patient, then somehow surreptitiously stole a five-shilling note from one of the guards. He scaled the wall of the asylum and made his way to a public-house in the town where he boasted of the money he had got and of his box. After enjoying a number of glasses of ale he then returned to the asylum in the same way he had left; over a wall. It was assumed to possibly steal more money. The authorities having been alerted to his escapade, Parsons

THE PRISONER.

was shackled to the wall of his cell with a heavy ankle ring made of iron and imprinted on it 'Bodmin Lunatic Asylum.' The restraint was doubly secured with four counter sunk rivets. This was no barrier to James though, as he had already previously nearly made good an escape after having picked the locks by which he was confined to a post, using wire torn from the rim of a saucepan. He was also said to have destroyed many double hand-bolts by striking them with a stone suspended from his mouth.

A few days later James Parsons yet again escaped after tearing down the cell door. He was seen later that evening by a member of the public hiding in a hedge at the side of a road about two miles from Bodmin on the Lostwithiel road. It was suspected that he might have been attempting to head for a seaport. Having been trained as a carpenter, James Parsons was very ingenious and could pick almost any lock. Some of his contrivances were said to be too clever for publication. It was thought that in his desperation to avoid capture, he was likely to make free without ceremony, with any money, clothes, or horses, that he may come across in his bid to stay a free man. It seems highly likely that James did make good his escape and perhaps changed his name.

SARAH STACKHOUSE WEDS.

On the 23rd of February 1830, Sarah Stackhouse, the eldest daughter of the Revered William Stackhouse, the vicar of St. George's Church, Modbury, wed Revered William James Pinwill, the curate of Bigbury.

THE UNION INN.

A now long forgotten ale house that unfortunately appears without address, though is thought to have been on Poundwell Street, was the Union Inn, where regular auctions were held in the 1820's and 30's. In 1825 Higher Yeo Farm situated in the parish of Woodleigh was auctioned off at the inn. The estate consisted of a farmhouse, barns, stables, and convenient outhouses. There were also eighty acres of arable, pasture, and orchard attached to it. It also included twenty-two acres of coppice which was well stocked with thriving trees. A footnote was added stating that the new road from Dartmouth to Modbury was likely to pass through a small part of the farmland.

In June 1830 'Bradridge' within the parish of Diptford and seven miles from Modbury was up for auction at the Union Inn. The estate consisted of an excellent farmhouse with all necessary outbuildings, and was within a mile of lime kilns and the Great Western Road leading to Totnes and Plymouth. In April 1831 three separate lots known as Ermington Mills were auctioned at the Union Inn.

TURNPIKE ROAD NEAR MODBURY.

A letter sent to the editor of the Exeter and Plymouth Gazette in March 1830…

Editor, I take this method of calling to the attention of the Turnpike Commissioners to the very bad state the road from Sacker's Bridge, Modbury, and at the same time to urge the necessity of immediate reparation of the same. I should be sorry to adopt the alternate open to all his Majesty's liege subjects, namely, the right of indicting the parishes in which the road is situated; for if travellers are expected to pay a toll (which tax I always bear without a murmur) it is but common justice to give them good roads for their accommodation. The hills are too steep and inconvenient, but from the nature of the ground and situation, a much to be desired improvement may be effected at trifling expense.
I am, Mr. Editor, yours obediently, a friend to improvement. 4th March 1830.
[*It seems many of the roads in the South Hams are still in the same state today!*]

TRANSPORTED FOR SEVEN YEARS.

Twenty-six-year-old George Manning was arrested for stealing some tools from both Ugborough and Modbury in August 1831. The following March at his trial at the Lent Assizes at Exeter he was sentenced to seven years transportation.

A DEATH FORETOLD.

James Prior, a Private with the 89th Regiment of Foot, which was stationed at Modbury during the Devonport elections, held in December 1832. He later told the story of how during their stay

in the town, a French peddling fortune-teller amused him and several of his comrades in a variety of ways with cards and tricks. In the course of their conversation, the seer informed them that one of their officers would drown before they could return to their quarters in Devonport. Prior taking offence at this remark got into a rage with the Frenchman and insisted upon hearing how he had acquired such knowledge. The seer declined to divulge anything further and the party soon broke up. Two days later, when the regiment returned to their base at Devonport, they learnt with extreme regret, that Ensign Dewes, a fine young man who was revered by the corps at large, had sure enough been drowned in attempting to swim to Drake's Island.

MODBURY REFORM DINNER.

The 'Friends of Reform' dined together at Mr. Stidworthy's, Exeter Inn on Tuesday the 18th of December 1832, and were honoured with the company of Lord John Russell and Mr. Bulteel. More than two-hundred people sat down dinner. The bells rang merrily, and it was said that even the oldest inhabitant of Modbury had never seen the town looking so vibrant before. The room was crowded after the dinner, owing to the intense concern of hearing Lord John Russell express his sentiments, that it was utterly impossible for the worthy host to send in supply of wine etc by the usual communication, and he was obliged to introduce the beverage through the windows, which were scaled up to by means of ladders.

CHRISTMAS BALL.

A rather belated Christmas Ball was held at the White Hart Inn on the 1st of February 1833. It seemed quite usual at that time in the South West to hold Christmas Balls after the event. In 1832 the Christmas Ball was held on the 10th of January, and the Exmouth Annual Christmas Ball took place on the 12th of January. In 1834 the Ilminster Christmas Ball in was held on the 21st of January.

Christmas Ball.

LOST AND FOUND.

A ladies gold watch was lost on the turnpike road between Totnes and Modbury in early September 1833, much to the distress of its owner who probably hunted high and low for it being such a valuable item. Thankfully, an honest carrier called Richard Lavers of Modbury found it. He placed an advert in numerous newspapers stating that if the rightful owner got in touch, he would happily return it in exchange for the cost of his expenses in advertising.

The same week another advert was placed in the Exeter Flying post offering a three guineas reward to the finder of a gold watch, lost either in Starcross Chapel or between there and Powderham boat-house. The finder was asked to deliver it to either Reverend Powley at Starcross, or to Mr. Adams, a silversmith of Exeter to claim their reward.

DIED IN LONDON.

William Langworthy, the twenty-one-year-old eldest son of William Southmead Langworthy, surgeon of Modbury, died at his lodgings at St. Bartholomew's Hospital in London of brain fever on the 21st of November 1833. His body was brought back to Modbury were it was interred in St. George's Churchyard.

THE RUN-AWAY.

'Ran away from her master.' - John Harris of Wakeham, Aveton Gifford, on the 2nd of March 1834 placed the following advert in a newspaper: TRIPHENA FURNEAUX, aged 20 years. Whoever harbours or employs the said apprentice after this notice, will be prosecuted – Wakeham Farm, Aveton Gifford, near Modbury.

[*It sounds as though Triphena probably had a very miserable life. I'm happy to tell you she later married in 1839 at Torquay.*]

A SILVER SALVER.

In June 1834 the inhabitants of Modbury sent an elegant silver salver to the Revered William Stackhouse of Trehane, near Truro in Cornwall, on the occasion of his retirement and as a testimonial of their esteem of the faithful, exemplary, and efficient manner in which he had carried out his pastoral and social duties in the town over the previous thirty-six years.

STOLEN SILK.

John Gadon, his wife Elizabeth, Charles Modley, James Stepson and Jane Mortimer, were together indicted for stealing on the 5th of May 1835, silk and other articles from the shop of John Williams in Modbury. Harriet Wilson was also indicted for having received the goods.

William Evans, the shopman for John Williams said that on the morning of Wednesday the 6th of May he went to open up the shop and found that a window had been broken and around sixty pounds worth of silk fabric and other goods to be missing. When making enquiries into the theft, Mr. Williams received information that led him to travel to Exeter with Philip Blight, a farmer from Ivybridge who had informed him that the thieves had turned up at his house with large bundles the previous evening and asked him to take them to Chudleigh. In Exeter they found Charles Modley and James Stepson. Having gained further information, they then went to Butcher's Row to a lodging house kept by Harriet Wilson, where John Gadon and his wife Elizabeth were staying. The constables were then called to make the arrests.

A few days earlier, Charles Modley had gone to a lodging-house in Ivybridge belonging to Mary Horswell. The following day Gadon and his wife joined him, and the next day Jane Mortimer came to stay. They all left together to attend Modbury Fair on the Tuesday morning, and returned at one o'clock the following morning. That evening they set off for Chudleigh and from there they made their way to Exeter and entered a public house belonging to Samuel Nicholls; the 'Pestle and Mortar,' and afterwards went to Harriet Wilson's lodging house.

John Gingham and W. Howard, the arresting constables at Exeter, on information given to them by Williams and Blight, went to the house of Harriet Wilson and found two bundles of silk in the room where the prisoners were staying. A neighbour hearing the commotion went outside and found two bundles of silk thrown into his backyard, which had been thrown there by Harriet Wilson, fearing them being found in her house. She later told the constables that Gadon and his wife had said she could have the silks for forty shillings. It also came to light that one of their accomplices; Jane Mortimer, had sold other lengths of silk to a lady called Anne Wynne and had asked her if she could also make her a dress with some other material she had.

At their trial, James Stepson, Jane Mortimer, and John Gadon were all found guilty of the crime and sentenced to transportation to the colonies for life. Harriet Wilson was found guilty of receiving stolen goods and sentenced to twelve months imprisonment. Elizabeth Gadon was found not guilty.

A DEARLY BOUGHT FANCY.

In 1835, the book 'Burkes History of the Commoners' stated that the Champernowne family lived in magnificent splendour at Court House, Modbury, and they had a particular liking to keeping very fine band of singers and musicians. This band it was said, was to become the ruin of the family.

Mr. Champernowne deciding to take his performers on a boat on the Thames in the time of Queen Elizabeth I, Her Majesty was said to be so delighted with the music that she requested the loan of the band for month. Mr. Champernowne, aware that it was very doubtful that the members would be allowed to return to Modbury, declined saying that he hoped Her Majesty would allow him to keep his fancy. The Queen was so highly infuriated at this refusal that she deliberately found some pretence to sue him at law, and brought him to ruin by obliging him in the course the proceedings to sell no fewer than eighteen of his manors.

ESTABLISHMENT OF THE AGRICULTURAL ASSOCIATION.

An Agricultural Association was established in Modbury in March 1839. A meeting of the neighbouring gentry having been held at the White Hart Inn for that purpose. W. J. Clarke Esq., chaired the meeting and Mr. T. Kelly, Esq., was requested to act as honorary secretary. It was decided that an annual show of cattle and other animals should be held in the town to encourage the spirit of industry and ingenuity amongst agriculturist in the South Hams in general.

THE UNFORTUNATE ACTIONS OF EDWARD PRETTYJOHN.

In September 1840, William Luscombe a farmer at Woodley near Kingsbridge, brought action against Mr. Edward Prettyjohn to recover from the defendant compensation and damages for the loss of the services of his daughter, by the means of the defendant having seduced her.

Seventeen-year-old Dorothy Luscombe was the youngest of nine children; two girls and seven boys, and was in the habit of attending Kingsbridge market where she sold poultry, eggs, and butter, on behalf of her father. During these trips she became acquainted with Edward Prettyjohn, who was in his mid-forties and worked as a cider merchant. They commenced a courtship in early January of 1838 and after a short space of time he asked her to marry him, whilst at the same time making an indecent proposal to her to which she gave way to, thinking he intended on making her his wife. She asked him to go to her father and gain his permission to wed, but Prettyjohn made various excuses to put off the meeting. Their courtship continued and they became intimate on a number of further occasions, the final time being on the 9th of February. Edward Prettyjohn had apparently told her that if she got 'in the family way' she should take some salts to procure a miscarriage.

In March of that year, Dorothy travelled to Plymouth with her cousin Mrs. Mary Ann Dennis, and before she left, she asked Edward PrettyJohn to meet her in Modbury, but he failed to turn up at the appointed hour. Some months later Dorothy discovered she was pregnant and again pressed Edward Prettjohn as to when he would marry her, but he kept putting off asking her father for her hand in marriage and there was no further intimacy between them. After the child was born on the 5th of December 1838, Mrs. Luscombe made contact with Edward Prettyjohn and urged him to make her daughter his wife. Prettyjohn told her mother in no uncertain terms that he had never intended to marry her daughter, and followed this up by making a serious attack upon her character by saying that he knew she had been intimate with other men, including a man named Foster. He said he was not the father of the child and named another man as being the potential father.

Dorothy's father William Luscombe decided to take a civil case against Prettyjohn, to pay towards the keep of the child that had now become a burden to him. At the hearing in September 1840, Dorothy insisted that she had never been intimate with any other man and that she was with her brother and her cousin the whole two weeks that she spent in Plymouth. She said that when she again challenged Edward Prettyjohn in mid-November 1838 to make her his wife, he refused, saying that she had been with other men and that a wife was of no use to him anyway as he had no house to take her to. He did though say he would visit her after her confinement and bring the child a handsome present.

Things didn't look good for Dorothy when other evidence came to light in regards to her behaviour around the time she had 'become with child.' Susan Luscombe, a cousin, said that a man named Francis Foster had come to live at her family home on the 1st of March 1838.

25

Dorothy had been on friendly terms with him, but one day when she [*Dorothy*] had come to the house on horseback, and on a number of other occasions when Foster was at home, he refused to go out and see her. Although she hadn't seen any improprieties between them, Dorothy had handed her a note to give to Mr. Foster, and she was aware of rumours that her cousin had been intimate with other men.

Francis Foster was then asked to give evidence and admitted that there had been intimacies between Dorothy Luscombe and himself, and that she had told others that he was the father of her child, even in front of her parents. He said he was introduced to her by a friend called Carpenter who said, "If you wish to have a bit of fun, I will introduce you to a girl." He said he had never mentioned his intimacy with Dorothy to anyone until the previous week when he had been summoned to give evidence.

Grace Hannaforth, who had been a servant for William Luscombe, said that she could recall seeing Dorothy in an improper position with a man called Robert Gill in 1837. A married man but separated from his wife. She also said that during the winter months Dorothy often stayed out all night, letting herself in with a key on her return. She said that she had been with the family for nine and a half years. When Dorothy was aged around twelve, she had begun to conduct herself improperly and was known to be going with men, and led a life of outrageous dissoluteness. When asked why she was no longer in the employment of Mr. Luscombe, Grace said she had left the Luscombe's farm because Mr. Luscombe would come into her bedroom at night.

The learned judge after hearing all the evidence, then proceeded to sum up the case. He said that this action had been brought by the plaintiff because of the defendant having debauched his daughter and occasioned the birth of a child, the plaintiff had sustained great loss through the loss of the daughter's services for which he wanted compensation. He said that he had approached the examination of the case with some degree of anxiety, because he could not fail to have observed that a great many things had been said which were very much calculated to mislead the minds of the jury as to whether the verdict should be for the plaintiff or the defendant, and if for the plaintiff whether the damages should be very heavy. He wished the jury to not find the verdict in favour of the plaintiff unless the evidence satisfied them not only that the defendant had been communicated with, but also that he was father of the child - because if not, he had not occasioned the injury with which he was charged. The judge pointed out that in 1838 the first day was a Monday, consequently the 6th of January would be the first Saturday – the day Dorothy said she first met Edward Prettyjohn. She saw him again the following week and the following Saturday he saw her home, made love to her in an apparently honourable manner and asked her if he may pay his addresses to her which she accepted. The judge then went on to give further dates and that the last time Dorothy saw Edward Prettyjohn was on February the 9th. Nine calendar months would bring the birth of the child to the 9th of November. The birth of the child had occurred nine calendar months, three weeks and five days later. He said he was rather inclined to believe that she had been 'unchaste' with some other man, rather than that the laws of nature had been altered for her accommodation. Touching on the alleged promise to marry her, he said that was the kind of thing which a woman expected to have said to her before she yielded to the solicitations of a man, and that they very often give way after it is said without believing it all. The man might acknowledge that he was father the child if he was taxed with it during her pregnancy - but if the child was not born until nearly two months after he expected it, he would then conclude that somebody else must have been the father. The child was fully grown at birth, of that there was no doubt as according to the mother's statement it was not born till three weeks and five days after the usual time. Her calling on Mr. Foster who refused to see her, was a strong indication that something occurred between them. If not, why did he not go out? With regard to the note; if the jury believed that she had written a note to Foster, it was strong in validation of his statement. He was anxious to go into consideration of Foster's evidence dispassionately. When Foster went into the witness box, he heard hissing in the court and on the face of it there was something very disgraceful and revolting in the idea of a man standing to state that he had enjoyed a lady's favours. The main thing was for them get over the difficulty believing that Prettyjohn was the father of the child.

After hearing the summing up by the judge, the jury sat for fifteen minutes considering their verdict before returning it in favour of the plaintiff William Luscombe, much to the shock and disbelief of many in the courtroom. The judge awarded William Luscombe one hundred and fifty pounds in damages to be paid by Edward Prettyjohn.

[*In the 1830's the age of consent for females was twelve and for males fourteen. If Dorothy Luscombe had conceived the child on the last occasion she had been intimate with Edward Prettyjohn, the child would have been due on or around the 2nd of November.*]

WHEN A JOKE GOES TOO FAR.

Mr. William Hallett, a farmer of Bigbury, was returning home from Modbury market in January 1841 when he stopped off at a public-house where several other people who had also been in attendance at the market were sitting in perfect harmony and minding their own business. By way of a joke, Hallett took from a table a pint of ale belonging to another man with whom he wasn't on the best of terms with and drank it down in one go. In consequence of this a fight broke out between them that lasted several minutes and Hallett was severely beaten – he died a few days later.

PUBLIC DINNER AT THE WHITE HART HOTEL.

A public dinner was given for the inhabitants of the Hundred of Ermington, one of the thirty-two, ancient administration units of Devon, on Friday the 15th of January 1841 at Mr. Roger Tarring's White Hart Hotel, to commemorate the establishment of a Petty Sessions in the town which was in the centre of the Hundred. J. C. Bulleel, Esq., of Langstone House presided, assisted by vice-president Nicholas B. Avent, Esq. The sessions for the division had previously been held at the extremity of the adjoining Hundred, a distance of fifteen miles.

The cloth having been removed and grace said by the Reverend F. Stephens who officiated in the absence from home of Reverend Nutcombe Oxenham, the vicar of the parish. The chairman then rose, and amidst a most enthusiastic cheering proposed the first toast, namely to the health of the Queen and Prince Albert. This was followed by a number of further toasts given by many of those gathered. Mr. Avent the vice-president said that he thought it would scarcely be believed in a few years' time that the people of the neighbourhood had been subjected to such gross and palpable injustice, as to be compelled to perform a journey of thirty-four miles even to get parish rate signed, and then on arriving at the house in which the magistrates were assembled, the overseers, way-wardens, and hundred constables, were compelled to wait on the staircases or in the passages, with a constable being stationed at the door to prevent their admission to witness the manner in which the public business of the division was transacted. That was a great evil; and no sooner was public attention directed to it, than an immense meeting of the inhabitants of the two Hundreds was held at the Exeter Inn where a memorial was prepared, which within a few days had some thousands of signatures, respectfully requesting the magistrates to discharge their door-keeper and admit the public. They had yielded to the appeal, and so far had given temporary satisfaction, but the distance was still too far, and notwithstanding the repeated and persevering applications which were made to the magistrates to confer on this particular Hundred the advantages of a local Sessions, they had invariably refused and stated that although it was inconvenient to the people of the Hundred on account of the distance, it was equally so to them. He said it was a matter of pride to honour those gentlemen who had been regular and punctual in their attendance at the Sessions and an honour to every inhabitant of the parish, and every other in the Hundred. He then proposed a toast to Mr. H.R. Roe Esq., of Gnaton Hall, Yealmpton, who he said the inhabitants of the Hundred were chiefly indebted for the success of the reason they had now gathered to celebrate. Mr. Roe responded saying that although he was suffering from a severe indisposition, he had attended the dinner as his paramount interest was always for the convenience and welfare of the inhabitants of the neighbourhood. Many more toasts were given and drank to before the dinner came to an end.

FALL FROM A WINDOW.

An inquest was held on the 22nd of September 1841 at the Maltman's Arms, Modbury, into the death of William Couch, the youngest child of John and Mary Couch of Brownson Street, who accidentally fell from the window of his house and died due to the injuries he received. He was just one-and-a-half-years-old.

LIFE EXPECTANCY.

Many people assume that in the nineteenth century people died young and that fifty was a good age. There certainly was a high mortality rate, mainly in new-born babies. Up to fifteen percent of children died before their first birthday. For people born in 1841 the average life expectancy was around forty to forty-five years. Survival past the first year of life increased their chances of a longer life, and once a child had reached five years of age, he or she was much more likely to reach a greater age. Living away from the overcrowded dirty towns and cities also increased the life expectancy somewhat, though Modbury like many other places also suffered from an inadequate water supply leading to poor sanitation.

The 1841 census showed the population of the town to be very young by today's standards; most inhabitants being under the age of forty, predominately under thirty. There were though a number of folk who had reached the grand old age of seventy and beyond – even a handful in their eighties, including Elizabeth and John Chapman of Brownston Street. John was then still working as an agricultural labourer. Grace Mortimore of Chapel Place was eighty-five, as was John Hills, a pauper of Galpin Street. Grace Lee and Grace Crocker, both of Brownston Street were aged eighty. Grace Crocker died the following year aged eighty-two, as did Grace Lee – though her death records show she was born in 1744, meaning she was actually ninety-seven or ninety-eight when she died!

[*The 1841 census rounded ages up or down to the nearest five. A seventy-eight-year-old would be rounded up to eighty and as a seventy-six-year-old would be rounded down to seventy-five.*]

TO LET.

Shearlangstone Farm at Kingston was available for rent in July 1842, for a term of fourteen years. The tenancy which was presently in the occupation of Mr. William Hooke was to be taken up on the following Lady Day [25th of March.] The farm was said to be situated two miles from Modbury and had eighty-three acres of excellent arable, meadow, pasture, and orchard land. Sea sand, seaweed and lime for manure was said to be easily available within two miles of the premises.

FOR SALE.

On Wednesday the 3ʳᵈ of August 1842, an auction was held at three in the afternoon at the Exeter Inn, Modbury, for the dwelling house, surgery, stabling, cow-house, garden, and courtyard with double access on Brownston Street, formerly the property of the late Mr. William Froude Langworthy, surgeon of that town.

THE COMPLETE SUFFRAGE UNION.

Letter dated October 12th 1842, Modbury.

Gentlemen, This day the town-crier of Modbury came to my house with a message from Major Hunt, one of Her Majesty's Justices of the Peace for the county of Devon, desiring that I would come to the office of J. Kelly, Esq., solicitor, to answer certain questions respecting bills posted in the town connected with the 'Complete Suffrage Union.' To which I replied I had no objection, and went carrying with me the rules of the society, its objects, and a card of membership which I laid on the table. There were present: Major Hunt, J. Kelly, Esq., the magistrate's clerk, and John Andrews Esq., solicitor.

Mr. Hunt addressed me in the following manner; "Is your name Cave" - Yes.
"Did you send this bill to the town crier (holding one of the addresses of the National Councils in his hand) - Yes.
"Did you pay the crier for posting?" - I shall see that he gets paid.
"Where did you get those bills from?" - Birmingham.
"Do you know that there is a special warrant issued by the Home Secretary for the apprehension of *Mr. Joseph Sturge?" - I do not.
"You know that this bill is seditious and inflammatory, calculated to cause the inhabitants to be dissatisfied when otherwise they would not?" - I am not possessed of sufficient knowledge to know that it is.
"The poor are wronged, are they not? For if they have not work there is the poor law to protect them." - We are not calling for charity, but our political rights which no man who is a patriot influenced by Christian principle can refuse, and for which we are determined to struggle by peaceable and legal means.
"Are you for physical force?" - No sir. We say 'sheath the sword' believing that our wise and good Creator never intended that one man should be trained to shoot another; our motto is 'Peace, Law, and Order.'
Mr Andrews; "How do you expect to obtain your object?" - By peaceful agitation, and by petitioning again and again, as we did for the Reform Bill.
"Are you the better for the Reform Bill?" - No, because we were disappointed by those who pretended to be our friends. But now we hope to have a government that will be responsible to the people.

Mr. Hunt; "I am of the opinion that every law ought to be obeyed while it is law, be it ever so bad, you must not endeavour to upset the government." - Sir, that is an everyday occurrence. For when the Tories are in office, the Whigs try whatever they can do to upset them; and when the Whigs are in office, the Tories are at the same game. We believing that both parties are dishonest and our object is to destroy them, and have a 'Complete Suffrage Parliament.'

Mr. Hunt. "You had better take care of what you are doing, for it is quite illegal to post such bills as this. I am going to write to Sir James Graham this evening, and I wish to get all the information I can. Perhaps you have no objection to taking this card?" - You are welcome by paying for it.

"What is the price of it?" - Sixpence.

"What you do with the money?" - Pay for the cards with it.

"What constitutes a member?" - Purchasing the card and keeping the rules.

"What oath do you take" - None.

"Then I will pay for this card." After which Mr. Kelly said to the Major, "You are now a member of the Complete Suffrage Union!"

Mr. Hunt; "Will you will please let me have the names those who have taken cards of membership from you?" - I do not know whether I am justified in doing so.

"Then I have no hesitation in saying yours is an illegal and secret society, and as I have been informed there is likely to be an outbreak in this neighbourhood, and if anything should happen, you will be the first taken." - Sir, as we wish to keep within the pale of the law and not to cause disturbance, but to do all we can to prevent it, I give you their names. At the same time, I have never heard that there was likely to be any disturbance in this neighbourhood until now, but I can assure you that myself along with those whose names I have given you will be ready at any time to render you all the assistance we can to prevent any breach of the peace.

With a great deal more which the limits of letter-paper will not allow to write. This conversation was closed and I left the office. Class legislation has received such a blow that I have no hesitation in saying it will never recover. They are getting very uneasy in Modbury; so uneasy that they have caused the crier to demolish all the bills and ordered him not to publish any more meetings.

> I am gentlemen, your obedient servant, Robert Cave.

*Joseph Sturge, a Quaker, was born into a farming family in Gloucestershire in 1793. During the 1830's he was a central player in the anti-slavery movement, both in Britain and abroad. In 1842 he began to work for Parliamentary reform. His 'Complete Suffrage Union' talks began in February 1842 in Birmingham, working towards reform through a unity of the middle and working classes. Eighty-seven delegates from across Britain met in Birmingham Town Hall between the 5th and 8th of April 1842. Sturge stressed class unity and peaceful means to gain their aims. During the summer of 1842 the second great Chartist Petition was presented to

Parliament - and was rejected. Huge strikes broke out around the country, as Chartists were angered by harsh prison sentences for Chartist leaders. A second conference was held in Birmingham in December 1842. Four hundred delegates attended. Middle class delegates wanted to drop the Chartist name, which had become associated with violence, but many Chartists who had worked, been imprisoned, and suffered in that name, refused to drop it. No agreement could be reached and the conference broke down. Sturge later stood for Parliament on a programme of Parliamentary Reform, but he failed to be elected.

A MUSICAL CHALLENGE.

In May 1843, the Totnes brass band having accepted a challenge from the Modbury reed band, a contest was played out in public at Newhouse, between Totnes and Modbury. Each band put five pounds aside which would be given to the winner, each band being known to be very talented.

Early on the morning of Monday the 8th of May, after word having been sent out across the county, great numbers of people from the neighbouring towns, villages, and farms, arrived at the appointed place. At eleven o'clock the performance began in a wide area formed by the junction of two turnpike roads, near to the Avon Inn. The bands were elevated on a platform so as to be heard by the vast numbers who were present. The Totnes band chose for their umpire John Caunter, Esq., of Wave House near Ashburton, but that gentleman not being able to attend, requested that his brother Henry Caunter, Esq., also of Ashburton attended in his place. Mr. Purton of the Marine band Plymouth was chosen to umpire by the Modbury band. Each band played ten pieces of music of their own selection alternately. The Totnes band played the 'Hallelujah Chorus' in excellent style, as well the other pieces of their choosing. The Modbury performers also excelled and the serpent player was said to be a first-rate performer and won the admiration of everyone. After the performance had concluded, the umpires (gentlemen both well-known in the musical world) conferred together, each having kept separate notes of the proceedings. After a patient investigation it was found that each band had performed five pieces so well that the umpires could not decide which band had outshone the other. It was then agreed that a gentleman called Captain Dennis should be a third umpire; but on account of the performances being so well balanced, he could not decide either. The wager was therefore withdrawn with both bands having added fresh honours to their well-known reputation.

FARMS FOR SALE.

The following farms were put up for sale in August 1844.
Lot 1 - Brownston Farm – consisting of a good farmhouse, outhouses and one hundred and six acres of arable, pasture and meadow. It also had a good water supply.

Lot 2 - Collywell Farm – consisting of two cottages with gardens and a small orchard, together with several fields. Also, Foxhole and Long Moor tenements which came with twenty-nine acres of arable land, two acres of orchard, and twenty-nine of pasture. The farms were at that time in the possession of Mr. Edward Jeans and ownership was to be taken the following Lady Day [25th March.]

Lot 3 – Bickham Farm, North Huish, consisting of a good farmhouse and outhouses. Fifty acres of arable land, three of orchard and fourteen of pasture. The land described as being superior. It was then tenanted by Robert Jonas whose term was due to expire the following Lady Day.

NEW RAILWAYS.

The expansion of the 'new' railway lines across Britain in the 1840's was huge, and the construction of a line in South Devon from Dartmouth to Plymouth was proposed in 1845. It was said that it would pass near or through Dittisham, Cornworthy, Stoke Fleming, Blackawton, Slapton, Stokenham, Chillington, Frogmore, Charlton, Dodbrooke, Kingsbridge, Salcombe, Aveton Gifford, Modbury, Yealmpton, and Plympton, from where it would proceed to Plymouth.

GLEANERS.

The members of the Modbury Agricultural Association met in August 1845 and came to a resolution as to the protection of their property, not to allow gleaners [*poor people who picked up grain left on the ground after the harvest*] to enter or remain on their land other than between the hours of seven in the morning and eight in the evening.

KIND FARMER LANG.

At a time when many people would possibly have made the most of such an opportunity to make a profit, Mr. Joseph Lang, a conscientious and kind farmer, on Thursday the 20th of May 1847, hearing of the intention of other corn-growers asking thirty shillings for a bag of wheat and an equally exorbitant price for barley; he took to Modbury market twenty bags of barley and retailed them himself in half bags at twelve shillings per bag. Had he not done so, there would not have been a grain in the marketplace for the poorer folk of the town. Mr. Lang and two other farmers said they were determined to continue supplying the poor at this price for the next three weeks. Mr. Lang also sold his wheat at eighteen shillings a bag.

A NEW COACH SERVICE.

A new coach, the Mazeppa, began its service in July 1848 from Kingsbridge to Plymouth and back on alternate days. Mr. William Foale, the proprietor of the old coach, was continuing to run his vehicle every day. As an additional attraction to the service of the new coach, Mr. Goodwin who played a melodious horn, had been employed to alert the inhabitants of its imminent arrival at stopping points on the route.

THE PROPHET OF MODBURY.

The town of Modbury and surrounding district had for many days been the scene of much excitement in October 1848, after Mr. John Dingle of Great Orcheton Farm, one of the better educated and well-known farmers in the neighbourhood, suddenly turned away from his normal course of living and became a totally different character. He said that God had called him, just as he had Paul on his way to Damascus, and that he must out of necessity preach the gospel. The power he said being irresistible and infinite. In consequence of this decision Dingle gave up his farm saying that he would never again buy or sell, or otherwise mix in business, and that he was leaving his wife and children to look after themselves whilst he travelled the counties of England, warning all at the near approach of the millennium, which he asserted would commence in 1850.

From some of the 'revelations' made to him and which he proclaimed to the townspeople; it was thought he was not now in his right mind. The previous week he had delivered a lecture on 'The Millennial reign of Christ on earth' at Modbury. The large room was found to be much too small to hold the crowd that attended and the meeting was therefore carried out in the street, where for about an hour he addressed the assembled throng with much fervour and fluency. Notwithstanding his incredible and ludicrous assertions, there were many who believed he would soon obtain many more. The bill announcing the meeting stated that the subject had been revealed to him in a vision the previous week. He soon after left, to spread the word across Devon and beyond.

John Dingle was back in Modbury the following year – see story below.

AGRICULTURAL DEPRESSION.

A public meeting was held at the White Hart Inn on the 10th of December 1849, to consider what steps should be taken to relieve the present depressed state agriculture in Devon. The room was crowded to excess with many tenant farmers being present. Mr. Cumming of Bigbury commenced the meeting stating that it was an open meeting and they wished to hear the opinions of all parties. He moved that Mr. Pearse, a tenant farmer, should preside - which was agreed to by all. The chairman then commenced by stating that the distress among the agriculturists was very great, and he believed that with the present prices it was impossible for the rents agreed to be paid. The question was, what was the remedy. If something wasn't done for the tenant farmer he must then surely go to the workhouse?

Mr. John Dingle of Modbury, 'the prophet' as he had become known, and a prime mover in calling the meeting, moved a resolution: "That the corn-laws (said to be made for the protection of the British farmer) had tended to raise the price of land above its real value, and to the injury of the tenant farmer. It was his opinion that nothing could save them but an immediate reduction in the present rental price of the land, to be levied according to the annual price of grain. He observed that the price of land had more than doubled within the last fifty to sixty years, whilst the price of agricultural produce was still about the same as at that time. A fact which conclusively showed that this was a question of rent. He then went into some matters of a personal nature, saying that he had been a tenant farmer forced to leave his estate. He had been compelled to pay his rent in advance, and because he could not from his then present distress do so, his stock had been taken to pay the money owing.

Mr. Gumming was next to speak, he said he was of the opinion that agriculturists were divided into three classes; first the landlords, who were born and bred landlords, and who did not care for rent so much as for the power and domination which they endeavoured to get over their tenants. Second the landowners, men who had laid out their money in the purchase of land, and by high rents and other burdens would endeavour to get for their money so laid out, as great a return as possible. Third the tenant farmer, whose object it was to get as much land as cheaply as he could. The interests of all these classes were directly opposed, and the tenant had to contend against the other two, with what success yet remained to be seen.

Mr. Bignell of Kingsbridge then read Lord Fortescue's letter to his tenantry and commented upon the several passages in as he proceeded. He advised the tenant farmers to unite together and combine to resist the tyranny and oppression they were at present suffering from the landlords. He said the tenants could easily punish the landlords by leaving their farms at Michaelmas. A long and stormy discussion then ensued which was ultimately set at rest by Mr. Lethbridge moving that 'a return to a fair and moderate protection is the only proper remedy to raise the tenant farmer and tradesman, but more particularly the agricultural labourers.' This amendment was put, but only a few hands were held up in its favour. The original resolution being carried by an immense majority. Three cheers were then given after which the meeting broke up.

A law introduced in 1813 had meant that grain was sold at a set price, so as not to let farmers suffer from the cheaper foreign imports being brought in to the country. Unfortunately, the landowners were taking the profits and leaving the farmers poorer and with grain they were unable to sell. This law was in force until 1846. John Dingle had become very disillusioned with farming since having taken over Great Orcheton, a two-hundred-and-ten-acre farm on Lady Day

1844. He quit the farm altogether in October 1849 having had enough of the poor prices he was paid for his crops, the high rents, and tithes. He had demanded that his landlord lowered the rent by fifteen percent but this was refused. He had also been heard to say he didn't think he would be working much longer in England as land prices abroad were much cheaper. In 1849 the price of corn was extremely low and John Dingle along with many other farmers found themselves struggling to pay their rents. His was three-hundred and sixty-five pounds a year. He therefore sold virtually every item on the property, leaving him unable to cultivate the land.

A FRIGHTENED HORSE.

In March 1849 Captain Nathaniel Francis Edwards of the Royal Navy, residing at Ludbrook Manor, Ermington, was charged before the magistrates at Modbury with an assault upon Mr. Samuel Widdicombe, son of Mr. Widdicombe of Hay, Ugborough. The alleged assault was committed on the 12th of February, by the defendant threatening to horsewhip the complainant at his father's residence on account of his having abused a savage dog kept by Widdicombe which had jumped out and frightened his horse. The bench fined Widdicombe six' pence with costs.

1850-1899

RETURNS OF MORTALITY.

According to the quarterly return of the Registrar General of Marriages, Births, and Deaths for the United Kingdom which has just been published in February 1850, the total number of deaths during the last quarter of 1849 had been 97,778, an increase of only five per cent on the corresponding quarter of the preceding year. In Modbury there had been twenty-six births and thirty-nine deaths. Some of the deaths were recorded as having had the following causes; Cholera - two males and one female. Small-pox – seven males, four females. Scarlatina maligna – two females. Cynanche maligna – two males and one female.

In the district of Newton Abbot deaths had increased from two-hundred and sixteen the previous quarter to three-hundred and fifty-four, and in Totnes from one-hundred and seventy-eight to two-hundred and forty-eight, owing in a great measure to the visitation of cholera in October 1849. In Woodbury there had been twenty-eight births and fourteen deaths. These deaths had not exceeded the average, although six had occurred in the village within the previous ten days due to smallpox - some after having the vaccination. In Stokenham there had been thirty-one births and eighteen deaths. A forty-four-year-old woman had died of cholera when seven months pregnant.

COACH CRASH OUTSIDE THE EXETER INN.

William Foale, a carrier of Kingsbridge was returning from Plymouth on the afternoon of Thursday the 5th of September 1850, when about midway down Church Street the chain on the drag of his carriage broke, and almost immediately the horses began to proceed at a rapid rate down the hill without the driver being able to have any proper control over them or the coach. The pole between the coach and horses then also snapped, and even with both drags full on there was nothing he could do. When opposite the Exeter Inn, the coach overturned and scattered the passengers in all directions. Mr. Foale and Mr. Bignall, who was sitting next to him were thrown clear. One of the outside passengers, a young woman had her foot almost severed and her ankle fractured. She was immediately taken into the Exeter Inn and a surgeon called. Unfortunately, he was unable to save her foot and carried out an amputation there and then. Another young lady had two fingers broken, and a number of other passengers were badly bruised.

A CHARGE OF FORGERY.

George Shepherd, who carried out his business as a linen draper in Modbury, and who also worked as a clerk in the offices of Mr. T. J. Savery, solicitor, as well as being a parish clerk, had recently been declared bankrupt. In October 1850 he was summonsed to appear in Exeter on the 23rd to be given his certificate of liquidation, but before that could take place, he was apprehended on a warrant charging him with having forged the name of John Mortimore, a builder and stone mason in the town, and was said to have drawn several bills at the Devon and Cornwall Bank in Kingsbridge in Mr. Mortimore's name.

At Shepherd's trial the following March, John Mortimore said that he had known George Shepherd since they were children and that he could neither read nor write very easily as he had never attended school. The two men had indeed been very close friends and George Shepherd was one of the executors of his will. They also both belonged to the same Friendly Society. A short while after being declared bankrupt, George Shepherd had approached him and said that the bills he had previously signed for him would be honoured. In 1848 and 1849 he had signed three bills of acceptance for Shepherd's creditors who were chasing him for money, with the promise of it being paid back. Then in 1850 whilst he was ill in bed with typhus, he was shown a bill which he said was not in his handwriting. There were three other bills later shown to him which he said he was sure he hadn't signed, amounting to one-hundred and twenty-seven-pounds. Another witness, Richard Lethbridge, stated that John Mortimore when signing his name made a clumsy 'J' rather like an 'I' which the cheques shown to him appeared to have on them, though admitted Mr. Mortimore's handwriting was very poor.

Mr Karslake acting on behalf of Shepherd, pointed out that the dates and amounts Mortimore had given for signing cheques were the dates on three of the cheques submitted, but he was now disclaiming it to be his signature on two of them. The two men had been very great friends, and Mr. Mortimore had even at one point during the trial stated that two of the signatures that he said wasn't his may well have been written by him many years ago.

As there was no evidence to prove clearly that John Mortimore was not the signatory, George Shepherd who up until his insolvency had been a very upstanding man in the town, was acquitted of all charges by the jury.

FIRE IN A LINHAY.

Some labourers working on the farm of Mr. Hodder at Edmeston, noticed smoke issuing from a linhay adjoining a detached barn on the farm on the Wednesday morning of the 23rd of October 1850. Going to investigate they found two tramps had kindled a fire with some straw and sticks and were preparing to roast a fowl which they had no doubt stolen. They were immediately taken into custody and were committed to prison for one month.

RUN OVER BY HIS OWN CART.

A steady and industrious workman named William Andrews aged fifty-eight, in the employment of Mr. Adams, a tanner of Week in the parish of Modbury, was proceeding with his horse and cart towards Bigbury on the 4th of January 1851 when the wheel of the cart ran up a hedge and the vehicle was upset throwing Mr. Andrews underneath. His body was discovered about an hour later; he was quite dead.

The previous day, Friday January the 3rd in the adjoining parish of Kingston, Mr. Lewis Brooking, a respectable farmer, was discovered suspended from a beam in his barn. His death was said to have been the fifth suicide in the locality within the past three months.

ATTEMPTED ROBBERY.

On the night of Thursday the 12th of April 1851, a robbery was attempted on the premises Mr. William Paddon, a watchmaker of 6, Church Street. The thieves succeeded in boring several holes with a gimlet through the shutter of the shop-window and cutting away a portion sufficiently large enough to allow a man's hand through. It was supposed the thieves must have directed a light through the opening, but finding there were no watches within reach, made off without doing further damage. Mr. Paddon was in the habit of taking his watches upstairs with him to his living quarters after he closed up the shop at night.

THROWN OVER A BRIDGE.

On the 21st of August 1851, a horse and cart carrying four children inexplicably fell into the waters below from Shipham Bridge near Modbury. The cart was smashed to pieces but the children and horse miraculously were uninjured.

LITERARY AND SCIENTIFIC EVENING.

The Kingsbridge correspondent for the Exeter and Plymouth Gazette wrote an article in regards to a trip which he made to the Modbury Literary and Scientific Institute on Brownston Street in October 1851 which I have condensed...

The building was founded in 1840 by Richard King Esq, who had made his fortune in New York. It was on a return visit to England that he purchased the site in Brownston Street and built the impressive Palladian style building. Throughout our county, on entering a town, one can predict with all but inevitable accuracy the intelligence and the literary and scientific advancement of the inhabitants from physical appearances. As a rule, in those towns in which a flourishing Mechanics' or Literary Institutions exist, there the spirit of progress and improvement prevails not merely as an element but as all-pervading principle. Education refines the taste, creates new wants and desires, and of necessity makes us dissatisfied with old fashioned, clumsy and inconvenient edifices. The very establishment of such Institutions is indicative of a desire to search deeper and to soar higher, to unlock those secret chambers where the great laws of nature are revealed, to seek new depths, new strata, and new productions.

In Modbury, an individual in quest of Literary or Scientific Intelligence, on observing the character of the buildings and the physical conformation of the town, would without doubt pass through without staying even to enquire of the existence of such an Institution, for not one spark of improvement is to be seen. The town presents the appearance of having been built by contract some two or three hundred years since, and by some local or other act the inhabitants agreed from making any alterations or improvements in the very many picturesque angles and projections of the houses. But, on entering the Institute and in mixing with its very intelligent members, how thoroughly did I become convinced of the folly of trusting my first impressions which were that I had arrived a literary Nazareth, out of which and in which was no good thing. Each member vied with his neighbour in giving hearty welcomes of such a character as one could feel to be genuine, to both friends and strangers.

In the Lecture Hall, in which about one-hundred and fifty members participated, the Reverend Nutcombe Oxenham was in the chair, and among those present were the Reverend F. W. Pulling, Reverend T. Purrier, Richard Peek Esq., John Andrews Esq., W. D. Walke Esq., Rev. James Fisher, etc. A delegation from the Kingsbridge Institute were also in attendance, consisting of the Reverend Prebendary Luney, Messrs. Jarvis, Bickford, Miller, Pulliblank, and Prowse. The celebrated Modbury band played some inspiring English airs. Ladies gathered in great numbers, and the room was well and tastefully ornamented by festoons of flowers and by appropriate emblems, interspersed with R. X. - the initials of the founder of the Institution, Richard King, Esq. The Reverend Oxenham said he was proud to see so large and respectable a body present, and he hoped those strangers who were in attendance would avail themselves of the opportunity to re-visit when a more intellectual character was the invited guest. He spoke of the value of the privilege afforded to them by having such an institute and those who were not yet - he encouraged to become members. An institution of this sort he said was a very useful and advantageous means of benefiting society at large, but of no use if the people being taught did not care to learn. No teaching was more practically useful than intelligent persons asking questions and drawing out from the lecturer the particular information they may require. He then gave some practical suggestions to test the qualifications of lecturers and the best manner in which the information may be obtained. He recommended that they should always be influenced by sound and honest motives and not in a captious spirit. In conclusion, the Reverend said "Get knowledge, and what you do not understand, get explained. Experience is the mistress of life." He said he wished the people of the town to try the institution, and he assured them they would benefit by it and be improved. This was followed by a performance by the Modbury band.

TWO DEATHS IN TWENTY-FOUR HOURS.

Two of the town's highly respected gentleman died within twenty-four hours of each other in October 1851. David Roberts a ninety-four-year-old widower, a former coal merchant – a trade he was still employed in at the age of eighty. He had latterly taken on a slightly more sedate role as a grocer. He died on the 23rd of October 1851 at his home 28, Church Street, where he lived with his widowed daughter Mary Liddy and a number of other residents who rented rooms in the property. Originally from Carnarvon in Wales, he was known in his younger days to walk the six-hundred-mile round trip to visit his family.
The following day, William Southmead Langworthy Esq., a surgeon of 8, Brownston Street died aged sixty-two. Both men were buried in St. George's Churchyard.

DEATH DUE TO WALL COLLAPSE.

A fatal accident befell a labourer named Richard Voysey aged forty-eight, in the parish of Kingston on Wednesday the 19th of November 1851. He along with several other workmen were employed in removing some cob walls on an old barn at the estate belonging to Mr. Elliott of Babland, when a large mass suddenly fell on him crushing him to death. His bones were said to have been shockingly fractured in almost every part of his body. The coroner's inquest returned a verdict of 'accidental death.'

Postcard of Brownston Street, courtesy of Pam Wilson.

LECTURES AT THE LOCAL INSTITUTE.

On Thursday the 20th of November 1851 at the Modbury Institute, Reverend James Fisher delivered a lecture on 'Milton and his Poetry.' The reverend was said to have gratified the admirers of the noble English poet with some excellent readings from several of his works, especially 'Paradise Lost.' The previous week Joseph Flashman had read a lecture on the 'Attainability of literature by the working classes.' It was the sequel to an earlier lecture he had given on the 'Compatibility of literature with physical labour.' The author stating that there was no station in life however humble, that offers any natural barrier to the acquisition of knowledge, the achievement of science, and the delights of literature.

A GREAT GALE.

The South West of England and Devonshire in particular was visited by a violent gale on the night of Saturday the 23rd of November 1851. Many apple trees were uprooted and slates were flung far and wide from roof tops. Torrents of rain then followed throughout the following day. Whereas on the Eastern coast, from Norfolk to Scotland, heavy snowstorms and piercing cold winds were felt.

RURAL POLICE.

A meeting was held in December 1851 at the White Hart Inn, pertaining to the establishment of a rural police and lock-up house in the town. There had been a significant rise in crimes being committed in the parish of Modbury and those surrounding it and recently there had been a number of sheep go missing. Thomas Pearse of Stoliford had recently had a breeding ewe slaughtered in the field and its hind quarters taken away. An agreement was reached and a subscription was set up to cover the expenses of an officer and a lock-up house, amounting to twenty-seven pounds fifteen shillings and six' pence.

NOT A HAPPY CHRISTMAS.

In the darkness of a winter's night, on Christmas Eve 1851 some scoundrel or scoundrels, wilfully destroyed a large quantity of glass in the windows of St. George's Church. The following morning, many stones, some weighing several pounds were found in the interior of the building. It was thought they must have been flung with great force, as the wood work of some of the pews was also damaged. Various other offences were committed in and around the town on the same night. A reward of five pounds was offered for the discovery of the offenders.

PAYING A HEAVY TOLL.

A gentleman who was said to be well-known in the commercial world, on the 27th of December 1852 whilst making his way westwards, passed through Kingsbridge and tendered the toll to the gatekeeper who said that the six' pence he had offered up was counterfeit and returned it. The gentleman, not liking the rebuke, threw the coin on the ground, whipped his horse and drove on. But before reaching Modbury he was overtaken by the gatekeeper who had ridden after him, followed by a policeman for the purpose of taking him into custody, who announced to the surprised commercial man, "You are now my prisoner. I having two charges against you. One for evading the toll at the turnpike, and the other for offering a base coin." The trio then proceeded on to Modbury, where an investigation took place before a respectable attorney who recommended a compromise, which Mr. Temple (the gatekeeper) consented to accept. On the traveller paying the expenses amounting to one pound seventeen shillings and six' pence, he was allowed on his way.

A FIGHT BETWEEN TWO TAILOR'S.

A Boxing match took place in 1852 between two tailors'; James Balson of Exeter and Peter Newland of Modbury – both putting up a sovereign for the winner. They fought ferociously for twenty-five minutes during which Balson suffered a broken and split nose and Newland was beaten blind, fighting two rounds totally unable to see. The consequence of the fight was that both men needed to be taken to hospital where they remained for a number of days; likely neither claiming the other man's sovereign.

MODBURY CRICKET CLUB.

A Cricket Club was formed in the town in 1852 which was supported by many of the leading gentlemen of the place, and since April of that year had been practicing twice week in a spacious field belonging to John Andrews, Esq. The club under the presidency of John Dawson Esq., of Church Street, convened at several meetings to discuss the formation of rules etc.

FATAL GUN ACCIDENT.

Ebenezer Lethbridge, the eighteen-year-old son of Richard and Sarah Lethbridge of Little Modbury, in January 1854 went out with a gun for the purpose of shooting rabbits. On his return he went into one of the outhouses of the farm, and whilst putting the gun down it exploded. The whole contents of shot became lodged in his upper part of his left thigh. He was immediately carried into the house by one of the labourers on the estate, and every attention was paid to him, but miserably without any effect. The poor lad who was in excruciating agonies, passed away the following morning.

No. 2 BROAD STREET FOR SALE.

Mr. Thomas Pearse, auctioneer, held a public sale on the 22nd of August 1856 at the White Hart Hotel offering two properties for sale. The first sale was for 'Little Modbury' which included the farmhouse, outbuildings, barns and land. The second sale was that of a spacious dwelling house with offices, courtyard and gardens, at number 2, Broad Street. The property was said to have for many years past been the drapery business of Messrs. Roper and Callard. Samuel Callard was the tenant rather than the owner, as he continued to trade at that address until his death in 1897, aged seventy-four.

AFFRAY AT SPRIDDLESCOMBE FARM.

Two roguish looking men knocked on the door of Mr. George Yabsley at Spriddlescombe Farm in early December 1859 and enquired if any chimneys needed sweeping. When he said that they didn't the men began to beg, and from begging to demanding, and supposing that no other men were in the house they commenced throwing stones at the doors and windows of the property. Fortunately, four of the farmhands who were on their way back to the farmhouse for dinner came to the rescue, and with the great difficulty managed to secure the ruffians. A policeman was then sent for, who handcuffed them before taking them to cells at the Ridgway, Plympton. During the skirmish Mr. Yabsley was wounded by a stone striking him on the eye. The policeman was also wounded when one of the men bit him on the hand.

MODBURY RIFLES.

A meeting was held in December 1859 at the White Hart Hotel, with the view of establishing a Rifle Corps in the town. Among those present were Messrs. Richard Andrews, John T. Savery, Alfred Pearce, John Widdicombe, Samuel Widdicombe, Richard Pearce, James Ford, William Hodder, Frances Wyatt, Richard Crocker, and many others. Mr. Richard Andrews opened the meeting by briefly stating the object, pointing out the necessity of a Rifle Corps being formed, and called to those present who were able and willing, to join. The appeal was well responded to and in a short space of time thirty members were enrolled. It was expected that within a week so, at least another fifty members would likely add their names to the list.

GAS LIGHTING NEEDED.

On the evening of the 26th of January 1860, Mr. Cole of Ridgeway, Plympton, an innkeeper was leaving a house in Modbury situated on a steep bank, when in the darkness and unfamiliar with the ground, he lost his footing and fell breaking his leg. This incident amongst many others had many residents protesting for the need of gas lighting in the streets of the town.

4TH DEVON MOUNTED RIFLES.

The newly and locally recruited 4th Devon (Modbury) Mounted Rifles on Sunday the 8th of July 1860 paraded through the town. The locals came out in significant numbers to watch them as they marched from the barracks to the church four deep and with the town's band leading the way, playing some favourite marches in true military style. Once the service was over and the corps were making their way back to the barracks their route was thronged with well-wishers. The dust caused by the tramping of such large number filled the air and caused the troops uniforms; which were grey with green facings trimmed with red, to become quite unsightly.

Captain, J. Bulteel Esq., of Flete, known for his kindness and hospitality invited the corps to meet at Flete the following Thursday evening to drill, and to bring with them to use his own words 'their sweethearts.' The following Thursday the Modbury Mounted Rifles assembled at five o'clock in the grounds of Flete House, accompanied by friends and family numbering around three hundred in total. The troops were put through a variety of manual and marching exercises for about hour which they were said to have carried out admirably. Parade over the corps were dismissed and were shortly afterwards to re-assemble with their wives and friends at tea-tables which had been set out on the lawns. After dining, the parties were encouraged to stroll through the gardens and grounds and enjoy the delightful walks and charming scenery. At eight o'clock dancing commenced to the sounds of the Modbury band, and at eleven they all sat down once more to a magnificent supper which had been prepared by Mr. W. Thomas of Devonport. After the meal was over the dancing re-commenced, and was kept up with unflagging spirit until five o'clock the following morning.

Postcard of Flete House, courtesy of Samuel Harrison.

THE RAMSHACKLE HOUSE.

One of the principal attractions in the town in September 1860, was said to be 25, Church Street, the former home of Cyprian Pearce, a surgeon, who died in 1853 aged seventy-six. The house was passed on to his sons and daughters, and it was still then in their possession, but from some disagreement between them the house had been allowed to fall into ruinous decay. Many offers were made to purchase it; however, the owners could not come to an agreement and it was left to decay and as many said – a disgrace to the town.

FIRE AT COTLASS GRIST MILL.

On the night of Tuesday the 13th of November 1860, a fire broke out in a small grist mill at Cotlass about a mile from the town and situated at the side of Aylestone Brook. The roof soon fell in, burying beneath its ruins a pipe of cider [*equivalent to one-hundred and five gallons*] and several bags of corn. The ferocity of the fire caused most of the stones belonging to the mill works to break. The damage was so severe that the mill had to be pulled down.

A CHRISTMAS PARTY AT RINGMORE.

On Thursday the 27th of December 1860, the school children of the village and surrounding cottages and farms, were treat to a Christmas party by the rector, Reverend Francis C. Hingeston and his wife Martha. The rectory barn was prettily decorated for the occasion with flags, bunting and evergreens, and by Egyptian lamps of various colours. The fifty-eight invited children assembled at six o'clock in the evening and enthusiastically indulged, after grace had been said, in the well laden tables of food provided by and presided over by Mrs. Hingeston. They then proceeded to the church where an evening service was held. Once this was over, the parishioners along with the children retired back to the barn where the remainder of the evening was occupied by the exhibition of large magic lantern show, which was a presentation of astronomical pictures followed by comic slides. This occupied nearly three hours, as every slide was illustrated by anecdotes and amusing stories by the rector which produced continuous roars of laughter from the eager audience.

Francis and Martha had married at Ringmore in 1860. They had five sons and six daughters, all born between 1861 and 1881.

A COLD WINTER.

The winter of 1860/ 1861 appeared to be a particularly harsh one in South Devon and the temperature dipped to four to five degrees below zero on a number of occasions in early

January. The old and infirm certainly suffered, and in Modbury death came and took by the hand a number of the vulnerable townsfolk. These are the burials that took place at St. George's Churchyard between December 1860 and March 1861.

Thomas Bunker, a mere baby at just one-year-old was taken on the 2nd of December 1860. The following day Samuel Williams a seventy-three-year-old yeoman of Little Modbury Farm passed away. Two days later on the 5th, Thomas Fox a forty-three-year-old carrier died. A few days later on the 9th, Irene, the ten-year-old daughter of John Denbow a butcher, and his wife also called Irene, was taken. Susanna Sambell aged forty-eight died on the 14th of December, and on the 22nd, sixty-three-year-old William Lugger a farmer of Titwells, Averton Gifford, passed away. A week later, Temperance Luscombe aged sixty-seven, a widow of Higher Brownston Farm died on the 28th December.

Mary Furzeland a fifty-seven-year-old widow died on 6th January 1861 at Aveton Gifford. Richard Foot aged sixty-two, a tailor, died on the 9th January, and on the 16th the oldest inhabitant of the town, Agnes Spinney aged ninety-two of 10, Galpin Street, a pauper, died. Richard Hosking, a grocer and postmaster of 32, Church Street passed away aged seventy-nine on the 21st of January.

In February of 1861 I can find only one funeral having taken place at St. George's Church, that of Eliza Mortimore aged sixteen, the daughter of John Mortimore a mason, and his wife Jane. In March there were two deaths; seventy-two-year-old Sarah Stoneman and eighty-four-year-old John Woolridge.

NOT SUCH A POOR WOMAN.

An old woman [*from Ancestry.co.uk records I presume her to be Mary Andrews aged seventy-nine*] who had for many years been receiving parish relief, died in early January 1862, but on examination of her boxes and papers after her death eighty pounds was found.

MODBURY WESLYAN CHAPEL.

The want of a vestry for the Weslyan Chapel had been long felt needed, and on the 29th of January 1862 a sale and entertainment were laid on at the White Hart Assembly Rooms arranged by the friends of the chapel. The weather on the day was rather unfavourable and it was feared the occasion would be a failure, but those fears were soon put to rest when a gathering of one hundred and fifty people crowded into the room. There were stalls of items both useful and ornamental, and three charmingly decorated Christmas trees were added which gave the room a very seasonal appearance. At five-thirty in the afternoon a tea was then served. The sale of goods raised twenty-three pounds towards a new vestry.

BLOCKING THE HIGHWAY.

In May 1862 John Camp, a twenty-two-year-old dairyman of Modbury, was summoned by P.C. Luscombe for being the driver and owner of a horse and cart that had been left for an unreasonable amount of time amounting to five hours in New Road and obstructing the thoroughfare. He admitted the charge and expressed his sincere regret. The Bench fined him five shillings with ten' pence costs. He was then charged with assaulting P.C. Luscombe on the same day after being arrested. Camp again pleaded guilty. The Bench fined him nine shillings for this offence with and eleven' pence costs.

VOLUNTEER FETE AND BAND CONTEST.

This annual event took place on Wednesday the 6th of August 1862 in the beautiful grounds of the Norman castle in Totnes. The South Devon Railway Company ran a special cheap train service for the occasion, and in consequence there was a large number of day-trippers to the town. At one o'clock the gates were thrown open, and very soon the grounds were filled with pleasure seekers.

Four bands engaged in the contest for the prizes, which as a collective came to twenty-pounds. They were Devonport Dockyard Volunteer Artillery; 17th Devon (Totnes) Volunteer Rifles; 4th Devon (Modbury) Mounted Rifles; and 1st Devon (Dawlish) Volunteer Rifles. The first competition was for the buglers who each played fifteen regulation calls. The competition lasted about an hour and the declared winner was Peter Watts of the Devon (Modbury) Mounted Rifles. The effect of the buglers was said to have been striking and the echoes reverberated from the old walls of the castle. An interval of three quarters of an hour was then spent where the guests were invited to walk the grounds and explore the ruins of the castle. An 'Aunt Sally' and 'Uncle Sara' along with a number of other amusements of a miscellaneous character were provided for the visitors, as well as a refreshment tent selling tea and cakes and another selling strong liquors.

The main contest commenced shortly after three o'clock. The band of the 4th Devon (Modbury) Mounted Rifle Volunteers first took up their position in the band stand, and performed a selection from 'Trovatore.' The band was composed of the following gentlemen and instruments: John Cove, leader, E flat clarinet; Peter Watts, cornet; Samuel Hawkins, cornet; William Crocker, cornet; John J. Shepheard, cornet; Jonathan Crocker, E flat tenor saxophone; Edward Pearse, B flat baritone horn; John Crocker jnr, B flat euphonium; James Shepherd, bass trombone; James Shepherd, bombardon; William Shepherd, bass drum.

After the competition, the bands were united, and played the contest piece composed for the occasion by Mr. W. Winterbottom who was judging the event. The contest ended at about six o'clock, when the secretary (Mr. John L. Winter) mounted the podium and announced that Mr. Winterbottom had decided on awarding the first prize of twelve pounds to the Devonport Dockyard Artillery band. The second prize of five pounds was awarded to the Modbury band, and the third prize of three pounds to the Dawlish band. At the conclusion of the contest the bands played 'God Save the Queen,' and marched off the ground. The Totnes Amateur Ethiopian Minstrels then gave and amusing performance and the proceedings terminated at eleven o'clock in the evening.

ARSONIST IN MODBURY.

A fire broke out on the night of Friday the 9th of January 1863, which did no small mischief. It originated in a barn at the Green. As with many other occasions when the fire engine was called out it was a long time in coming, and when it did arrive there was no water to supply it. The fire continued to burn until about one o'clock on the Saturday morning, and in the meantime, besides destroying the building, it consumed or injured the greater part of thirty bags of barley, a quantity of carrots and mangold wurtzel, some wood, and a winnowing machine. The articles destroyed belonged to several people. There had been a fire at the same premises five years previously and it was supposed that case had been arson. The same opinion was assumed with this fire, as the previous night an attempt was made to burn the outbuildings of a tradesman of the town.

LIFE IN DEVON IN THE EARLY 1860'S.

The population of Devon taken from the 1861 census was collated and made available in 1863. It looked at ages, occupations, and the civil and social conditions of the inhabitants of the county. Devonshire it said contained an area of 1,643,700 statute acres, and in April 1861 had population of 589,385, of which 307,728 were females. The inhabitants of the county were reputedly known for their longevity, with 3 males and 5 females over the age of 100. 23 males and 35 females were 95 years and older; 78 males and 184 females were between 90 and 94; 440 males and 681 females had reached 85 years, and 1,391 males and 1,878 females were 80 or older. The unmarried males in the county numbered 172,153, of whom 150,139 were aged 20 and under. 18,340 were in their prime -aged between 20 and 45. Only one bachelor had reached 95, whereas 23 married men had done so, and three of them were centenarians [*the only men to still be alive who had reached the grand old age of 100*]. The unmarried females numbered 179,680. 19,977 of them aged 20 and under and 9,677 of 25 and over. The wives of all ages numbered 102,958, of whom 625 were just 15 years of age; 22,177 were 30 years and under, and 3,804 above 70.

There were no fewer than 10,611 widowers, and 25,090 widows in the county; of the latter there were 15 who had been deprived of their husbands before they (the wives) had reached the age of 15! [*The age at which a person could marry and at which they would require consent changed in 1929. Before that marriage could be at twelve for a girl and fourteen for a boy, but consent of the parent(s) was required for both up to the age of twenty-one.*] Of the total population, 37, 684 males and 36,989 females were under the age of 5 years old. 77 males and 443 females were described as being foreigners. In Modbury the population was 1,839 males and 1,840 females.

Referencing the occupations of the male population of Devon, it was interesting to see that there were 93 barristers and 366 solicitors, 77 physicians and 431 surgeons and apothecaries (as distinct from druggists). Authors, editors, and other writers numbered 29. There were 99 people who described themselves as painters and 10 as sculptors. Another 59 were bankers, 96 shipowners, 855 landed proprietors, 10,771 farmers and graziers, 28,688 agricultural labourers, besides 12,601 in-door farm servants. 16 people were honest enough to enter themselves as 'dependent on relatives.'

Employed female returns showed that 1,067 were tailors, clothes dealers or outfitters, 46 were milliners and dressmakers, 12,463 shirtmakers and seamstresses, 2,374; stay makers, 2,289 glove knitters, 4 shoemakers and bootmakers, 1,496; shoemakers' wives, 2,378; umbrella makers, 29; laundresses and 5,913, amongst numerous other home-worker occupations.

An old house, Modbury, painting by William Henry Pike RBA

CLOCK AND WATCHMAKER DIES.

William Paddon, a clock and watchmaker of 6, Church Street, died on the 12th of June 1863 aged seventy-one. The following year his wife Elizabeth put the business premises and part of their dwelling house up for sale. William's longcase clocks are still very collectable items today and occasionally come up for sale.

BURGLARY AT BROWNSTON STREET.

On the night of the 2nd of June 1867, George Atkins, a twenty-nine-year-old hatter broke into the house of Richard Ashley, a tanner of Brownston Street, and whilst Mr. Ashley was in bed asleep, Atkins crept into the room and stole a gold watch and two coats. Hearing a sound, Mr. Ashley awoke and challenged the thief and pinned him to the floor and with the use of some leather straps, bound the thieves' legs and arms so that he couldn't escape. Calling out he sent a family member to fetch the local constable who arrested the intruder. At his trial it was said Atkins had committed a number of previous offences and it was feared that he was one of a gang who had recently infested the county. He was sentenced to seven years' penal servitude.

Addressing Mr. Ashley, the judge said the mode in which he had carried out the capture of the burglar was very creditable to him.

ANNUAL MEETING AT MODBURY.

In early November 1867 the annual cattle show with its show of stock was held in the Barrack Field, then in the occupation of Mr. T. Mitchelmore. The show consisted of South Hams and other breeds of cattle, sheep, horses, and pigs. There was a supplementary contest for prizes offered for malting barley.

At four o'clock, two-hundred and fifty gentlemen sat down to dinner at the White Hart Hotel Assembly Rooms. Mr. S.T Kekewich Esq, M.P. acted as chairman. In the course of the proceedings Mr. Tucker, one of the judges, congratulated the gentlemen on continued prosperity of agriculture. They had had a good harvest. The year had been remarkable for its abundant pasturage and root crops, and the general health of their herds and flocks had been a cause great thankfulness; for not only had the rinderpest [*cattle plague*] disappeared, but other foreign and fatal diseases which for many years had devastated their stock, had under the cattle plague restrictions been entirely removed. It was true that the number of head of cattle destroyed in the country by rinderpest was enormous; but if they knew how many cattle had annually fallen victims to pleuro-pneumonia during the previous thirty years in the country, the number would be found to be nearly as frightful. In the year 1865 in Cornwall, many hundreds of cattle were destroyed by pleuro-pneumonia, and the farmer had borne the loss in silence. He had no doubt whatsoever that pleuro-pneumonia, like the rinderpest, instead of having a spontaneous origin in England, was the result of infection from diseased animals imported from abroad. [*Hear, hear! called the seated gentlemen.*] The state of their flocks had been satisfactory. He believed the year had given them additional proof of the great value of the recent discoveries in connection with the lamb disease and its prevention, for he never remembered so few dying of that disease. He had spoken to a friend who had found rape-seed beneficial in the treatment of the lamb disease.

Mr. Kekewich then gave a speech in which he mentioned the movement to abolish the turnpike tolls, something to which he was very much for. Out of the whole sum gathered from turnpike tolls he said, which amounted to more than a million pounds a year, much of it was paid out in the expenses of collection, in bills before Parliament, and in payment of the persons engaged in running the trusts. It was his opinion that if they got rid of the tolls, the ratepayers would manage the whole of the repairs the roads and that the highway board should administer funds for the repairs which would likely be cheaper than the present way in which it was run.

THE PLYMOUTH WITCH.

At Plymouth Guildhall on Monday the 9th of December 1867, Mary Catherine Murray, a respectably dressed woman aged around fifty, was charged with witchcraft. Five months previously, Mary, the sixty-one-year-old wife of Thomas Rendle of 28 Galpin Street, a farm labourer, had taken ill and was now paralysed. Telling his nephew who lived in Bigbury that his wife had been 'ill-wished' Mr. Rendle's nephew recommended that he visit Mrs. Murray in Plymouth, as she would be able to cure his wife. Thomas made his way on the 7th of August to the address he had been given; 18, William Street in Devonport. Answering the door Mrs. Murray queried as to why he had come, and Mr. Rendle said it was because people had told him that his wife had been ill-wished and he knew she could help him. Mrs. Murray invited him in and asked him a number of questions. She then took out a large book and after leafing through the pages said she could cure his wife in two or three weeks, provided he paid her one guinea to begin with, and that if his wife was not cured, she would reimburse him all the money for the herbs and services she was about to provide him with. She took down his address and Mr. Rendle quite satisfied left and returned to Modbury. A week later he received a letter from Mrs. Murray detailing some powders, potions, and articles she was going to send him, and also included an explanation as how and when they were to be used. But before she could put them together, she said she would need the money by return of post as she couldn't afford the outlay and she had to collect the items that week. Thomas Rendle duly sent the money she requested through his daughter-in-law Elizabeth, and received in return the items promised. His wife took the herbal mixtures with a glass of water every morning and evening and the packets of powder were burnt in the fire as directed. His wife though got no better and if anything grew worse.

About two months later Mrs. Murray came to Modbury to visit the Rendle's, and asking for a glass of water she looking into it and said she saw some shadows. At Mrs. Murray's bidding, Mary Rendle took up a poker and smashed the glass. Mrs. Murray then said she had seen a man and a woman in the water, and the woman was the worst; meaning that she felt this was who had ill-willed her. She then gave her a piece of parchment on which were drawings of the planets and extracts of writing in a strange language. This Mary Rendle was to wear about her person at all times. Mr. Rendle again paid Mrs. Murray for her services; a total of four pounds and ten shillings.

After going over the evidence, the Bench sent Mary Murray to prison for three months with hard labour for taking money under false pretences. Undeterred, Thomas Rendle, desperate to heal his wife, had already turned to another white witch/healer called Gribble who also said he could heal her, and if not would return all monies given. Mary Rendle passed away on the 26th April 1868.

ACCIDENT AT KINGSBRIDGE ROAD.

George Little, the engine-driver of a train who was dreadfully injured by scalding water at Kingsbridge Road Station on the 21st of March 1868, was too ill to be moved from the local area for a number of weeks and was attended to at a local hotel until early May when he was finally removed to his house in Red Cow village, Exeter. Although well enough to be removed he was still very ill, and had be conveyed from the railway carriage to his house on a stretcher.

Wishing to thank those who had helped him, Mr. Little wrote to the editor of the 'Western Times' on the 8th of May, asking if his letter could be published in the paper, thanking Mr. Cornish of Modbury for the medical attention he had received. Also Mrs. Crispin, the hotel-keeper at Kingsbridge Road, and the South Devon Railway Company, who kindly paid every attention to promote his recovery.

DWELLING HOUSES AND WORKSHOP FOR SALE.

On the 1st of July 1868 at four o'clock in the afternoon, No's: 13 and 14, Broad Street were auctioned at the White Hart Hotel by Mr. William Pearse, auctioneer. Immediately adjoining the Market Cross, the properties were described as being in the best situation in the town, containing a frontage of one-hundred and twenty feet and ample premises behind. The property at number 14 comprised on the ground floor of an excellent and roomy shop, counting-house, parlour, and kitchen. On the first and second floors were many rooms of good dimensions. The courtyard was said to cover about six poles of land and was complete with coal and other stores. It also had a smithy and a stable, and everything was adapted for carrying on a large wholesale and hardware business. The house at number 13 was conveniently arranged for a small family, and was then in the occupancy of Mrs. Elizabeth Pearse. The whole of the two premises was then in the tenancy of Mr. Edmund George Lakeman; ironmonger, stamp distributor and stationer. Viewings were available between the hours of ten a.m. and four p.m. Tuesdays and Fridays. Anyone requesting further particulars were to contact Mr. Richard Andrews, solicitor of Modbury.

Elizabeth Pearse, the widow of Thomas Pearse a cordwainer, continued to live at number 13, Broad Street and died on the 10th of April 1891, aged the old age of eighty-four.

FLETE HOUSE SOLD – OR NOT?

Many newspapers across the country printed the story of Flete House and estate, said to be one of the most desirable in the Kingdom, the ancestral seat of the Bulteel family, of whom Mr. John Bulteel of Pamflete was the then owner, had in March 1869 been sold to Lord Dorchester for one hundred and sixty thousand pounds. Lord Dorchester was said to have recently sold his Hampshire property 'Greywell Hill House' near Hook, and was looking forward to taking up his new residency. This was news to William F. Splatt Esq., who had been the exclusive owner of Flete House since 1864 and said he had no intention of parting with it. [*He did eventually sell the house in 1876 and moved to 'The Elms' Torre, Torquay.*]

ANTI-RITUALISTS OUTRAGE.

A sacrilegious outrage occurred in Modbury when at sometime between the morning and afternoon services on Sunday the 6th of September 1869, someone or some people, entered the church by the belfry door, all the others being closed, and proceeding to the altar where they tore down the floral decorations, removed many of the ornaments and carried away the altar cloth, candles and flowers. They then left by the same way they had entered, where the remains of the vases were found; evidently having been wilfully smashed. The damage was thought to have been carried out by 'anti-ritualists.' The perpetrators were never found.

MAINTENANCE PLEASE.

Thomas Luckcraft of the Kingsbridge Road Inn [*also known as the California Inn*], was summoned to court by Ellen Guest, of Loddiswell, to ask why he would not contribute towards the maintenance of her female illegitimate child which had been born the 17th June of that year. The Bench, without hearing the defence, dismissed the case saying there wasn't sufficient evidence to prove he was the father of the child.

SUDDEN DEATH.

On Thursday the 28th of October 1869, at sometime between six and seven in the evening, two agricultural labourers were returning home from their days work, when at Shilston they overtook an old man named John Walke, a sixty-seven-year-old sailor from Dartmouth. Having alighted at the Kingsbridge Road Station Walke was intent on walking to Modbury to visit his brother. He was seen to stagger and called out to the two men saying he didn't feel very well and asked if one of them would kindly carry his bundle for him. The men came to his aid, but within moments Mr. Walke said he felt a curious giddy sensation come over him. Taking his bundle, the trio set off at a slow pace. They had only got as far as Mary Cross turnpike gate on the Dartmouth road when John Walke suddenly collapsed into a hedge. In a panic one of the men ran to Mrs. Shepheard's house nearby to ask for a light, but before it could be procured his life had expired.

Postcard of Modbury, courtesy of Graham Ferguson.

BIRTHS...AND DEATHS.

Two babies, a boy and a girl were born less than twenty-four hours apart in Modbury in 1870. Twenty-nine-year-old Mary, the wife of Joseph Ralph a dividend and property agent of 29, Church Street, gave birth to her second child William on the 15th of February. Hours later, Sarah aged thirty-eight, the wife of Henry Meathrell a plumber and licenced victualler of the Dartmouth Inn at 9, Broad Street, gave birth to a daughter Alice – Sarah's eighth [*at least*] child on the 16th. Sadly, little Alice died on the 2nd of December that year. William didn't have a long life either. He was drowned at sea aged nineteen when he fell overboard from the Merchant Naval vessel on which he was serving, just off Cape Horn on the Chilean coast. Incredibly sadly the following year on March the 28th, Sarah and Henry Meathrell lost their second born daughter, Emma, who was just thirteen-years-old.

BABY BORN AT POUNDWELL HOUSE.

Richard C. Andrews, the second son and fifth child of Richard Andrews a solicitor, and his wife Elizabeth was born at their residence Poundwell House. The house had been the former residence of Henry Legassicke. The magistrates court had also been previously held there and had its own cells.

FIRE ON CHURCH STREET.

A dreadful fire occurred in early August 1870 at the premises of Mr. Joseph T, Foale, a draper of Church Street. The fire was discovered at eleven o'clock in the evening when the inhabitants; Mr. and Mrs. Foale, along with their three young children, Mr. Foale's mother, the Reverend Mr. Langdon (a Wesleyan minister) and Mr. Langdon's servant were just about to retire to bed. The fire spread rapidly and without difficulty through the shop and dwelling-house. They all managed to get out unharmed, though hadn't been able to save any of their belongings in their escape. A fire engine was soon on the scene, and with the help of neighbours were able to finally extinguish the flames, but not before the house had been completely destroyed along with its contents. A messenger was despatched to Ivybridge from where two engines were sent, but arrived too late to be of any help. The house was insured as was the drapery store goods. A meeting was held the following evening at the White Hart Hotel, and a subscription list opened to help the now destitute family. Records show that by the following year Joseph Foale had managed to secure a new premises at Broad Street.

ANOTHER OLDEST INHABITANT.

Richard Toms Esq., of 18, Church Street, a landed proprietor and one of the oldest inhabitants of the town, passed away aged ninety-two on the 2nd of September 1870. He was said to have had his full faculties right up till near to his passing.

THEFT FROM HER MASTER.

Seventeen-year-old Elizabeth Treeby, in January 1871, was convicted of having, on October the 27th 1870, stolen fourteen pounds belonging to Mr. Thomas Lakeman, her master. She pleaded guilty to having taken only five pounds and was sentenced to four months' imprisonment with hard labour at HM Prison Swansea.

AMY BALL.

Holbeton's oldest inhabitant, ninety-six-year-old Amy Ball died on the 31st of March 1871. Amy Harvey had married Thomas Ball at Holbeton is 1806. Thomas passed away in 1843 aged fifty-seven, and Amy had lived with her widowed daughter, seventy-three-year-old Sarah Penwill for the past twenty-four years. Previous to that she had lived with another daughter; Amy Nichols.

ATTACK BY HORSE.

At the Modbury Cattle Fair held on the 4th of May 1871, a carthorse called 'Young Oxford' who was being exhibited turned upon its owner, Mr. Hannaford of South Battisborough, who was leading the animal at the time and most viciously attacked him. It seized him by the arm, and raising him the air threw him violently to the ground and endeavoured to kneel upon his chest. It was said that the horse would undoubtedly have killed its owner had not bystanders rescued him in almost the nick of time. He was immediately attended to by Dr. Langworthy, who found Mr. Hannaford's arm to be badly lacerated and it was feared that amputation would likely have to be resorted to. Apparently, this wasn't the first time the horse had attacked his master.

THE LOST COW.

On Friday the 7th November 1871 a spotty cow, giving milk from three teats, and with a halfpenny in each ear as a mark, was reported missing near Modbury. A reward was offered for her recovery and anyone with information as to her whereabouts was asked to contact Mr. N.P. Oldrieve of 'Southwood House' near Dartmouth, or Charles Ferris of 'Dunstone,' Yealmpton.

SHOOTING COMPETITION AT FLETE.

On Wednesday the 3rd of April 1872, the members of the 3rd Devon (Modbury) Light Horse Volunteers, competed in a shooting competition at the range within the grounds of Flete House. That evening the prizes were distributed at the White Hart Assembly Rooms. The usual toasts were disposed of and a pleasant evening was spent eating, drinking, and dancing, as the town band was also in attendance.

The prizes handed out were as follows: A silver fruit knife and fork presented by Private J. H. Gills was won by Private Stevenson. A riding whip presented by Private Andrews was won by Private Stevenson. An electro-plated goblet presented by J. T. Savery, Esq., was won by Sergeant May. A bronze ink-stand presented by Mr. E. G. Lakeman was won by Bugler Watts. A riding whip given by Cornet player J. Hodder was won by Private Davis. He also presented a riding whip to Private Smerdon. A pearl tea caddy presented by Mr. N. Lakeman was won by Sergeant Gill. A travelling rug presented by Private Gee was won by Sergeant May - his second prize in the event. One pound and ten shillings was presented by John Bulteel Esq., to Corporal Codd. Richard Andrews Esq., presented Sergeant Gill with the same. James Bulteel Esq., then presented Private Stevenson with his ten-shillings prize.

THE STORMS.

On Tuesday the 17th and Wednesday the 18th of June 1872 the British Isles were battered by swathes of continuous and violent thunderstorms. In Newcastle-upon-Tyne five people were killed and four injured by lightning, whilst two people at least were carried away by floods in the streets. In Cheshire a child was washed out of its house and drowned, the other members of the family were rescued by men going into the property with ropes tied round their waists. A fisherwoman was struck by lightning and instantaneously killed whilst gathering bait on the Mussel Scalp, near Fisherrow Links in Scotland, and a mother and child were killed by lightning near Walsall in the West Midlands.

In the South West the storm lasted for twelve hours in Plymouth. From six o'clock on the Tuesday evening until the same hour on the Wednesday morning. A horse belonging to Mr. Batson a mail contractor, while carrying the London mail from the railway station to the post-office was killed by the lightning, and several minor casualties were reported. The Plymouth correspondent for the Pall Mall Gazette telegraphed London saying; "During the terrific thunderstorm on Wednesday at Plymouth, over inch of rain fell in less than an hour. Some curious incidents are recorded from country districts. At Malborough near Kingsbridge, the lightning struck a thatched cottage which it set on fire and caused the occupant to become paralysed. The electric fluid descended the chimney, entered the bedroom, and shook a wooden bedstead to splinters. It then ran through the kitchen obtaining egress through the back door where it killed a pig. The chimney of the dwelling-house of Mr. Moule at Newton Abbot was very much damaged by the lightning and a candlestick standing upon the bedroom table was hurled with great force across the room. Considerable damage was done to the telegraph wires. At Modbury post-office, the telegraph instrument was smashed to pieces with a noise similar to the explosion of a gun. Telegraphic communication between Kingsbridge and Prawle is still impeded. No such storm has been known in the west for many years."

EXTRAORDINARY LONGEVITY IN KINGSTON.

In January 1873 it was reported that there were twelve people, of whom two were married, five widows, and three widowers, whose combined ages came to nine hundred and seventy years. The average age being eighty-one. The eldest was eighty-seven and the youngest being seventy-six. There were also several residents over the age of seventy who were still active and attending to their work daily.

POOR HORSE.

A strange accident befell a horse belonging to Mr. John Crocker a farmer of Modbury, in late August 1873. The animal had been kept in Barrack Field and next to it were some houses.

Underneath one of the properties was a cellar which was entered from the ground outside; the ingress which was covered by a wooden board. The horse happened to step on the board, which unfortunately gave way under the weight and the poor animal was precipitated into the cellar below. When it was eventually found, after having been noticed missing from the field, it was thankfully only slightly injured despite the traumatic experience.

The report doesn't say how the poor animal was extricated – most probably by ropes and pulleys and lots of manual labour. The board had likely weakened due to the terrible rains that Devon had been experiencing that month, as the article also went on to state that much of the corn crops had been lost and that which had been saved was likely to have been spoilt. The inclement weather was forecast to continue in the coming days and hundreds of acres of crops would more than likely be ruined. Some farmers had lost nearly all of their corn, and portions of which had been saved were turning quite black.

GOING TO AMERICA.

William Bunker, a farm labourer, along with his wife and several of his children, like many others at that period in time looked towards making a new life in America. In 1873 the family upped sticks and sailed to America where they made their way to Cleveland, Ohio, and then on to Kansas in 1878 where they made their home. Sons Mark and Matthew decided to stay in England. Mark who is mentioned later on in this book, was then serving in the Royal Navy. Matthew Bunker went on to become a Baptist minister as well as running a drapery business in Modbury.

Between 1870 and 1900, twelve million immigrants, mainly from England, Ireland and Germany travelled to America in search of a better life; fleeing from job and land shortages, crop failures, rising taxes, and political and religious persecution.

ATTEMPTED ROBBERY.

A daring robbery took place on the night of the 7th of May 1873 at Whympston House, the residence of Mr. Nicholas Pitts Esq., He, his wife, and daughter, were spending the evening in Modbury and only the servants were home. A sound was heard coming from one of the unoccupied rooms and so a search of the property was made. On entering the drawing-room, a man was seen making his escape from the window. The alarm was raised and Mr. Pitts and P.C. Cornish were both sent for. They soon arrived at the property but no trace of the intruder could be found. It was supposed that the thief or thieves had entered the drawing-room through the same window they exited, and had been in the property for some time before being discovered. The annual fair had been held in the town that day and several suspicious characters had been seen loitering in the neighbourhood.

THE UN-NAMED ECCENTRIC.

In May 1874, two hoax fire alarms were raised in Modbury causing great excitement as a consequence. The perpetrator was said to be a man whose recent eccentricities had caused great anxiety to his friends. His last irrational act was to leave the town on a donkey cart and not return. A search over a wide area was made, but by the following day he had still not been found.

BITTEN BY A DOG AT AVETON GIFFORD.

In September 1874, the Western Times reported that a man named Hingston was drinking in a public house at Aveton Gifford. Also present was the landlord of the Bell Inn at Modbury who was accompanied by his bulldog. A fight ensued between the two men and Hingston was knocked down. Getting to his feet he received another blow with the same result. The dog which had been earnestly watching the fight now sprang upon his master's foe, and seizing him by the leg kept him on the ground where he held on to Higston's leg tearing at the flesh. Determined to defend his master it was with great difficulty that he was forced to loosen his fangs. Kingston was so badly bitten that he was confined to his bed and had to apply to the Kingsbridge Board of Guardians for relief. Legal proceedings were said to be taken against the Modbury landlord.

A week later the newspaper printed an apology to the landlord of the Bell Inn, having erroneously named him as the owner of the dog who attacked Mr. Hingston.

SAVAGERY AT KINGSTON.

During the night of Saturday the 5th of December 1874, an intruder entered the stable of Mrs. Ann Goss near Kingston. They turned one of her horses out onto the road and stabbed the other deeply in the throat. The following morning when Mrs. Goss's son went attend to the animals he found one having nearly bled to death and the other missing. Mr. Richard Fox, a farrier, was hastily on the scene and attended to and dressed the wound but gave little hope of the poor animal's recovery. In his opinion he said that it was someone who knew what they were doing as the wound was about inch from the jugular vein. It was likely that the miscreant felt for the vein, but it being dark he missed his aim. The horse was said to have been the best on the farm.

SORROW AT SEA.

Through a telegram received in early January 1875, news reached Modbury that the 'Transvaal' a wooden barque cargo ship on her maiden voyage from London, having left in December 1874, had been wrecked. She had dragged her anchor and having become stranded was driven ashore south of the Umgeni River in South Africa. All hands onboard were lost except the captain who happened to be on shore carrying out business. Twenty-four-year-old William Dobell, the eldest son of Mr. William Dobell, a solicitor's managing clerk of Traine, was a midshipman onboard the vessel.

MURDEROUS ASSAULT NEAR MODBURY.

John Robert Ward, a thirty-year-old farm labourer, was brutally kicked to death at Brownston

Cross on the night of Sunday the 30th of July 1876. The inquest into his death was held the following day by the coroner Mr. Mitchelmore at Mr. Tribble's farmhouse at Lupbridge, where John Ward had been employed. Mr. Davies of Kingsbridge appeared on behalf of the police authorities, and Mr. Nepean of Ugborough watched the proceedings on behalf of the accused attacker; Robert Cocker.

Around eight months previously the two men had a petty quarrel at the Kingsbridge Road Inn, where nineteen-year-old Cocker had accused Ward of calling him a liar. He challenged Ward to a fight, but was told by others who were with him to sit down and be quiet, and that appeared to be the end of the spat. On Sunday the 30th of July, Ward stopped off at the Kingsbridge Road Inn again, better known locally as the 'California Inn,' and bought a pint of beer which he took outside and sat drinking with friends. A short while later,

Cocker, who happened to be at the inn saw Ward sitting outside, and going over to him and again offered him to a fight saying, "Ain't you the man I owe a grudge?" Ward responded by saying, "Why, you don't want bring that up now do you?" Cocker replied, "I'll give you a punch in the head." To which Ward retorted, "I'm not going to fall out with you tonight because of my clothes." meaning his Sunday best clothes. Un-deterred Cocker took off his jacket and hat and struck Ward with one fist to the chest and with the other punched him in the face, felling him to the ground. Whilst John Ward was lying on the roadway, Cocker began to kick him as hard as he could with his large hob-nailed boots. Ward managed to pull himself onto his knees and it was at this point one of the young men with whom he had been talking to; Charles Clark, took fright and went inside the inn but failed to tell anyone what had happened. Cocker continued his vicious assault on Ward leaving him for dead. The other friend and only other witness to the assault; Richard Matthews, at this point ran away. Cocker pursued him for a short distance before returning to his original victim and kicked Ward's dead body several times more before returning to the inn where he boasted to all who could hear him that he had "murdered the b_____."

At The inquest, Elias Andrews, a thirty-two-year-old farm labourer residing at Lupbridge, with whose family the victim lived with, said the last time he had seen John Ward alive was on the Sunday night at about nine o'clock at Brownston Cross. Ward was standing outside of the California inn with George Soper, Charles Clarke, and Richard Matthews. They each had a pint of beer in their hand. Ward called out to him and he came over and joined them, but stayed only a few minutes before proceeding on his way. About half-an-hour later he returned to Brownston Cross and saw Ward lying by the side of the road, seemingly dead. He obtained a horse and cart and conveyed the body back to his house. He said no-one was near Ward when he arrived back at the inn, but he noticed several men who were some distance away talking together. He asked them to help in assisting him to load his friend's body onto the cart.

Hannah Edwards, the wife of Edward Edwards, a farmer residing at Beerscombe Farm, Modbury, said that the deceased was her brother. He had been at her house on the Sunday and stayed for both dinner and tea. He arrived about eleven o'clock in the morning, and at half-past five she, her husband, and her two children left with him to go to Chapel. Her brother didn't attend Chapel but when they came out after the service, she saw him coming down Brownston Lane near the Cross. They all then went to the California Inn where another of her brother's, George, ordered a pint beer and between them they drank it. John then called for another pint of beer which again they shared. After having some conversation, she and her family set off for home.

Robert Cocker had been arrested at Fowelscombe Gate, Ugborough in the early hours of the Monday morning. When he later gave a statement to the police, he said that it was Ward and his friends who had challenged him in regards to the previous quarrel and that one of them hit him in the face and then caught him by the waistcoat. The other friend tore his shirt and the now deceased Ward had kicked him on the leg. He said that one of the men then ran into the public house and it was at that point he left and walked home with his brother.

Mr. Philip Alfred Cornish from Modbury, the surgeon who carried out the post mortem on John Ward found great extravasation of blood in the pancreas caused no doubt by a heavy blow. All the organs he said were healthy, but in the heart the aortic valve was almost closed with ossific deposit, the result of rheumatic disease. He considered that death had resulted from a blow causing such a shock to the system as to stop the action of the heart. The disease was not sufficient to account for death without the blow.

At his trial on the 13th of December 1876, Robert Cocker was acquitted of murder but found guilty of manslaughter and sentenced to twenty-years in prison. The jury, in addition to their verdict, said they could not separate without expressing their indignation that any Englishmen, like Clarke and Matthews, should have run away when such a brutal attack was being made upon an inoffensive man. The judge agreed with the jury and said that these men deserved the reprobation of all Englishmen, and he could only hope that if ever they were implicated in such an affair again, they would show more manliness and not run away and leave a poor man, as they did, to be the victim of the brutal attack made upon him.

A CHRISTMAS GHOST.

On the morning of the 21st of December 1876, whilst the choir was engaged in practising for the Christmas services at St. James the Less Church in Kingston, the main door suddenly opened and through the dimly light church a figure draped in white slowly made its way down the aisle and mounted the pulpit. No one dared challenge the apparition which stayed silent before slowly retracing its steps and vanishing through the same door from which it had entered.

The terrified choir fled in horror at witnessing the ghostly spectre. Some later said they thought they recognised the features of the ghost, of those of a deceased popular former minister of the church. The following day at least one member of the choir required medical assistance due to the shock of the sighting.

AN EXTRAORDINARY HARE HUNT.

A hunt was started at the Mary Cross turnpike gate, half a mile from the town in the midst of very hilly countryside on Tuesday the 9th of January 1877. At eleven o'clock there mustered an array of farmers and gentlemen of the neighbourhood. The sport did not start well; a hare was soon found, but was lost again after a short run near Shilston Farm. Then word was sent round that another hare was sitting in a hedge near the brook which runs through the valley. She was soon started, and ran towards Mr Rowells farm at Spriddlescombe. She then turned upwards, and ran over the hills towards Ugborough as far as Dunswell and back towards where she was first sighted. She then set off over the fields of Sheepham near the top of the hill, giving those who preferred it an opportunity of riding a long gallop along the ridge road, with the hounds alongside them. At last, on reaching Crown Hill Cross, she took to the road and raced down the hill towards Modbury, across Sheepham Bridge. Here she turned to the right and went up the hill and ran round the old barracks. From there she crossed the road and made for the garden at the back of a house in Brownston Street. Here she tried to find a little rest after such a long run, amongst the cabbages in Dr. Roger's garden. Being dislodged, she ran behind the house at Mr. Coyte's orchard and garden. Here again she tried to hide among the greens. By this time the inhabitants of the town were called out onto the streets by the noise and excitement. Ladies and gentlemen, rich and poor, old and young, were all hurrying to see what was the matter. "I see her! I shall have her," exclaimed a very stout old gentleman who plunged forward to grab her. But she was too alert, and his own portly front was the only thing to suffer, as he rose from the soil with rueful expression and muddy clothes amidst roars of laughter. The same fate awaited a shoemaker, who thought himself more active. The hare, thinking it quite time to be gone, rushed through Mr Coyte's coal-house, jumped a six-foot wall, went through the house and out the front into the open street.

Such a scene – with hare, hounds, horsemen and footmen, all racing down the steep hill towards the market place. Just before reaching the bottom of the hill the hare shot off to the left and ran under Mr. Webber's archway and through a very narrow' passage into the gardens at the back of Broad Street. Mr. Nicholas Lakeman was sitting in his parlour at the back of his house, and hearing the commotion opened the window to see what was the matter. As he did so the hare tried to jump in, but being too exhausted fell backwards to the ground. However, some of the hounds thinking the hare had jumped through the window followed suit, and after running wildly round the room, knocking over furniture and causing quite a mess, jumped back through where they had entered. The hare having had a slight reprieve, crossed Bakehouse Lane where she entered Mr. Hopkins's garden and jumped against a young lad who happened to be standing there. The collision made the lad fall, but he caught the hare and killed it with his bare hands.

FATAL FALL DOWNSTAIRS.

John Walke, a wheelwright aged fifty-five, died after falling down the stairs at his home in Church Street. The previous evening, the 22nd of May 1877, he had attended a public dinner and returned home at about midnight. He was put to bed very much the worse for drink and the following morning was found lying at the foot of the stairs. Mr. Langworthy, the local surgeon was called and found Walke to be quite dead. He had a contused wound on the left side of his cheek and another over the eyebrow. There were several other bruises and marks elsewhere about the body. His death was recorded as 'accidental,' likely having tumbled down the stairs in a drunken stupor.

John Walke was the cousin of John Walke who died at the roadside near Shilston in 1869. Both are buried in St. George's Churchyard, Modbury.

RICHARD CUMMINGS.

On Friday the 10th August 1877, Mr. John White of Okenbury Farm, was travelling home from a sale when he was brought to a sudden halt by the sight of a youth stretched out on the roadway with his faithful dogs sitting by his side guarding him. Attentive to their master, it proved quite difficult to quieten the animals so that he could see to the youth who he recognised as Richard, the son of Mr. G. Cumming, of Cumery Farm, Bigbury. Richard was eventually lifted into the trap and brought to Modbury for medical assistance. He was then placed in lodgings with one of Mr. White's labourers overnight and was removed to his home next day where he lay in a very precarious state. Richard was unconscious when found, and had been in a semi-conscious state ever since and unable to explain how the accident had occurred. He had been riding his horse at the time, and it was supposed the horse had been spooked, and Richard losing control of the frightened animal had fallen with the horse landing on top of him, because when it arrived home alone, the animal was said to be badly bruised on the right-hand side, as was Richard and his dogs.

MODBURY CHRISTMAS CATTLE SHOW.

The annual sale of cattle and sheep held under the auspices of the Modbury Fat Stock Society, was held on the 10th of December 1877 and was said to be the most successful sale that had taken place since the society's formation. There was an excellent show of fat stock and a large amount of business was done during the day. It had been hoped that Sir. Massey Lopes M.P. and Mr. Carpenter-Garnier would been present to represent the county of Devon, however, they were unfortunately prevented from attending and the proceedings were thus deprived of much of their importance.

Prizes were awarded as follows:

Cows – First prize to Mr. F. Coaker of Stokenham, second to Mr. John Wroth of Coombe, third to Mr. William Pearse of Stoliford, fourth to Mr. John Luscombe of Coarsewell, Ugborough.
Steers - All four prizes were awarded to Mr. John Wroth of Coombe.
Sheep (Wethers) – First prize to Mr. W. S. Wroth of Folly, Bigbury, second to Mr. May of Ermington, third to Mr. Wroth of Lapthorn.
Wether Hoggets – First to Mr. James Adams of Stodbury, Aveton Gifford, second to Mr. W. S. Wroth of Folly.

In the afternoon the annual dinner of the society was held at the White Hart Hotel where over one hundred people sat down to a hearty meal, presided over by Mr. Thomas Pitts junior of Plymouth. In proposing 'success to the society,' he made reference to the supply of food to the people, remarking that in spite of all the efforts that had been made to prevent the spread of cattle disease and in other ways to increase the quantity of animal food, recent statistics showed that the number of cattle had significantly decreased during the past year. He said they couldn't disguise the fact that they had on the other side of the Atlantic, a formidable competitor so far as to the supply of meat to the country was concerned, and therefore it was down to the agriculturists of England, and the consumers as well, to encourage in every possible way the increase in animal food for the country. Several other speakers who followed spoke strongly against the prevailing system of pampering animals for years for the mere sake of winning prizes, and declared that some of the cattle exhibited in the county shows created a feeling of disgust amongst practical farmers due to the over-fattened condition to which they were brought.

JAMES DAVIS – LICENSED VICTUALLER.

James S. Davis, the fifty-seven-year-old proprietor of the White Hart Hotel died in June 1880. He had been running the business on and off since at least 1861. Although in 1871 the census showed another gentleman, Mr. Gard, was the then landlord of the inn and James was a farmer of twenty-five acres. Possibly he returned to running the inn sometime later that decade. His wife Elizabeth continued to run the White Hart for a further number of years.

There appears to be another hotel called 'Davis's Hotel' or sometimes referred to as Mr. Davis's Hotel in Modbury, at 7/8 and possibly 9, Broad Street. Elizabeth was definitely running this hotel in 1884 and in 1891. In 1900 William Rowland had recently acquired the business and described it as having a spacious function room, private rooms and stabling. Davis's Hotel appeared to be in business between the 1877 and well into the 20th century. In 1911 the hotel had changed its name to the Great Western Hotel. It had fourteen rooms and was run by Mr. Harry Dennis. It was still in business under that name in the 1930's.

WHIPPED AND SENT TO A REFORMATORY.

William Jones alias William Parkley, a thirteen-year-old boy sailor, pleaded guilty to stealing a pair of boots and a cap, the property of Charles Roker, on the 14th March 1878, at Modbury. William was sentenced to be imprisoned for one month, then to be privately whipped once, and receive twenty strokes with a birch rod. After which he was to be detained in a reformatory school for five years.

SIR WILLIAM MITCHELL.

Sir. William Mitchell, journalist, editor, and proprietor of the 'Shipping and Mercantile Gazette' died on the 1st of May 1878 at his home Strode House, after a short illness. Sir William was born in Modbury in 1811 and moved to London at a young age to pursue a career in journalism. He first worked for the 'True Sun' newspaper before beginning a long career in 1836 with the 'Shipping and Mercantile Gazette.' He was said to have been instrumental in causing the adoption of what became 'the international code of signals for all nations' – which has since 1855 been used by the principal maritime states. For this and other services to maritime commerce he was knighted by patent in 1867. There is a memorial to Sir William inside of St George's Church.

THE SUDDEN DEATH OF JOHN FERRIS.

John Ferris a fifty-year-old carpenter, died suddenly on Wednesday the 19th of January 1881. He had been engaged earlier that morning assisting in the killing of a pig. After this was done, he went home and immediately exclaimed to his wife; "Oh, my side!" and sinking into a kneeling position, he expired. His death was thought to have been caused by heart disease and spasms, from which he had recently been suffering. He left behind a widow and four children to mourn his sudden passing.

FOOT AND MOUTH DISEASE.

There were four fresh outbreaks of foot-and-mouth disease reported in Modbury in August 1881, two in pigs and two in cattle. By mid-September eighteen cattle at Modbury were suffering from the disease and eight at Kingston. Other farms across the country were suffering too, often with much larger numbers. Early October saw nine cattle at Modbury and seven at Kingston with the disease. Also, fifty-one sheep at Kingston. At Holbeton two sheep were suffering from scab.

ROBBERY BY A WAITRESS.

Ellen Rogers a married woman in her early-fifties and working as a waitress at the Modbury Inn, was charged before the Yealmpton magistrates in January 1883 with stealing sixteen pounds from Richard Atwill, a seventy-one-year-old farmer of Ermington. Atwill had entered the inn on the 8th of January at about quarter to eleven in the evening and called for some liquor. In payment he gave Mrs. Rogers a sovereign, and in his change, he received a half sovereign and some silver. He put the half sovereign in a bag which already had in it two five-pound notes and some gold. The silver he put in his waistcoat pocket. The bag containing the notes he then put in his trouser pocket.

Postcard of the Modbury Inn on Brownston Street, courtesy of Pam Wilson.

As he was leaving, Ellen Rogers came up to Mr. Atwill and linking arms with him she chatted as she walked him to the door. Outside, putting his hand into his pocket he found the bag of money to be missing. He went back inside the inn and told the landlady that he thought Mrs. Rogers had taken his money. Ellen had by now left the premise and returned to her own house nearby. She was immediately sent for and told to return to the inn. When the accusation was put to her that she had taken the money, she vehemently denied it and in consequence P.C. Dunsford was called to attend the scene of the alleged theft. John Blight, who had also been drinking at the inn saw the exchange of money at the bar, and thinking that Mr. Atwill may have been mistaken through intoxication, made a search of his clothing in front of Ellen Rogers and P.C. Dunsford, but no money was found. Ellen was then taken into custody. It was at this point she made a confession and said that she had taken the money and it was in her house. P.C. Dunsford escorted her to her home where she handed him the bag of money that she had hidden under an old cushion on an armchair. She professed to having found the money where Mr. Atwill had been sitting and had only taken it home with her to look after until she could return it. Brought before the magistrates, the Bench didn't believe Ellen's excuse as she had previously been convicted of stealing a bottle of rum in 1879, and had been sentenced to one month in prison with hard labour. However, they were prepared to give her another chance and leniently gave her a lighter sentence than they normally would have. She was sent to prison for two months with hard labour.

What they were possibly unaware of at the time was that Ellen was rather a habitual offender. In January 1883 she had been imprisoned for stealing sixteen pounds and was sentenced to two months imprisonment with hard labour. In June of the same year, she was imprisoned for a further three months, again with hard labour for stealing one pound. Not having learned her lesson, Ellen was within weeks of her release again brought before the Bench, this time for having stolen one pound at Woodbury. She was sentenced to three months in prison, again with hard labour. In 1887 she stole money from the till of Samuel Wyatt at the Modbury Inn [see: **THEFT FROM THE MODBURY INN]** and then in 1888 she was again sent to prison, this time for twelve calendar months, for stealing costume cloth, six lengths of Russel cord, two and a half lengths of cashmere, and some three lengths of French merino wool from Elizabeth Little.

THREE BROTHERS CHARGED.

Three brothers; John, William, and Andrew Rogers, all farmers of Heath Farm, Aveton Gifford, were charged at Modbury in December 1883 with having cut off and sold the manes and tails of a number of horses and colts belonging to Mrs. Pearse of Chantry, and Mr. John Baker of Ashford Mills, Aveton Gifford. Enough evidence was given to justify remanding them until the 31st of the month, but was forestalled on condition they paid ten pounds bail money each and their father thirty-pounds.

There doesn't appear to be any further action taken against the brothers – maybe they weren't the guilty parties after all?

THE DANGERS OF BENZOLINE.

Henry Pearce a seventy-seven-year-old gardener of 36, Brownston Street was sitting by the side of his fire at about ten in the evening of the 5th of February 1884 with his wife Emma alongside him. He poured some benzoline into a small lamp, when it exploded and caught both himself and his wife alight. Hearing their screams, a neighbour, Mrs. Barns, rushed in and put the fire out, but his poor wife was severely burnt, and lingered until the 16th when she died.

TOTAL ABSTENINCE SOCIETY.

Mr. Tom Horrocks, known as the 'Converted Clown,' visited Modbury in April 1884 and gave a speech at the Gospel Temperance Mission lecture hall in Galpin Street, which was well attended. Mr. Horrocks appeared to generate a great impression on his attentive audience when he spoke of the many amusing adventures he had before becoming a total abstainer, and

described in detail the effect drinking alcohol had at times made upon him – sometimes pathetic and other times entertaining. He also spoke of the absurdity of some of the numerous drinking customs in our country. Twenty-five people in the audience were moved enough to signed the pledge. Hopes were expressed that at some future date, Mr. Horrocks would again visit Modbury.

Tom Horrocks spent many years travelling the breadth of the country giving talks on abstaining from alcohol. He died in Blackpool aged seventy-four on the 19th of October 1908.

THE EXTRAORDINARY DEATH OF LAURA DIMES.

Hugh Shortland, who had recently returned to England from New Zealand where he had been practising as a barrister, was apprehended at Modbury in May 1884 charged with having murdered his recently betrothed wife; Laura Dimes. Miss. Dimes was the twenty-two-year-old daughter of William and Martha Dimes of Oldstone House at Blackawton near Totnes, and had married Mr. Shortland a month previously on the 8th of April at the Registrar's Office in Kingsbridge. After the ceremony Laura returned to Olsdtone House where her husband visited her, but they did not cohabit. Two days later on the 10th of April, Hugh Shortland unexpectedly told his wife that he had to return to New Zealand and would return to England as soon as possible.

On Monday the 28th of April, the new Mrs. Shortland who was still residing with her parents at Oldstone House went out for a ride on her horse at ten o'clock in the morning and returned two hours later. She then changed from her riding habit into a walking dress and went out again without saying where she was going. When she didn't return home that evening no alarm was raised as it was known that Mr. Shortland was said to be still residing in the area prior to his departure to New Zealand, and it was thought the couple may have gone away for the night to say goodbye to each other.

The following morning Mrs. Elizabeth Luckraft, the wife of Mr. Dimes land agent, went in search of the missing woman, having her suspicions that something was amiss, and in a pond in the grounds of the property, she was horrified to discover the body of the unfortunate young woman standing upright in the water and about three feet from the edge; her hands held up in front of her and the water covering her hat by an inch or two. She at once called to her husband and a man who was nearby named Langworthy, who helped drag the body from the water.

Laura's body was examined by Police Sergeant Mills of Blackawton and also by Mr. R. W. Soper a surgeon of Dartmouth. Both men agreed that the deceased's clothing showed no indications of a struggle having taken place. A close scrutiny of the path around the wall of the pond also failed to detect any traces of a scuffle. The only marks of violence on her body were slight scratches on the left temple and on the right tip of her nose. These the surgeon thought might have been caused by contact with the wall of the pond. His theory was that Laura possibly fainted when standing near the edge and had fallen in. He said he could not say positively that death had been caused by drowning as the body had been too long in the water, but by appearances it was consistent with the theory that Laura Shortland was still alive at the time of immersion. An inquest into her death was held and a verdict of 'found drowned' was returned.

The same morning as her body having been discovered, a letter addressed to the newly-wed Mrs. Shortland was received at Oldstone House purporting to come from her husband who was at the time of writing allegedly in Brindisi, Italy. It said, "I am hurrying on at the fastest rate and shall soon be home again." The envelope bore a Plymouth postmark, but this was explained by Mr. Shortland who said he was enclosing the letter with some other documents to his solicitors in Plymouth and had asked those gentlemen to post it on to Oldstone. It later transpired that this was simply a ruse and that Mr. Shortland had not left England at all but had all the time been within a few miles from his wife's home. His later arrest along with a man named William Ryder; also known as 'Modbury Bill,' who was suspected of being associated with him in the crime, caused considerable excitement throughout the whole district.

At Kingsbridge Magistrates Court on Wednesday the 7th of May 1884, Mr. Hugh Shortland was charged with the wilful murder his wife Laura Shortland. The Superintendent of Police said that when the inquest into her death had been held, two letters had been produced; one of them was in the prisoner's handwriting which had arrived at Oldstone on the morning Laura's body was found in the pond. It stated that he was then at Brindisi on his way to Australia, and that his wife might next expect to hear from him from Sydney where his father Dr. Shortland was in practice. The officer said that on information he'd received, he went that morning to Back Street Cottage, the home of a labourer named William Ryder, and there found Mr. Shortland, where he had been staying since the 10th of April. It was said to be common knowledge that whenever Hugh Shortland visited Modbury rather than stay in one of the respectable hotels there, he would lodge with his friend William Ryder who lived near to a tannery where he worked. He went on to say that a witness had seen Hugh Shortland walking through some fields early in the morning of the day his wife's body was found. He also alleged that the letter supposedly sent from Brindisi, had been written in Ryder's house and that William Ryder had sent his son to Plymouth to post it. William Ryder, whom Shortland sometimes called his clerk, and sometimes his solicitor, had been driven handcuffed from Modbury to Kingsbridge in the custody of the police. He was then brought before Mr. Herbert the magistrate and charged with being an accessory both before and after the murder of Mrs. Shortland by having an awareness and been complicit in the posting of the fictitious letters.

Constable Dunford stated that on May the 4th he had interviewed William Ryder at his house in Modbury, where it was later found that Shortland had been hiding. Ryder told him that Mr. Shortland had gone to New Zealand via Brindisi, and that he'd received a letter from him addressed from the latter place. He further stated that the postmarks on the envelopes were Brindisi, London, and Plymouth. The constable also said that after the inquest into Mrs. Shortland's death he had shown a report from a newspaper to Ryder, who said he knew all about it and appeared rather distressed. When asked, William Ryder said he had no questions to ask the policeman; but he then commenced to make a statement where he admitted that he had told the officer a lie when saying that there was a Brindisi postmark on the letter. Police Superintendent Dore applied for a remand, but the magistrates decided that although Ryder had placed himself in a questionable position with regards to the letter there was not sufficient evidence to justify remanding him. The decision was received with loud applause and the prisoner was discharged.

On the 1st of June 1884 before the Kingsbridge magistrates, Hugh Shortland was again brought before the Bench and charged with the murder of his wife, but where surprisingly the Treasury solicitor stated that after an exhaustive analysis, they were of the opinion that there was no evidence Mr. Shortland had been involved in her death and therefore he would withdraw from the case. The Bench said they had no knowledge of any letters [*produced at the original hearing but had been handed over to the Treasury by the police*] and therefore could give no evidence. Hugh Shortland was a free man.

Aware of the suspicions and accusations made against him, Hugh Shortland went on to afterwards express his views as to the domestic arrangements at Oldstone, and stated that in his opinion, his wife was treated in an unnatural manner after her body was found. He said he fully appreciated the principal cause of suspicion against him was that he remained in concealment after his wife's body was discovered, and he had become aware of the fact of her death. Furthermore, he acknowledged that his intention of proceeding to New Zealand so soon after the marriage would appear strange. He said he had a double motive for lying in concealment for the two to three weeks before his planned departure. In the first place, when he left Oldstone, he told his wife that he had made arrangements for staying away for that period of time as he was concerned as to how her father would treat her after he had left due to their 'sudden' marriage. His second reason was that he had doubts as to how his new wife would be able to stand his absence. He stayed at William Ryder's cottage because Ryder was acquainted with both his and her families, having been employed as a servant to the Savery's [family solicitors.] He said he first heard of the death of his wife when a newspaper was given to Mrs. Ryder by Mrs. Wakeham, a woman living in the same lane. Mrs. Ryder he said was perfectly stunned when she heard the news. Mrs. Wakeham had said, "Here, don't faint Mrs. Ryder." Mrs. Ryder had given him the paper immediately after reading the news, saying; "I have very sad news for you. Mrs. Shortland has been drowned." When he read the article, he assumed it had been an accident. Then the Ryder's eldest son returned from buying some wood and said he had also heard of the death of Mrs. Shortland from a person called Luckraft.

Apparently forty-eight hours before his arrest, Shortland had sent the Ryder's younger son into Plymouth to purchase flowers to put upon his wife's grave, and to consult with a lawyer who he wanted to come and speak with him in Modbury. At that time, he [Shortland] anticipated as a lawyer himself, that from the simple fact of the Brindisi letter, he had exposed himself to suspicion and would be arrested. He told the lawyer that he recognised that one of the principal questions arising against him was why he hadn't attended the inquest on his wife and to the subsequent funeral? He knew that the two things he had done - remaining in concealment and writing a letter purporting to come from Brindisi, constituted a *prima facie* case of murder against him. He also alleged that in letters he had received from his wife [*presumably sent to the Ryder's address, but never shown to the courts*] he considered that his wife may have committed suicide. The general tone of them being despondent, she allegedly said she was very depressed and unhappy; in which she said "You are my own good angel darling Hugh. If there were no Hugh, I really think I should die." He said the reason they had not co-habited was because there was the desire that nothing should occur during his absence from England which would cast suspicion upon the virtue of his wife or that the marriage really had taken place. Subsequently however, he heard through his wife that her parents were not angry at all that they had wed in secret and all was well at home.

In September that year, Hugh Shortland sailed to a new life in New Zealand.

A follow-on strange tale…This is an abridged version of an article that appeared in the Totnes Weekly Times in November 1891.

In the spring of 1884, I met Hugh Rutherford Shortland for the first time. He had suddenly made his appearance in the neighbourhood of Modbury, where he created much discussion about the schemes he was supposed to be promoting, no less than by his eccentric manner which led me to doubt his sanity. It was in connection with these plans and projects that I came into contact with Shortland. He was anxious to secure the support of the press, but it was very difficult to take his proposals seriously. He wanted to form one company to run a tram line from Plymouth to Modbury, and to form another for the purchase of land to raise and grow meat and cereals for Australia. Whilst he was actively engaged in making speeches and writing letters on these subjects, and generally advertising himself freely and as cheaply as possible, Shortland was no less busy in affairs of gallantry, with the too obvious object of capturing an heiress. His family was one the best in the district. His father had emigrated to New Zealand many years before, but the Shortland's were so well-known throughout the South Hams that Hugh had no difficulty in securing access to the society of the county. He soon commenced a policy of pursuing eligible young ladies with good financial prospects. In one case, as admitted to me afterwards, the friends of one such lady sought the protection of a ward of Chancery appeal to the Lord Chancellor; Shortland was not easily discouraged.

He came to know in the manner that will be described hereafter Miss. Laura Dimes, the pleasant but guileless daughter of a county gentleman who lived at Oldstone near Blackawton. It was difficult to understand how Miss. Dimes fell as to the wiles even of Shortland. He was not a fine or attractive man in any sense. He was gentlemanly in demeanour but was lean favoured with a sharp face and shrewd expression, strongly flavoured with cunning. He was very far from being the Adonis with whom an impressionable young lady might fall distractedly in love with at first sight.

A visit to Oldstone House for which I made later accounted for much that was otherwise inexplicable. An olde-worlde mansion to which admission could only be gained after heavy locks and bars had been removed. Then there was a large quadrangle to be passed, and after that, more locks and bars which admitted one to a hall, dingy in itself and rendered gloomier by its armour and antler-clad walls. It was here that Miss. Dimes had lived with her aged father and mother and a still more aged housekeeper, receiving no visitors and visiting no one. Miss Dimes was possessed of property in her own right and Shortland prevailed upon her to accompany him one day to Kingsbridge. Here they married at the registry office. Miss. Dimes returned to her home and Shortland went back to his lodgings in Modbury. He next caused it to be given out that he was about to leave the country to develop his plans in New Zealand, and simultaneously the body of his young bride was found drowned in a pond in the grounds around Oldstone House. Her body was buried without internal examination. Later it was exhumed on the order of the Home Secretary after it was discovered that a letter in her possession which her husband had purported to have despatch in Brindisi, Italy, had really been posted in England.

On the day of the trial, I journeyed to Kingsbridge and was present in court. Hugh Shortland was placed in the dock accused of the murder of his wife. He looked a little haggard but was impassive and apparently indifferent. There was no touch of sorrow about him. Ever and on he stared steadily at me but there was no symptom of recognition. The proceedings lasted only a few minutes. The detective confessed himself as baffled, and Shortland was dismissed from custody. He left court in the company of his solicitor and if he despatched a look in my direction, it was one of curiosity rather than of acquaintance. Shortland was determined not to know me that day. The following evening, Sunday, I went to the Mercury office in Plymouth shortly after six o'clock. I found Shortland patiently sitting in my editorial room - the only other person in the establishment. The front door had been left unlocked for the employees and he had entered. I took Shortland's presence in very matter of fact way and jocularly twitted him for not recognising me at Kingsbridge Court. "That would never have done," he remarked with a laugh. "Well, and what can I do for you?" I asked. "I want you to communicate the case to the public" he responded. "But tell me, what do people think of the charge against me?"

"So far as I can gather, they think that you pushed your wife into the water" I said. Shortland looked at me with his hard foxy expression and then said; "And what do you think about it?"

"It looked very much like it, does it not?" was my reply. Shortland laughed and remarked; "Well, we will publish a story that will make the others [newspapers] wild to think they have not got it. Their reporters will be hunting me all over the town tomorrow."

My impression at this time was that Shortland feared that I knew and suspected more than I cared to reveal, and that he might bribe me into silence by furnishing me with material for a journalistic 'boom.' "Tell me then, I asked, how you first met Miss Dime?"

"Oh, it was in a lane near Oldstone, a nice little Devonshire lane with overhanging brambles. She was riding through on horseback and I was going the same way. Her hair caught in the brambles and fell in a cloud over her shoulders. I went to her assistance and then we rode on together. Quite romantic, wasn't it?" Shortland laughed out loud. With that a shiver went through me; for the man who could laugh under such circumstances was evidently insane or callous to the point of madness.

"And so, you were married soon afterwards?"

"Yes, we were married, clandestinely of course, for I wanted to be married before my departure to New Zealand. The marriage was never consummated for that would have led to discovery and I told my wife that there must be no evidence of that kind for the world to look on." Shortland laughed again that weird harsh laugh and then he produced a painting from his pocket; a picture of his wife which he passed to me for inspection. "Charming girl don't you think so? If you'd have asked me, I would have lent that to you so that you might put a sketch of her in your paper. My cell at Kingsbridge looked out on to the churchyard and if you had slipped in at the back and tapped at my window, I would have supplied you with all kinds of copy."

"What do you wish me to say in the paper?" I asked.

"You may begin this way, take it down in shorthand if you please; We are in position to give this morning, on authority which our readers need not question, certain information in reference to this remarkable case which adds considerably to that already in possession of the public." Reciting a passage from a letter sent from his wife, Shortland said "You are your own good angel. Hugh, if there were no Hugh, I think I should die, because I love you so dearly." He was not in the least moved as he recited this pathetic passage to me.

"But what am I to say about the death of your wife?"

"Put it down this way; with regard to the circumstances under which Mrs. Shortland met her death, Mr. Shortland has repeatedly asserted that the absence of all marks of a struggle in the pond, or in the locality of the pond, disproves the theory of the accident and the suggestion of suicide. He declines to hazard any theory as to the cause of death but says he has been struck by the fact that the body was found upright in the water. Upon this he wants to know if the body was found suspended in the water, at what point did the body start from and where there any footmarks? If it was murder, where were the marks to the body ever touching the ground? I understand that in Mr. Shortland's opinion, the chloroform theory would best reconcile with the circumstances under which the deceased met her death. The first time Shortland heard anything of chloroform was when he saw allusion to its possible use in one of the daily papers, and it struck him at the time very acutely indeed."

"You believe your wife was really murdered?" I asked. Shortland jumped from his chair, stretched out his arms and shouted across the table; "You have put that down in shorthand. Strike it out, strike it out!" He resumed his seat calm and impassive as before, recovering immediately his subtle and icy demeanour. Bidding I resume writing, he continued; "Mr. Shortland believes an accident has not been proved, he believes a suicide has not been proved, and to use a phrase that has been attributed to him, he believes murder has not been disproved." Shortland then told the journalist he had more to tell him and could they meet the following evening at eleven p.m. by the hollow at Compton, near to some trees and his aunt's residence, adding that it would be quiet and no one would be about. The writer turning down the offer was then informed that Shortland would instead return to the office the following evening, which he did. Exalted with the sensation of the statements he had already made he went on to come up with further ingenious ideas for diverting public attention from the beaten tract. On one occasion he asked the writer to state that; "a hooded, young, and beautiful widow who bears title showed considerable feeling towards Mr. Shortland near the turnpike at

Kingsbridge shortly after his release…… Mr. Shortland will shortly be on his way to Rome, to take a course of training at the Holy College, preparatory to being admitted to the ministry of the Holy Father. The Holy Roman Church is always clever and prompt to enlist talent and energy in her service."

Such was the man who married Miss. Dimes, such was the husband who believed that she was murdered, such were his views on the subject of her death. He hung about my office like a nightmare; suddenly and noiselessly entering my room and renewing the familiar theme - until at length he vanished without the formality of leave-taking, and I learnt, not without relief, that he had booked his long-deferred passage to New Zealand.

[*The fact his first wife had died in suspicious circumstances in England and that he had been tried for her murder, was again brought to the fore when eight years later Hugh Shortland was found guilty of criminal libel and sentenced to two years in prison. He was said to have lived the life of a libertine in New Zealand and had taken advantage of a young woman in Auckland. He had endeavoured to seduce her to gain possession of her savings, and not succeeding, he deliberately defamed her.*]

FIRE AT WHYMPSTON FARM.

Sometime between eleven o'clock and midnight on the 26th of May 1884, a fire broke out in a building at Whympston Farm, a short distance from Whympston House, the residence of Mr. N.W. Pitts, the county magistrate. The farm labourer and his wife who lived in the cottage adjoining the building, were just about to retire to bed when they thought they heard a crackling noise coming from the building. Going to check, they discovered flames issuing from the roof. They immediately gave the alarm and a man was sent to Modbury for assistance.

Many of the towns' inhabitants hearing of the fire proceeded to the farm and rendered valuable assistance until the fire engine arrived, which unfortunately wasn't until half past two in the morning. The fire had quickly spread through the buildings attached to it, and all except the labourer's cottage and some detached cowhouses were burned to the ground. Valuable machinery which was worked by a water-wheel, implements all kinds together with five carts, eighty bags of grain, and the produce of four or five acres of straw were also consumed. Fortunately, most the cattle were in the fields and there were only two bulls, six calves, and some pigs in the sheds, and these were easily removed to a place of safety. The household furniture of the labourer was also taken from the house and moved a safe distance away. The fire engine, when it did arrive, prevented the flames from spreading further.

The reason for the engine taking so long to arrive had been because the man who was in charge of it at the gashouse, which was situated a little outside of the town, didn't hear the ringing of the alarm bell, though everyone present was sure he had been called. After waiting until after one o'clock, Mr. Pitts despatched a horse ready harnessed, to bring the engine to the farm. When it arrived at the gashouse, the occupant was fast asleep. It was afterwards suggested that in hindsight there should be a meeting arranged for the better management of the engine in future. The origin of the fire was at first thought to be in some of the machinery that may have been in heavy use the previous day had become over heated, but on further examination it was supposed that the fire was the work of an incendiary. The machinery not having been used for at least week, could not have caused the fire.

SUNDAY SCHOOL TEA PARTY.

Modbury Baptist Church Sunday School held its annual treat on the afternoon of Wednesday the 29th of July 1884. The children first paraded through the town singing several hymns, and afterwards adjourned to a field at 'Fancy House' the residence of Mr L. H. Price. Games were played and a tea was provided for the children. This was followed later in the afternoon by a public tea to which a large number of the townsfolk sat down to and enjoyed.

IVYBRIDGE POLICE COURT.

At the Ivybridge Police court on Monday the 11th of August 1884, John Camp and Ann Woods, both of Modbury, were fined for being drunk and disorderly in Galpin Street. Richard Lego of Bittaford, a thirteen-year-old boy, was sentenced fourteen days' imprisonment without hard labour, and then to be detained for two-years in a reformatory school, for stealing a pair trousers the property of Mr. Brooks a local farmer.

DISTRESSING SUICIDE OF A SERVANT.

Elizabeth Jane Pate [or Pote] known to all by her middle name Jane, was a twenty-four-year-old general servant to Mr. and Mrs. Nelder at Butland Farm. She committed suicide on the 1st of December 1884 by hanging herself from a beam in the hay-loft of one of the farms outbuildings.

Mrs. Nelder had spent some time looking for Jane, and unable to find her appealed to a farmhand called William Shepherd to ask if he had seen her, stating that she had been missing for over an hour and she was quite concerned. Shepherd said he hadn't and continued with his work. Soon after he went to the loft to get some hay for the horses, and found poor Jane hanging from a beam which she had tied herself to by means of a plough rein. He called out to his fellow workmates who were occupied in the yard nearby. They rushed to his aid and helped cut Jane down, but it was too late and life was now extinct. A message was sent to Mr. William. F. Langworthy, surgeon of Modbury, who arrived at the farm as quickly as he was able, but of course his services were of no avail. A tearful Mrs. Nelder told him she knew of no reason why Jane would have chosen to end her life in such a rash manner, and that she had always been a very good servant and had been with the family about a year and a half.

Elizabeth Jane Pate was buried in St. George's Churchyard on the 4th of December 1884.

SAD CASE OF ATTEMPTED SUICIDE.

George Shepherd, a forty-four-year-old solicitor's clerk of Billericay, Essex, was brought before the magistrates at Modbury, charged with having attempted suicide on the 25th January 1885.

George had unexpectedly turned up at his brother Charles house in Brownston Street on the morning of Saturday the 24th. He had been in the habit of visiting his brother at Christmas for a short holiday each year, but the last time he had visited had been a little over twelve months previously. However, this time things seemed a little strange as he had arrived without any prior notification, only saying that he had caught the train the previous evening from London and as it didn't stop at Ivybridge, he had gone on to Plymouth and returned to Ivybridge on the first train the following morning. From Ivybridge he had engaged the services of man called Phillips to drive him to Modbury and who he had asked to return the same evening so that he could catch the mail train back to London. Later in the day George remarked that a night's rest in Modbury would probably do him good, and on the suggestion of his brother he sent a telegram to Mr. Phillips telling him not to bring the trap that evening. He spent the day walking about the town and drank two or three glasses of ale at different places, as well as treating some of his old friends to a drink. Although he appeared a little excited, his family saw no reason to suppose he was not in full possession of his senses. On the Saturday evening he purchased some meat for the following morning's breakfast, and retired to bed at a reasonable hour.

On the Sunday morning at about seven o'clock, and before it was light, George rose from his bed and went to St George's Churchyard where his father and several members of his family were buried. He returned to his brother's house before eight o'clock, and standing outside of Charles's bedroom told him it was time to get up and light the fire and to have a cup of tea. But by the time Charles and his wife had gotten up, George had taken off his clothes and gone back to bed. He declined to join them for breakfast, but took a cup of tea that Charles brought up to his room.

Shortly before dinner, Charles Shepherd again went to his brother's room and told him that the meal was nearly ready and that he had better get up. Mrs. Shepherd also called up to him from the kitchen. In reply he called back saying he could hear she had not yet put the cabbage on the fire, and some joke passed between them about the sharpness of his hearing. A few minutes later, Charles and his wife were startled when they heard the report of a gunshot come from their visitor's bedroom. Rushing upstairs and bursting in the bedroom door, they found George with his head hanging over the side of the bed and with blood around his mouth. Next to him was a small, inexpensive muzzle loading pistol. Dr. George. V. Langworthy was quickly summoned, and discovered the pistol had been loaded with small shot, and that George had held the muzzle to his mouth and discharged it. His tongue was blackened and lacerated, and the soft parts of the roof and back of the mouth were completely shot away. He wasn't able to make a proper examination of the injury until the following day, when he found a lacerated wound with very jagged edges in the soft palate. He presumed the pistol must have contained a slight charge of powder, and asked George Shepherd if that was so. Unable to speak Shepherd wrote down, 'not much powder, full of shot.' He still appeared in an excitable state and the doctor thought he had likely been taking stimulants. Up until the Monday evening, George was unable to eat or speak, but retained full possession of his faculties and spent most of his time in writing. Later that evening he felt something slip from his throat, and he immediately recovered his speech, and afterwards partook freely of nourishment.

The following morning, Tuesday, P.C. Dunsford visited George Shepherd and took from him the pistol, along with three caps and a few rounds of shot which he found in his jacket pocket. George told him that he now felt very guilty for having carried out the act, but had been very overworked and had great family trouble. The day before the incident he had received a letter which had troubled him greatly; he scarcely knew what he was doing. He said that before he left Billericay, he had written to his employer telling him that he was going to Modbury. This was true, as on the Saturday a telegram had arrived at Brownston Street from Mr. Hood his employer, saying that Shepherd was to ensure he returned to work on the Monday morning. On the Monday, Shepherd wrote a telegram asking it to be forwarded to Mr. Hood, telling him what had occurred and expressing his regret. Another telegram was sent to his wife asking her to come to Modbury at once.

When brought before the magistrates, George Shepherd expressed how truly sorry he was for what had occurred. He said he hoped they would deal with him leniently and not send him to prison because he would lose his job and he had a wife and family dependent upon him. The Bench retired for consultation, and on their return the chairman said that they had very carefully considered the case and they scarcely felt justified deciding on such a serious charge; but, if he was truly penitent and would promise that nothing of the kind should occur again, they said they would discharge him in the hope that this would be a warning to him and they hoped that his wife Jane (who was present) would look after him.

[On the 1891 census, George was living in Haverhill, Essex, with one of his children and described himself as a widower; Jane having died in January 1888. Was possibly the news of his wife's poor health the reason George took such drastic action? George died on the 3rd of June 1892 after being hit by a train on 'Rede's Crossing,' a level crossing just outside of Haverhill Station. At the inquest into his death, his youngest son John aged seventeen, said that his father had suffered a fit some time previously and often complained of dizziness. A railway signalman and a goods foreman who saw the incident said George appeared to rush at the engine as it got close to him and he headbutted it. The jury though after hearing all the evidence, decided that his death had been accidental after having falling in a fit of giddiness. They added a rider that the crossing was dangerous and needed to be looked at. A number of people wrote to their local paper and the Great Eastern Railway Company, stating that a footbridge needed to be built over the crossing. One of George's brothers; Joseph, his employer, and those who knew him well, described him as having a cheerful disposition.]

MODBURY HARRIERS ANNUAL DINNER.

On Friday evening, the 6th of February 1885, a dinner for the Modbury Hunt was held at the London Inn, Brent Mill, where around twenty resident farmers and other gentlemen sat down to excellent feast supplied by the host, Mr. Maunder. Once every year the Modbury Harriers were invited to South Brent where the Misses. Carew of Marley Hall gave permission for the hunt to go across their grounds. That same day, about thirty-five took advantage of this privilege and an excellent day's sport was enjoyed although the weather was somewhat boisterous.

POLITICAL SKIRMISH.

Political differences have often led to cross words and scuffles, but nothing as bad had ever been seen in Modbury as in September 1885 when Mr. Henry Lopes, the Conservative representative visited the town to make a speech in support of his candidature for the Totnes Parliamentary Division. Arriving in the town he was met by the town's band and several prominent supporters. A number of boys were soon clinging to the vehicle he was in and commenced shouting 'Mildmay for ever.' Mr. Henry Bingham Mildmay being the local Labour candidate. As the carriage passed through the main street some missiles were thrown and the coachman was struck on the head by a turnip.

In taking his seat on the platform in a marquee belonging to Mr. Davis, hissing and booing could be heard from an angry mob of boys and young men; said to have been encouraged by violent speeches and articles written in radical newspapers. Then, when he and his fellow Conservative members were making their way to the White Hart Hotel to meet with Mr. N. Pitts and Mr. Harris Pitts who were going to take them back to Whympston where they intended to spend the night, the mob began to throw stones, potatoes, rotten eggs, apples, bags of flour and rabbit skins at his carriage, causing Mr. Lopes and his fellow companions to take cover by crouching on the floor of the vehicle. Mr. Lopes was said to have been injured and his carriage badly damaged. They only managed to escape the town by driving at a very fast pace. Many of the people standing nearby were also pelted with the make-shift weapons, and a young woman, Miss. Emma Wyatt, had three teeth knocked out and was severely cut about the face when hit by a large stone. A ten-pounds reward was offer for the conviction of the culprit that threw the stone that injured her, but unfortunately no-one came forward with a name.

FINED FOR ASSAULTING A TEACHER.

At the Modbury Petty Sessions held on the 7th of December 1885, Samuel Marks, a thirty-one-year-old labourer of Galpin Street, was summoned for assaulting Charlotte Williams, a teacher at Modbury Infant School. He was charged with having entered the schoolroom and accusing her of striking his seven-year-old daughter. When Miss. Williams denied the accusation, he was said to have struck her on each side of her head before storming out of the classroom. In his defence Mr. Marks said that his daughter had come home from school crying, stating the Miss. Williams had boxed her ears. He said he went to the school to remonstrate with her and when she denied having struck the child, he put up his hands to her head to illustrate how she had hit the child; admitting that one of his hands had touched her head. Mrs. Pearse the head-mistress of the school, stated that there was no truth in the little girl's accusation and that she had been in the schoolroom with Miss. Williams the whole time and she would have witnessed the child having been hit. The chairman of the panel said that it was necessary that the school authorities (by whom the prosecution was ordered) should be upheld and the teachers protected in the discharge of their duties. Samuel Marks was fined one pound including costs.

DRUNKARDS.

At the Modbury Petty Sessions held on Monday the 2nd of August 1886, William Kerswill a labourer, was summoned to answer two charges of drunkenness and disorderly conduct, one taking place on the 7th of June in Bigbury and another on the 12th of July in Modbury. He pleaded guilty in both instances and was fined twelve shillings and six' pence including costs in each case.

John Camp, an old offender, was in his absence sentenced to twelve days imprisonment with hard labour for a similar offence on the 12th July in Modbury. He had however since left the town.

THE TOWN'S WATER SUPPLY.

For some years past, Modbury had suffered from an insufficient supply of water. This shortage had never been more keenly felt since a well from which many took their daily supply was closed due to sewage contamination. In August 1886 it was decided at a meeting of the Parochial Committee to recommend the Sanitary Authority to increase the length of piping by connecting the main supply to the town and carrying it through Church Street and Back Street, which would considerably expand the supply. Tenders for carrying out the work were asked to be put forward.

A DAMP GUY FAWKES.

The 5th of November revelries in Modbury passed off a little more quietly than usual in 1886 as heavy rain fell throughout most of the day and evening. A Guy carried by people bearing lighted torches was though carried in procession through the town, and was afterwards set fire to and carried to the Green. A tar barrel was burnt and several fireworks were let off in the street.

FRESH STRAWBERRIES.

In early November 1886, Mr F. Wilton, the driver for Messrs. Pearse and Andrews, solicitors of Modbury, came across a bunch of wild strawberries growing at the side of the road near Kingston on the road between Ivybridge and Modbury. The fruits were so plentiful that he was able to pick a large bunch.

A CHRISTMAS STORM.

A snowstorm blanketed the central and southern counties of England on Boxing Day 1886. It was so heavy that it pulled down telegraph wires, causing a total loss in communication between London and the South West. Trains were delayed and great inconveniences were caused to thousands of people. By the time the squall reached Devon it had turned to rain which fell in torrents.

In Modbury the morning had started off with heavy rain, but as the day went on it became even heavier and all the water courses overflowed and began pouring down the streets. The bottom of Church Street and Poundwell Street were soon flooded. The two brooks that ran through the town burst their banks within minutes, flooding nearby buildings. The lower portion of Back Street flooded as did some of the gardens at the back of Brownston Street. The malthouse and stables of Mr. Matthews filled with water, as did the Exeter Inn where the water flowed through a back parlour, out of the front door, and across the street and into Mr Gee's shop. By the afternoon the water had risen to four feet in places, where at this point it burst through the window of Mr. Gee's shop and poured into his parlour and over the stove in the kitchen. The lower basement of his house was soon filled with water which then flowed out of the back door in a torrent powerful enough to drive a mill. Next door Mr. Brown's bakery was also flooded, as was Mr. Sullivan's printer's business which was next door to the Exeter Inn.

Once the flood waters had abated, it was found that much damage had been done, especially to the Exeter Inn run by Mr. Mortimore, where the floor had been ripped up in several places and the hearthstone had been lifted in the parlour. The other inhabitants of Church Street who had their premises badly damaged were; Mr. Nicholas Lakeman the post master; Mr. Henry King, butcher; Mr Francis, draper; Mr. Charles Curson, tailor; Mr Francis Brown, baker and grocer; Mr. Edmund Lakeman, ironmonger; and Mr. George Hosking a carrier and farmer whose premises adjoined one of the brooks and was completely flooded. The cottages in Bakehouse Lane and Mr. Ellery's house at the bottom of Galpin Street were also flooded to the depth of nearly two feet. In Poundwell Street considerable damage was also done - Mr. Choake having had every lightweight item washed out of his fellmonger and wool shop. All the cottages in the street were said to have flooded when the brook burst through two large holes and almost completely destroyed the roadway. Furniture and belongings in many houses were all but destroyed. In a nearby meadow where the brook entered a common sewer, the force of the water was so great that it opened up creating two large holes.

At Swanbridge Mill many poultry drowned and pigs and other livestock were saved with difficulty. About a quarter of mile from Modbury at Prigdon Mill, Mr. Hingston, a maltster, was returning from Bigbury, and when near the bridge he was joined by Mr. John Roberts of Poundwell Street. They proceeded on their journey together. Reaching the bridge, they found the roadway of it completely covered with water but proceeded through it having no alternative route. Suddenly Mr. Hingston who was a few paces ahead, disappeared. He was carried along by the current and was eventually able to grab hold of some bushes, where Mr. Roberts was then able to pull him from the water. Unbeknown to them the bridge had collapsed under the immense weight of the pressure of water, and the stones of the bridge, some weighing several hundredweight had been hurled many hundreds of feet into the meadow below.

A gentleman in Torquay noted that the rainfall in the town from nine a.m. until ten p.m. measured 2.69 inches. At Yealmpton two cottages at Bowden Hill were flooded from the overflow at a reservoir behind the properties. The terrified occupants having to take refuge in the upstairs rooms. The town of Kingsbridge was completely under water to the extent of a quarter a mile area and in some places the flood waters were five to six feet deep. Stables near to the quay were under water and it had been necessary to move the horses to higher ground. Dr. Webb of Kingsbridge reported that the rainfall there had been 1.91 inches.

[*In 2012 Modbury was once again flooded and twenty-seven properties and businesses were badly damaged.*]

Postcard of Galpin Street, courtesy of Samuel Harrison.

TEMPORARY LICENSE.

Permission was given to Samuel Chubb of the White Hart Inn, to keep open his public-house until four a.m., on the occasion of the Harriers Hunt Ball which was held on the 5th of January 1887. He laid on a sumptuous supper for the many guests and dancing to music supplied by the Modbury band continued through-out the night until the early hours.

THE PRICE OF BREAD.

Mr. James Rendle, a baker of High Street, Modbury, who two to three times every week made visits to Kingston to sell his produce, was set upon by the inhabitants in March 1887 for having raised the price of an eight-pound loaf of bread from nine' pence to ten' pence. When he told the angry mob that his next visit to the village was going to be under the protection of a policeman even further threats were made.

THEFT FROM THE MODBURY INN.

Ellen Rogers, who we first met back in 1883, a former barmaid at the Modbury Inn who was caught stealing, was once again caught thieving from the same place. At the Modbury Police Court on Thursday the 16th of June 1887, before Messrs. E. Allen, and N. W. Pitts, Ellen, the wife of George Rogers of Modbury, was brought up on remand charged with stealing money from the till of Mr. Charles Wyatt of the Modbury Inn on Brownston street the previous Sunday.

At around nine-thirty p.m. Samuel Wyatt, the landlords' son was in the kitchen when he heard someone in the bar. He went to see who it was and on the way he heard the till rattle. Finding Ellen Rogers there looking very confused, he accused her of having been in the till and told her to hand over the money. She denied having stolen any, but on his insistence, she took a handful of silver from her pocket and gave it to him. Going to the till he noticed four pounds in gold which was wrapped in paper to be missing and which he again demanded she return. Mrs. Rogers again denied having taken it, but when another son of Mr. Wyatt came into the bar having heard the heated exchange of words, she thought it best to hand it over. She was then asked to leave; taking with her some ale that she had legitimately purchased.

Samuel Wyatt Snr, subsequently being told what had happened sent for Ellen to return to the bar, and on Mrs. Wyatt searching her clothing, found another six' pence in her pocket and some silver coins in her hand. P.C. Dunsford was sent for and into whose custody she was given.

Pleading guilty to the offence, Ellen Rogers was committed for trial at the following Quarter Sessions held at Exeter. Having previously made an admission of guilt, at her trial Ellen changed her plea to not guilty, totally denying her earlier admissions of guilt and said that the money snatched from her hand by Mrs. Wyatt had been her own, having been given to her by her son. A verdict of guilty was returned and Ellen was sent to prison for nine months, with hard labour.

ASSAULT ON A LITTLE GIRL.

Thirteen-year-old Bessie White lived with her grandparents at Ludbrooke Cottage, Ermington. On the afternoon of the 20th of June 1887, she left the cottage at four o'clock and walked into Modbury to run some errands for her grandmother. Having purchased the goods she was sent to buy, she set off for home. Whilst walking up Brownston Street at around five o'clock, with a basket in her hand and a two-pound loaf of bread under her arm, she noticed a young man wearing a sailor's uniform come up from behind and overtake her. When he reached the entrance to Dark Lane he stopped and waited for her to catch up. As she approached him, he asked where she was going - then out of the blue he asked her to kiss him, to which she point-blank refused. Without saying another word, he turned away and walked off along the lane. Now very frightened she hurried on her way, but when she got to Barrack Road she saw him again. This time he was standing by a gate waiting for her. As she tried to hurry past him, he grabbed hold of her arm and said she should go into the field with him. She again refused his advances and tried to fight him off. It was at this point he assaulted her before letting her go. As she ran away back down Dark Lane, she dropping the loaf of bread she was carrying but was too scared to stop to pick it up as the sailor was gaining ground on her, but seeing a woman coming towards them he turned around and walked briskly back in the direction he had come from.

Poor little Bessie was now shaking with fear and fright and had tears pouring down her face. William Coyte a wheelwright, who was coming up the lane on his trap saw the distressed child whom he recognised. He stopped to ask what had happened and Bessie told him that she said she had been "ill-treated by a sailor." He told her to climb in to the trap and took her home to Ermington.

Having explained to her grandparents what had occurred, her grandfather passed on the information to P.C. Mortimore who made his way to Modbury that evening and found the loaf of bread in Dark Lane which Bessie said she had dropped during the fracas. Having gathered further information, the following day he travelled to Devonport and arrested Thomas Davis, a twenty-four-year-old sailor serving on board H.M.S. Royal Adelaide. In reply to the charge made against him, Thomas Davis denied having been to Modbury since the previous Christmas holidays when he had last visited his mother. However, the following day whilst being held in custody and knowing that he had been seen in the town he admitted to having been in Modbury on the day in question. Brought before the magistrates at Modbury, a number of witnesses were called to give evidence. Mary Wyatt of Church Street, the old woman who had seen the sailor briskly walking away as she approached, said that she couldn't positively identify Thomas Davis as the man she had seen leaving the scene as she was too far away to at the time to make a clear identification. John Mildren a retired coastguard, said he had seen Davis shortly after five o'clock in the afternoon of June the 20th, and William Ash, a stonemason, said that he had also seen Davis that evening at the bottom Sheepham Hill at quarter-past six. Richard Ford, a cow-keeper and the grandfather of Bessie White, spoke of the distress of his granddaughter when she was brought home by Mr. Coyte. He described how she was crying and trembling, and in consequence of what she told him he passed on the information to the police. Dr. George V. Langworthy was then called to give evidence and said that when he examined Bessie two days after the alleged assault he saw no traces violence, though didn't deny that an assault could have taken place.

Mr. Thorne acting for the defence, said that he didn't deny that the girl had been assaulted by somebody, but he refuted the claim that his client was the guilty party and he was prepared with strong evidence of an alibi. Thomas Davis was then called forward. He stated his name and age and said that he was an able seaman in the Royal Navy. On the 20th of June he was not wearing a moustache [*as had been claimed by Bessie White*.] He said he was on his way to Ivybridge and did not see Bessie or any other girl. At Ivybridge he went to an ale house kept by Mrs. Tickler. He arrived there at around half-past six or twenty to seven. His mother had walked with him as far as the top of Sheepham Hill where they went their separate ways. Cross-examined, it was said that if Mr. Ash had met him at quarter past six that evening on Sheepham Hill, it must have been a mistake as the distance from Modbury to Ivybridge was four and a half miles over the fields, which is the way Thomas Davis said he went. Davis said that it was five o'clock when he met with Mr. Ash and not quarter past six as Mr. Ash had stated. Mary Jane Davis, the mother of the prisoner was then called to give evidence on behalf of her son and spoke of accompanying him as far as Sheepham Hill where they parted at a quarter to five o'clock. Mrs. Tickler the landlady of a public-house at Ivybridge said she recalled Davis arriving at about half-past six that evening.

The jury deliberated for a short while before finding Thomas Davis 'not guilty' on the grounds of insufficient identity...

Davis had possibly given shore leave, as Britain celebrated Queen Victoria's Golden Jubilee on the 21st of June 1887 – see story below.

THE TOWN CELEBRATES HER MAJESTY'S GOLDEN JUBILEE.

Queen Victoria celebrated her Golden Jubilee over a two-day period in June 1887, on the 20th and 21st of the month. The actual date of her ascension to the throne had been on the 20th June which she celebrated with family, diplomatic representatives, and European Royalty at Buckingham Palace. The public celebrated the event the following day; it being the first day of the fifty-first-year of her reign.

Modbury was attractively decorated with flags and bunting, and the church bells rang out early in the morning and at intervals throughout the day. The brass band enlivened the proceedings of the celebration, and people of all ages enjoyed a party dinner and tea. The Baptist and Wesleyan denominations were invited to St. George's church for a Thanksgiving service, and a most hearty service was the result. The curate officiated in the absence through illness of the vicar. After the service there was procession through the town followed by a number of sporting events. In the evening there was a firework display accompanied by a bonfire, followed by dancing.

Previous to the celebration, a meeting had been held to make arrangements for a commemorative party to be held in the town. A high tea consisting of beef, ham, cake etc was to be provided for six hundred people, each bringing their own knife, fork, cup, saucer, and plate. Stamped tickets (non-transferable) would be issued to those wishing to partake. A subscription had already been set up and it was hoped more people would join. A provision committee, sports committee, and decoration committee were also arranged, and it was suggested that to enliven proceedings the Modbury band should be engaged for the day. There was also talk of asking the School Board to allow the large hall to be used for dancing in the evening. It was also suggested that the townsfolk be asked to hang a flag of some sort from their upper windows and a string of flags be strung between houses opposite. It was expected that the cost to participants would be no more than two or three pence each.

The Queen later wrote a letter of thanks to her people which was published in the London Gazette and shared in newspapers across the country.... *"I am anxious to express to my people my warm thanks for the kind and more than kind reception I met with on going to and returning from Westminster Abbey, with all my Children & Grand Children. The enthusiastic reception I met*

with then, as well as on all these eventful days in London, as well as in Windsor on the occasion of my Jubilee has touched me most deeply. It has shown that the labour and anxiety of fifty long years – twenty-two of which I spent in unclouded happiness, shared and cheered by my beloved Husband, while an equal number were full of sorrows and trials, borne without his sheltering arm and wise help have been appreciated by my people. This feeling and the cause of duty towards my dear Country and subjects, who are so inseparably bound up with my life, will encourage me in my task often a very difficult and arduous one, during the remainder of my life. The wonderful order preserved on this occasion and the good behaviours of the enormous multitudes assembled merits my highest admiration. That God may protect and abundantly bless my Country is my fervent prayer."

— Queen Victoria

MODBURY BAND CONCERT.

The annual concert held on behalf of the Modbury band took place at the Assembly Rooms on the evening of Wednesday the 11th of January 1888. The band, both collectively and individually

under the leadership of Mr. James Shepheard played a choice of tunes. A piccolo solo by Master. John Coleman was so well executed that he was asked to repeat it. Mr. Alick Mildmay and Mr Alfred. Mildmay each gave a solo on the pianoforte. A duet on piano by Mr. Alfred Davis the organist at Modbury Church was also well received, as were the march and valse of the full string band. The singing of Mrs. A Pitman was without doubt the feature of the evening, and Miss. Shepheard and Miss. Pitts; both old favourites with Modbury audiences, did well and were encored. The Rev G. C. Green, Mr C. Green, Mr Browning, and others contributed to the evening's enjoyment.

EMPEROR WILHELM OF GERMANY.

References were made on Sunday the 11th of March 1888 in St George's Church to the death of Emperor William [*Wilhelm I of Germany*] who had died two days earlier, and the prayers of the congregation were asked for on behalf of Emperor Frederick and the Royal Family. The Rev H. Connolly preached at both morning and evening services and pointed out how the events of the past week called upon all true Christians to ensure preparation for their own hour of death. Chopin's Funeral March and the Dead March in 'Saul' were played on the organ and burial hymns were sung at both services.

FUNERAL OF A WELL-RESPECTED MAN.

The funeral of Mr Edwin Andrews, a sixty-eight-year-old seed merchant and saddler of 58, Church Street, took place on the afternoon of Tuesday the 17th of April 1888. The deceased had only been ill for few days previous to his passing. He was connected both by family and business within the neighbourhood. The funeral was said to have been the largest held in Modbury for several years. Nearly all of the local gentry, farmers, and tradesmen of the parish were in attendance, besides many from the adjoining towns and parishes.

Mr. Andrews had previously held the position of Portreeve, and the funeral service was conducted by the present Portreeve - the Reverend G. C. Green who was assisted the Reverend

C. W. H. Connolly. The organist played the Dead March as the funeral cortege entered the church, and two appropriate hymns were expressively sung by the choir. Mr. Andrews left behind a widow and a large family of grown-up children, besides great many friends, to mourn his passing.

[*The Portreeve, as well as overseeing the towns markets and fairs, was the leader of the town community. The appointment was for one year.*]

SUMMER STORM.

On Friday the 6th of July 1888 several parts of Devonshire were visited by a severe storm of thunder, lightning, and hail. The following day another thunderstorm of great severity arrived in the county. At Chaddlewood near Plympton, the ground in places was white with hailstones, so large that vegetation was cut down by them. In other places water ran like a river to the depth of two feet. Hedges were washed away and a piece of shrubbery weighing around two tons was carried bodily for several yards. A farmer at Langage stated that much of the soil had been washed from one of his fields, through a wood and into another farm, destroying his mangold and turnip crop. At Modbury the storm was severely felt from about eleven o'clock in the morning until one in the afternoon. The streets became rivers; the thunder startlingly loud and the lightning very vivid. Workmen in the Devon Rosery grounds of Messrs. Curtis, Sandford, and Co. at Torquay, were just beginning to cut rose blooms ready to send to London for the Crystal Palace show when the storm burst with such terrific force that the whole field of roses was utterly destroyed - flowers and foliage being cut to pieces. The consequence was that the firm were unable to exhibit. In the locality of St. Marychurch and Babbacombe, the effects of the storm were also felt severely. The hailstones were said to be extremely large and fell with such force that they beat through the canvas covering of a waggon. One of these stones was put on some weighing scales just after it had fallen and was said to have weighed thirty-one ounces.

DAY TRIP TO SLAPTON SANDS.

The members of the Royal Marine Light infantry band based in Plymouth, had their annual outing on Monday the 13th of August 1888, with a day trip to Slapton Sands. The party first proceeded to Modbury where a hearty lunch was enjoyed at Mr. Davis's hotel. From there they continued their journey to the beach where a most enjoyable afternoon was said to have been spent.

FALL FROM A SCAFFOLD.

John Roberts, a fifty-eight-year-old carpenter, met with his death through falling from a scaffold whilst repairing the roof at Ermington Church on the 15th of October 1888. Walking across the scaffold he tripped and struck his foot against a stool which resulted in both he and the stool falling a distance of twenty feet to the ground. John unfortunately landed on a pile of timber which caused a terrible wound to his head. He was carried home by fellow workmates, where he died the following day.

At the inquest into his death held at the White Hart Hotel, before Mr. R. R. Rodd the county coroner and a jury of whom Mr. E.W. Bickford was chosen as foreman, Mr. William. F. Langworthy, surgeon of Modbury, stated that he was informed of the accident and met with the trap bringing Mr. Roberts back from Ermington to Modbury. He found him to be badly injured but conscious. Mr. Roberts asked him to break the news of his accident to his wife, after which he fell into unconsciousness and stayed that way until he died.

George Tiddy, a fellow carpenter who was working with Mr. Roberts that day, said they had just finished eating breakfast and were making their way back to their place of work; he was following closely behind Mr. Roberts as they made their way back up the scaffold. He saw his companion trip on the stool and then fall forwards, plummeting to the ground. It all happened so fast that there was nothing he could do to stop him. He said the scaffold was very sturdy and three to four feet wide at its narrowest part. It was his opinion that the fall was simply an accident. The foreman of the work agreed with George Tiddy and said the scaffold was everything it should have been and was very secure. He had worked on church restoration work for the past twenty-six years and this was the first accident of that sort he had come across. The jury unanimously reached a verdict of 'accidental death' and added a rider that no-one should hold any blame.

John Roberts had been a very popular man in Modbury and almost every shop closed their shutters on the day of his funeral, which was attended by large number of the town's inhabitants and by all of his fellow workmates who had been employed in the restoration of Ermington Church.

ARGUMENT OVER A CLOTHES LINE.

At the Ivybridge Petty Sessions held on Monday the 22nd of October 1888, Sarah Freeman of Poundwell Street, charged Emily Wilton with assaulting her on the 3rd of that month. A dispute arose between them in regards to a clothes line, during which Emily Wilton was said to have thrown a rocking-chair at Sarah Freeman, cutting the side of her face. Emily Wilton said that Mrs. Freeman had called her an offensive name, and that the cut on her face was not caused by herself but by a bucket Mrs. Freeman was chasing her with which struck a doorway and glanced off, hitting her in the face. A witness corroborated the evidence of Mrs. Freeman and Emily Wilton was fined one pound with an added five shillings costs.

ATTEMPTED HIGHWAY ROBBERY.

At Modbury Police Court on Monday the 29th of October 1888, before Mr N. W. P. Pitts and the Rev. D. Pitman, a tramp named Robert Shaw from Worcester, a chairmaker by trade, was charged with attempting to rob and assault Miss. Ethel Pearse of Stoliford, the daughter of Mr. William Pearse, auctioneer and land owner, on the 23rd of the month.

Miss. Pearce stated that at about half-past three in the afternoon, as she was walking along the road from Stoliford to Modbury eating some nuts, she saw the prisoner approaching her, and at the same time heard a carriage coming from the direction of Kingsbridge, though still some distance off. As the prisoner got near, she stepped in to the lower hedge to let him pass. After he passed, he turned around and grabbing hold of her from behind threw her into the ditch and pinned her down. She struggled violently but the man had a tight hold on her and placing his hand over her mouth menacingly told her to keep quiet. Forcing the nuts from her hand he demanded that she give him her money. Ethel said if he allowed her to get up she would give him all she had. Allowing her to rise to a sitting position, she managed to get her hand into her pocket to take out the few coins she had, but was so terribly frightened and shaking that she could only fumble and couldn't grasp the coins. In fear she began to scream loudly. Her attacker again threw her down and lifting up her skirts, tried to cover her head with her them. She begged him to let her get up promising she would give him all her money. He once again let her

95

sit up, but hearing the approach of the carriage from Kingsbridge he ran off along the ditch and broke through the hedge.

Ethel managed to clamber from the ditch and ran towards the approaching carriage which was then about fifty yards off. Grabbing hold of the door she clung on until it stopped. Soon after the carriage of Mr. Richard Andrews, solicitor of Modbury, also drove up and seeing her in such a distressed state he told her to climb onboard and conveyed her home. The police were informed and a search was made for the perpetrator. That evening the prisoner was brought to her residence by a constable, where she immediately identified him saying she had not the slightest doubt that the man he had in his custody was the man who had assaulted her.

A witness, Mr Ephraim Townsend, of Norma Villa, Portland Square, Plymouth, told the court that he was riding on the box seat of a coach when he saw Miss. Pearse get up from the ground by the side of the hedge and come running towards his carriage calling for help. She had no hat on and her hair was falling loose around her shoulders. She appeared to have been badly treated. He said he got down from his carriage and searched over and around the hedge, but couldn't see the attacker. He did though pick up a hat and umbrella belonging to the young lady. Another witness, William Watts, a farm labourer who was working near to where the assault took place, said that on the afternoon of the 23rd he passed Robert Shaw on the road coming out of Modbury.

P.C. George Howard who was stationed at Modbury, stated that on being informed of what had taken place and having been given a description of the perpetrator, he went to Kingsbridge and apprehended the prisoner in the casual ward of the workhouse. He brought him to Stoliford the same night and Miss. Pearce positively identified him. He then took him to Modbury and where he charged him. The next morning, he searched the area where the struggle had taken place and found a penknife [produced in court] which was the property of Miss. Pearse. He also found that the prisoner's boots corresponded with imprints on the ground near the spot. Robert Shaw, when asked if he had anything to say, replied in the negative and was committed to take his trial the next assizes at Exeter. On the 4th of December 1888 he was found guilty of attempted robbery and outrage and was sent to prison for two years. The judge characterised Shaw's conduct as a most cowardly and brutal act.

The assault on Miss. Pearse, was said to have played upon the minds of many young folk in the area, especially females. Young people from outlying parishes had been put off walking to Kingsbridge. It was said that the attack by a tramp had put off many well intentioned and benevolent people who at one time would scarcely ever turn them away without a gift of some kind, would rarely now give anything at all.

JACK THE RIPPER.

The main effigy at the 5th of November 'Guy Fawkes' revelries in Modbury in 1888, was an image of the character known as 'Jack the Ripper' who was at that time terrifying the inhabitants of Whitechapel in London with his murderous activities which had become the talk of the country. A tar barrel was set alight and the Modbury Band enlivened the proceedings.

[*Jack the Ripper was the name given to a still unknown killer who between 3rd April 1888 and 13th February 1891 murdered at least five women before mutilating their bodies.*]

HUNT BALL 1889.

The sixth annual Modbury Harriers hunt ball took place in the assembly rooms of the White Hart Hotel on Wednesday the 2nd of January 1889, and was said to have been a great success. The room was tastefully decorated with evergreens and flags, and the guests included almost all of the gentry of the area along with a large contingent of tenant farmers and their families. The supper was supplied by Mr. and Mrs. Chubb, and dancing was kept up to the strains of the Modbury Quadrille Band until four a.m. the following morning.

TRAGIC ACCIDENT NEAR ORCHETON MILL.

On Monday the 14th of January 1889, two lime carts belonging to Mr. Henry Helmer of Langstone Farm, Kingston, were proceeding along a road near Orcheton Mill, when the shaft horse of the first vehicle became unmanageable when the breeching broke and the boy in charge had to abandon it. The driver of the pair of horses, twenty-eight-year-old George Southern ran to render assistance, but when trying to stop the horses he was dragged under the cart and died soon after from the injuries he received. He left behind a wife and three young children, all aged under five.

FLETE HOUSE ILLUMINATED.

It was reported in February 1889 that Flete House was to be lit throughout by electricity, and would be the first country seat in the west of England into which this improvement has been introduced. The estate had been sold twenty-five years previously to Mr. William Splatt, an Australian merchant, from whom it passed into the hands of its present possessor Mr. Bingham

Mildmay, who was connected by marriage with the Bulteel family; the original owners of the property and who lived there for several centuries. The house was said to have been enlarged and carefully restored since Mr. Mildmay bought the estate, and was now one of the finest country seats in Devonshire.

Kingston Torr, near Modbury. Postcard courtesy of Marina Walsh.

HOMING PIGEON LOST.

Mr. William Hodder of Edmeston Farm, whilst crossing a field in June 1889, found the headless body and plumage of a pigeon. On one of the wing feathers was stamped 'South Wales District Homing Society 608.' It was believed that the pigeon had been attacked by a hawk.

SPELL OR SUPERSTITION.

Edwin, the son of Mr. John Davis, a wheelwright of Galpin Street, was cutting down an ash tree in November 1889 at Shipham Hill, when he noticed one of the branches he was cutting begin to shake. He split the wood in two and from the centre fell a very old-fashioned half-ounce phial. The bottle was hidden in a cavity of the tree about an inch in diameter and three inches deep. It contained some black hair, which on examination appeared to human, several pieces of nail clippings, and some liquid emitting a strong smell. The hole in which the bottle was placed was in the centre of the tree and about twenty inches from the ground.

[*Was the phial placed there many years previously as part of a spell. Ash trees were at one time known as the 'tree of life.' Was this possibly a ritual in hope of healing a sick person? There were many old superstitions in Devonshire and it would be interesting to know if anyone could solve this very old mystery.*]

DEATH WHEN FELLING A TREE.

In April 1890, George Wyatt, a sixty-year-old labourer in the employment of Edmond Hicks of Leigh Farm, was asked to fell a tree in the shrubbery on his land. An hour or so later Wyatt was found lying dead on the ground near to the partially felled tree. An autopsy found his death was due to syncope, the result of overstraining when felling the tree, the deceased was said to already be in a delicate state of health.

OLDEST TOWNSMAN.

The Totnes Weekly Times was happy to report on Saturday the 18th of January 1890, that Mr.

Thomas Gill, formerly well-known in the area as a stationer and bookseller, was still living a hale and hearty life and possessing all his faculties at the ripe old age of ninety-six. In previous years Mr. Gill was known to travel across the South Hams visiting houses and shops with various books and take orders for new publications, frequently walking very long distances. Sadly, this news was to be short lived as Thomas died less than a month later on the 15th of February.

DEATH OF A HUNTSMAN.

Twenty-nine-year-old James Doney, the huntsman for the Modbury Harriers, was fatally injured when out hunting with Sir. Watkin William-Wynn's hounds during Ivybridge Hunt Week on Tuesday the 15th of April 1890.

While waiting at the Western Beacon, Doney observed the pack of hounds on the opposite side of the vale, and so he rode off with the intention of picking them up. Shortly afterwards his horse was seen on the turnpike road near Torr Hill, riderless. Meanwhile, the stricken Doney was found lying on the road by a passing gentleman who had him conveyed to the London Hotel in Ivybridge, and from there to his home in Modbury. Mr. Doney had suffered severe injuries to the head from which he succumbed the following morning. The horse from which had been thrown was found to be weak in the near foreleg, and it was supposed that the mare had tripped, pitching him on to his head. James Doney left behind a young widow and two children, the youngest being just three-weeks-old. Only a week previously he had told Mr. Pitts, the master of the Harriers, that the horse was all right when running in the field, but unsafe on a turnpike road.

THE UGLY DUCKLING.

Samuel Shute, a carpenter of Brownston, caused excitement in June 1890 when one of his ducklings was born with three legs and four feet, one of the legs being divided and having two feet attached to it. Someone was said to have promised him a sovereign for this 'freak of nature' if the poor little mite reached three-weeks-old.

THEFT OF COAL.

Mary Grace Marsh, a married woman and the caretaker of the Modbury Board Schools, was charged with stealing fifteen pounds in weight of coal valued at three' pence on the evening of the 5th of January 1891. P.C. Crook whilst on his beat met with her near the school, and noticing she had something hidden beneath her shawl he stopped her and found her to be concealing a quantity of coal. She said she was on her way to the infants' school and that she was taking the coals for the fire there. Thinking her movements suspicious he took her into custody. The master of the boy's school from which the coal was  taken was questioned the following day and said that his scuttle had been filled with coal before he left that evening, but noticed some of it to be missing when he arrived that morning. Mary pleaded not guilty to the charge, stating that she was simply carrying the coal from one school to the other. The Bench took a lenient view of the case as it couldn't be proven whether she was actually taking the coal for her own use or taking it to the infant school, though they still chose to fine her ten shillings.

THE BLIZZARD OF 1891.

In March 1891 a violent blizzard blanketed Devon. Mr. Sherrell of Little Modbury Farm lost between fifty and sixty sheep including a number of lambs, with many more missing. He also lost several head of cattle. It was estimated that in the Modbury postal district that up to a thousand sheep and a good number of cattle had perished in the storm.

From Monday the 9th of March, until the evening of Thursday the 12th, Modbury was completely cut off from rest of the world. Snow had commenced to fall on the Monday evening just after the market had closed, and many farmers who had started for home were compelled to return to the town and remain there at the numerous inns until the roads became passable once more. The wind blew with such terrific force throughout the night that the following morning it was found that there were drifts on the roads measuring between ten and fifteen feet deep, and in the fields cattle and sheep had become completely buried. Some houses had also entirely disappeared from view, including that of labourer Nicholas Furzeland at Fancy. In other places it was not uncommon to see drifts up to the bedroom windows. At the top of Sheepham Hill near the barrack wall, there was a drift that extended nearly to Ermington. A glass roof at the Exeter Inn caved in under the weight of snow and filled the bar and parlour. Telegraph wires were down and scores of trees uprooted.

On the Wednesday morning gangs of men were set to work to clear the snow from the roads as business in the town had been almost entirely suspended. Dead sheep were dug out in their hundreds. On the Thursday evening, a gentleman who had walked from Plymouth brought with him a copy of the 'Western Morning News' and information was then circulated as to what was transpiring in the world beyond the town. The following day, Friday, several more inches of snow fell as the large number of men continued to try and clear the roads.

One of the towns bakers, Mr. George Rendle, had sent a boy with a horse and trap on the Monday to deliver bread to Kingston, Ringmore, and Bigbury, was feared lost or possibly worse. Some farmers driving home that evening found the lad seated in the trap which was almost buried in snow. He was almost insensible from cold. They succeeded in releasing the horse and the boy, and along with the animal he was taken to the nearest house at Chapel where he soon recovered.

At Bottle-hill, Plympton, fifty-five-year-old Ann Farley had ventured out to visit her aged and ill father at Hemerdon on the Monday evening. Nothing more was heard of her until her body was found on the Thursday by James Locke a neighbour, in a field near to her house buried in a snow drift. At Malborough, a fifteen-year-old farm boy called Thomas Arnold who was in the employment of Mr. John Ford of Fursedown; anxious about some sheep, Ford sent the boy to his uncle also called John Ford, at Southdown a distance of about half a mile away, to find out if he had seen anything of them. The snow was falling heavily and it was impossible to see any distance. The boy lost his way and wandered on for mile upon mile and hour after hour. When he had still not returned to the farmhouse at four o'clock, Mr. Ford became anxious for his safety and went out in search of him but could find no trace of the lad. Darkness fell and the snow kept falling and John Ford was forced to give up his search. Early the next morning about ninety men set out from Malborough in search of the missing boy, but thankfully he had already been found by one of the coastguards at Bolt Head near to the signal station. Thomas Arnold told him that he had wandered about for hours unable to find his way back the farmhouse, and being worn out and exhausted he lay down under a furze bush and placing his oilskin coat over his head had settled down for the night.

ACCIDENTAL FALL FROM A CART.

On the evening of Saturday the 18th of April 1891, sixty-three-year-old George Hosking, a carrier of 60, Broad Street, met with a serious accident. He had been brushing out a cart that he'd been using to transport goods, and just as he was about to climb out he leant on the broom handle to balance himself - and it snapped. Falling heavily against the broken handle, it entered the lower part of his bowel causing a severe wound. Mr. William. F. Langworthy, surgeon, attended to Mr. Hosking, but gave little hope of recovery. George Hosking suffered a lingering demise and passed away from his injuries on the 13th of July that year.

FOUND DEAD IN A WEIR.

In September 1891, when the hatches at Flete Weir were raised for fishing purposes, with the rush of water into the river came the body of a man aged about forty years of age, with sandy hair and a moustache. He was removed to the river bank where it was discovered he was carrying a silver watch and had two pounds in money in his pockets but no identifying papers. The body had evidently been in the water for some days, and his head had been frightfully battered.

[*There is no record of the man having been later identified, but hopefully he was and the perpetrator arrested.*]

MODBURY BAPTISTS.

Modbury Baptist Church on Wednesday the 2nd of December 1891, celebrated the centenary of it having been formally recognised as a place of worship. Reverend A. Brice of Devonport oversaw the service which was followed by a very well attended public tea. At a meeting in the evening, the senior Deacon Mr. Samuel Callard read an historical account of the church; it having been compiled by himself and Mr. Henry Nicholson of Plymouth. He said that in 1770 there were nine members who walked from Modbury to Kingsbridge to meet in fellowship, a distance there and back of fourteen miles. Finding the distance too far, especially in inclement weather, they instead began to meet in a small room in the town. The numbers who came to hear the Gospel gradually began to increase and they were soon looking for a larger place to meet. Unable to find anywhere, they stopped meeting for twelve months, then on October the 16th 1791 they again began to meet up, though it wasn't until 1805 that it was decided to build a church and attention was directed to a site in Church Street known as 'Old Walls.' The building was completed in August 1806, and opened on the 26th the same month.

Postcard, unknown year. Courtesy of Samuel Harrison.

In 1815 one hundred pounds was paid for the site of the present chapel. Galleries were later added in 1826, and in 1845 schoolrooms. In 1866 the church was re-seated at a cost of two hundred pounds and since then another three-hundred-pounds had been spent on alterations.

A minister's house was also built at a cost of two-hundred and fifty pounds. In 1911 the church underwent further renovation work and re-opened in January 1912.The opening sermon was delivered by Reverend Charles Joseph of the George Street Baptist Church in Plymouth, and following this was a well-attended tea in the schoolroom. The church had again been badly in needed of repair, the greatest defect being in the ceiling which was positively dangerous to persons worshipping in the building. The whole the interior had been cleaned and decorated, and new lighting had been installed. The cost of the renovation work amounted to one-hundred and seventy-six pounds and fifteen shillings. The repairs took three months to complete and during that period the services were held in the Public Hall. Modbury Baptist Church was said to be one of the oldest in the West of England.

JACKDAWS AT THE VICARAGE.

Reverend George Clark Green recorded in some of his notes in April 1892, a reminiscence of twenty or so years previously when a pair of jackdaws kept by him at the Vicarage had been taken from their nest in the summer and their wings slightly clipped. After this their wings were allowed to grow and they lived at full liberty in the garden. They were perfectly tame and would come and feed out of his hand and also come into the house. In the mornings they would knock at the window with their beaks to ask for breakfast.

The following spring they flew away to join their companions, make their nests, and rear a family. In the autumn they returned to the garden and again fed from his hand and were still as tame as ever. But the curious thing he found was that a couple of seasons later they brought with them another jackdaw - presumably the young of one of them and which was just as tame, although nothing had ever been done to make it so. It was impossible to tell which were the original birds and which was the new one. Moreover, when after few years one the jackdaws was accidentally killed, a replacement bird was brought to the garden by the other two.

WATERED DOWN GIN AT THE BELL INN.

George Treeby the landlord of the Bell Inn, was charged in August 1892 with having sold a pint of gin thirty-nine degrees under-proof the previous June. Superintendent Ryall had visited the inn on the 22nd of the month and purchased the gin. He then told the landlady (Mrs. Treeby), that he was going to have it analysed and asked whether she understood what he had said. She said she did and watched as he split the gin into three bottles. One he gave back to Mrs. Treeby, another he sent to a public analyst to have it examined, and the third he kept with a certificate stating that the gin was thirty-nine degrees under proof, which was four degrees under the level that was acceptable for publicans to sell. Mr. Treeby was fined ten shillings, with eleven shillings added on to cover costs.

A FARMER'S WIFE KILLED AT TOTNES.

Annie Wroth, the wife of Mr. Alfred Wroth of Ley Farm, Aveton Gifford, on the 2nd of December 1893 visited her sister Mary Sherwill at Wonton Farm, South Brent, as a stop off on her way to Totnes. Mr. Alfred Sherwill, Mary's husband, said he was also going to Totnes and offered to take Annie with him, leaving her horse and trap at the farm until her return. As they neared Totnes Workhouse, Mr. Sherwill's young horse caught itself on a wheelbarrow at the side of the road and ran against the kerb. Mr. Sherwill was pitched out and rendered partially insensible. With Mrs. Wroth still onboard, the horse bolted towards the High Street, and it was believed that Mrs. Wroth in fear for her safety jumped out. Mr. R. E. Bourne, seeing the un-manned horse and trap dashing past his house, he rushed out and found Mrs. Wroth lying in the road bleeding and insensible. She was taken to Dr. Smith's house close by and died there that evening without having recovered consciousness. She was forty-three-years old and left behind three children.

The horse was later secured after dashing in to the shop of Mr. Harris, a confectioner in the High Street, breaking a large pane of plate glass.

FIRE AT DAVIS'S HOTEL.

A fire broke out in the commercial room of Davis's Hotel on Broad Street when a lamp was left too close to a curtain on the evening of the 23rd of December 1893. Thanks to three young gentleman who were on the premises at the time; William Leigh, Edward Roberts and Ben Toms, the fire was quickly extinguished and the fire engine didn't need to be called out to assist.

OPPOSITION OF A RAILWAY TO MODBURY.

At the House of Lords on the 12th of June 1894, the Plymouth and Dartmoor Railway Company's Bill to run a railway from Plymouth to Modbury was read before a Select Committee. There was only one opposition to it; from Mr. Baldwin J.P. Bastard of Kitley.

In his petition against it he referred to his comfort and privacy. It was pointed out that Devon was filled with gentlemen's estates and all were only too pleased to have a railway line accessible near to them. It was also stated the line would not be visible from Mr. Bastard's house. Unfortunately, Mr. Bastard was unavailable at the reading of the bill having recently been injured in a carriage accident. Mr. William E.P. Bastard, his nephew, stated that his uncle said if the proposed line were to be built it would be visible for some considerable distance close to his mansion and would cross the ornamental waters, private grounds and carriage drive to his estate. He also said that his uncle felt there was no local or public necessity for the railway.

Kitley House 1829 engraving.

The Bill was finally passed in July with clauses added that if the construction was to go across the lake on Mr. Bastard's property, an embankment would be constructed to allow fresh and salt water to pass freely to and from the Yealm estuary.

LANGWORTHY MARRIES LANGWORTHY.

William Southmead Langworthy, a surgeon of London, the only son of the late Southmead Langworthy of Modbury, also a surgeon, married Miss. Ethelind Marion Langwothy, the daughter of the late Mr. John. M. B. Langworthy of Salcombe. Their marriage took place in St. George's Church on Tuesday the 11th of September 1894. The day was said to have been exceptionally sunny and warm, and as the bride came up the aisle on the arm of her uncle Mr. William Froude Langworthy, the choir sang the hymn 'The voice that breathed o'er Eden.' Ethelind wore a cream-coloured silk dress with a long train and tulle veil. She also wore a pearl brooch - a gift of the bridegroom, and her bouquet was a shower of seasonal flowers. Ethelind was attended to by one bridesmaid; Miss Mary Langworthy (the sister of the bridegroom) who also wore a cream-coloured dress and carried a pink and white bouquet - also a gift from the bridegroom. After the ceremony, the party were received at the house of Mr. and Mrs. William Froude Langworthy, the invitations being limited to near relations of both families. The bride and bridegroom then left by an afternoon train for Torquay, en-route for London. The wedding gifts were said to be numerous and costly. The bells of St. George's continued to ring merrily at intervals for the rest of the day.

BOARD SCHOOL CHRISTMAS SHOW.

The Modbury Board School, put on a highly entertaining Christmas show on the 20th of December 1894. The school hall was filled to overflowing, and the audience included many of the leading gentry of the neighbourhood. The programme was described as varied and excellent. Many of the girls who made up the chorus were dressed as 'little mothers' and carried baby dolls in their arms. Emily King who was ten-years-old showed remarkable talent in her recitation of 'Barbara Fretchie.'

Nine-year-old Edith Lavers sang a solo of 'Buy a broom,' and her voice was said to have far surpassed that of an older child and her performance quite remarkable. Charles Shepherd aged twelve, said to be the nestle-bird of a very musical family, sang 'The marmot' with much purity, affording evidence that he was a talent awaiting development. Great praise was also given to the teachers who had given the children such excellent training, especially Mrs. Salway the wife the head master. Also Miss. Husband the head mistress. Mrs. M Shepherd and her daughters; Miss. Martha Shepherd and Miss. Beatrice Shepherd, along with the help of Mr. Sharland Coleman and Miss. E. Geatches. The proceeds of the evening were donated to the Teachers' Benevolent Society.

TILL DEATH US DO PART.

Edward Ward of 7, Brownston Street, died on the 7th of March 1895 after a short illness. He was seventy-two. Just two days later his wife Susan aged sixty-one also died, again after a short illness.

EXPENSIVE DRUNKEN BOUT.

A special Petty Sessions was held at the White Hart Hotel on Tuesday the 8th of January 1895 before Messrs. N. W. P. Pitt and Mr. R. Ashley; county magistrates. Samuel Edgcombe and Henry Willcocks, two seamen, along with Edward Luggar, a labourer of Aveton Gifford, were charged with being drunk and disorderly in New Road the previous Sunday evening. Also, with assaulting Mr. Nicholas Lakeman, a chemist of Broad Street. Samuel Edgcombe was separately charged with assaulting Miss. Irene Pearce, the daughter of Mr. William Pearse, auctioneer, at the same time.

Mr. Lakeman said on the Sunday evening at about nine o'clock, he was walking Miss. Ethel Pearse to her home at Stoliford Farm. Her three sisters; Irene, Florence, and Blanche, were walking a little way ahead. Suddenly one of the sisters came running towards him and said that two sailors and another man were assaulting Irene. He hastened to her assistance where he found twenty-two-year-old Irene lying in a ditch next to Samuel Edgcombe who appeared to be helplessly drunk. He tried to help her to her feet but was prevented by Luggar and Willcocks. The men then turned on Mr. Lakeman and all three of them fell to ground. No actual blows were struck but a scuffle ensued. Mr. Robert Sherrell, a local farmer who was passing along the road came to Mr. Lakeman's assistance and freed him from the men.

Irene Pearse stated that on the evening in question she along with her sisters were returning home after church when they met with two sailors and another man who appeared very drunk. They passed them by quickly but found the men to be following them. They slackened off their pace in hope the men would pass them by, but instead of so doing Edgcombe stepped in front of her and opening his arms said "Come with me!" She struck him with her umbrella to try and ward him off but he stumbled and fell, and she fell underneath him.

Having heard the evidence the magistrates retired, and on returning to court fined all three men fifteen shillings each for being drunk and disorderly. Samuel Edgcombe was found guilty of assaulting Miss. Pearse and Mr. Lakeman, and was fined an additional four pounds for that offence. Edward Luggar was also fined one pound for assaulting Mr. Lakeman. Henry Willcocks was found not guilty of assaulting either Miss Pearse or Mr. Lakeman. Including costs, the total fines came to six pounds and fourteen shillings.

SHIPPING DISASTER IN THE CHANNEL.

The discovery of several bodies at different points along the South Devon coast left no doubts in the minds of everyone that a serious disaster has occurred in the Channel. In late April 1895, a boat bottom side up with the name 'S.S. Marie' on the stern was washed ashore near Thurlestone Sands in Bigbury Bay. At Challaborough a ship's lifeboat and a body lashed to a plank was picked up. Also, the body of a merchant seaman wearing a life-belt was found under the cliffs at Mothercombe. The following day the body of another merchant seaman was found floating in the water near to the Plymouth Breakwater. Another body was recovered at East Hollacombe, about a mile from the mouth of the Yealm River. The body of a young man carrying a rosary and other Catholic talismans was recovered by a fisherman and towed into the Yealm. He was wearing a cork life-belt, and from the appearance of his dress it was assumed he was the ships engineer. Among the considerable trail of wreckage picked up were a set of drawers, a door marked Boatswain's store, and an oar with 'Marie' painted on it. On April 21st 1895, the vessel which was registered in London had left St. Valery-En-Caux in France for Runcorn in Cheshire with a cargo of flints.

A VERY STRANGE CODFISH FIND.

Revered George Clark Green of the Vicarage, Modbury, in 1895 received a letter from his son Arthur, who was then working as a surgeon at Ripon in North Yorkshire, which included the following curious particulars: "A very large cod was on sale at a fishmonger's stall in the open market. The fishmonger went to cut the fish up for a purchaser, and as he laid it open to clean it a guillemot appeared. The fishmonger threw it to one side with the rest of the offal, but a boy begged to have it to take home to his father. The bird was in a great mess and covered with slime, but quite perfect and in no way digested showing that its captor must have been itself captured soon after its heavy meal. The bird was at once taken to the local bird-stuffer who identified it and weighed it after cleaning it from the dirt with which it was covered. It weighed exactly three and a half pounds."

A GENTLEMAN'S DOWNFALL.

The Marylebone (London) Board of Guardians applied to the Kingsbridge Board of Guardians in September 1895, stating that they had an elderly man named John Dawson staying at the workhouse who said he was a native of Modbury.

Now aged sixty-five, John Dawson had been brought up by a great-uncle, the Reverend Isaac Dawson, who was said to have as well as a lump-sum, left him all his property valued at about one-hundred-thousand pounds. He had been educated at Kingsbridge Grammar School, and afterwards went to Oxford where he took a Master of Arts degree at Brasenose College. He became engaged to the daughter of a titled gentleman, but the engagement for whatever reason was broken off. At that time, he had been associated with all the best families and was said to have been one of the leading figures in society. Intemperance and overindulgence were said to have led to the commencement of his downward course, and for many years he continued to live the high-life. In 1886 he left Modbury and went to Plymouth where he lived in a hotel for three years, visiting Modbury every Sunday to attend church. He would take the train

to Ivybridge, and no matter what the weather was he would walk from Ivybridge to Modbury to attend divine service, and would then walk back to Ivybridge and return to Plymouth even though he had plenty of means to provide a carriage. After that he went to Keighley in Yorkshire where he had been born and also owned considerable property. He then spent some time in Oxford in 1891 where he had at one time gone to university. He was recorded as living at lodgings at 132, High Street, Modbury on the 1891 census. Having left Modbury in 1886 and was not seen again, all his properties in the town as well as his residence, 16 Church Street, were eventually sold off as no trace of his whereabouts was known. Dawson was remembered as a learned and accomplished man, and Mr. Edgecumbe of the Kingsbridge Guardians said it would be better to keep him in London as it would hard for him to meet those of the upper classes with whom he was once on such familiar terms.

Unfortunately, the Marylebone Board of Guardians refused to keep Mr. Dawson and he was removed to the Kingsbridge workhouse. Some of his old acquaintances from Modbury and Plymouth started a fund for him, hoping to provide a small annuity so that he could be removed from the workhouse and live out his days in some form of comfort.

A LACK OF STREETLIGHTING.

At Modbury Petty Sessions on the 8th of October 1895, Richard Wakeham and Robert Williams were charged by Mr. E. W. Bickford the town's rate collector, with refusing to pay their gas rates. They upheld their objection by saying there were no gas lamps in the street in which they lived. The magistrates (Mr. E. Allen and Mr. K. Ashley) said they could not dictate to the Gas Company where they should put their lamps. He said the ratepayers were liable for the lighting of the town and must pay  the rate. Wakeham was ordered to pay two shillings and three' pence in costs, and Williams one shilling and two' pence costs.

CENSURE FOR A FAKE MEDICINE MAN.

Mr. R. R. Rodd the county coroner held an inquest Modbury in January 1899 into the death of James Wood, a forty-nine-year-old quarryman of Church Street. His widow said her husband had been suffering for some months from diabetes and had been attended to by Dr. Lakeman up until the end of the previous September when he then consulted with Dr. Fox of the Plymouth Dispensary. Soon after he saw an advertisement in a newspaper and as a result consulted Mr. W. H. Roberts of Plymouth, whom he met by arrangement at the Noah's Ark Inn on Saltash Street, Plymouth. Roberts gave him several powders for which he paid two pounds and ten shillings. Following this initial purchase further 'powders' were obtained and another one pound and two shillings was handed over. To begin with her husband said he felt better, but two days before his death he became quite ill and she sent for Dr. Lakeman.

William Henry Roberts who described himself as a gentleman with no occupation, except that of a former agent in Johannesburg, and residing 2 Barton Crescent, Mutley, Plymouth, said he was not a qualified medical practitioner although he did advertise that he could cure cancer and diabetes. He went on to say James Wood had consulted with him after reading that he had cured a lady of a similar disease. They had met at a public-house in Plymouth, but he did not physically examine Mr. Woods. Instead asked him to write down an account of his habits and mode of conduct. The powders he said were merely table salt for removing constipation. Had the deceased lived he would have continued to treat him and the amount demanded was to cover the whole course of treatment. He also said that Mr. Woods had told him a doctor in Plymouth had told him his disease was incurable, and that he personally had neither treat nor prescribed anything for Mr. Woods – he simply sold him the powders.

Dr. Thomas Lakeman of Modbury was next to give his evidence. He said he had last attended to Mr. Woods the previous September for diabetes. As Mr. Woods said he was unable pay for his treatment, Dr. Lakeman advised him to go to hospital where he would have a better chance of recovery. When he next saw him in the January, he was in a state of collapse and almost pulseless, as well as extremely weak and cold. Having been informed by Mrs. Woods that her husband was now being treat by a Mr. Roberts of Plymouth, and not knowing that he wasn't registered as a medical man, he advised her to send him a telegram immediately. In reply to the letter she sent, Mr. Roberts responded by saying that he had not treat Mr. Woods condition, as he was careful not to treat any case. After the death of James Woods, he carried out a post-mortem examination which showed that he ought to have lived for several years longer had he chosen to take the proper treatment. The coma he suffered and which attributed to his death had been caused by his diabetes. If the powders were simply table salt, then it was not injurious and Mr. Roberts's treatment had not accelerated his death.

The jury asked to have one of the powders which Mr. Roberts had given to Mr. Woods at their first meeting to be analysed, as well as one now in the possession of his widow. The inquiry was adjourned for a couple of hours whilst the investigation took place. On the inquest being resumed, Mr. Nicholas F. Lakeman, analytical chemist of Modbury, stated that the two packets of white powder proved to be as Mr. Roberts had said: common table salt. The coroner remarked that the inquiry had done good in exposing the wicked fraud practised on the deceased and on the public. He added that in view of the suddenness of Mr. Wood's death, he hoped persons requiring medical aid would consult no one other than a qualified medical practitioner. The jury returned a verdict of 'death from natural causes,' and through the coroner expressed strongly that the treatment given by Mr. Roberts was absolutely useless and was nothing more than a fraud. They severely censured him and warned him to be very cautious as to his future actions.

SHOT IN THE FACE.

Arthur Wroth, the sixteen-year-old son of Arthur Wroth of Ley Farm, was accidently shot in January 1899 by Mr. Hodder of Bennick Farm, who was out rabbiting and fired through a hedge at a rabbit that had sprung out from a hole. The shot hit Arthur full in the face and in the chest. He unfortunately lost his sight in one eye and after consultation with a specialist in Devonport the eye was removed to save the sight in the other.

This was the second tragedy to hit the Wroth family, as six years previously Arthur's mother had been killed when the horse pulling the trap she was travelling in lost control in Totnes. [See: **A FARMER'S WIFE KILLED AT TOTNES**.] A further tragedy was to follow later in the year when his father passed away aged fifty-one.

CAUGHT STEALING GUNS.

Henry Hill and Ernest Rundle, both boys, were brought before Modbury Police Court in March 1899 charged with stealing six rabbit guns from the property of Mr J. Proust of West Leigh Farm, East Allington. They admitted to taking the firearms. The Bench gave them words of advice, and told them that if they behaved themselves for the next twelve months, they would not hear anything more about it.

A RACE DOWN CHURCH STREET.

On the evening of Saturday the 1st of April 1899, Mr. William Pearse of Stoliford, along with his eldest son, were descending the steep hill leading into Modbury in their cart when the harness gave way. The horse at once sprang into a fast gallop, and before it had proceeded very far Mr. Pearse was pitched out on to his head, just outside the entrance to the church. His son however was able to jump out and was unhurt. The animal carried on down Church Street until it came into contact with a house and knocked down a little girl who was standing outside. Thankfully she was only slightly injured; the trap however was smashed to pieces. The horse continued on its mad journey into the centre of town where it was stopped after knocking over a man.

Back up the hill, Mr. Pearse was picked up unconscious and at once taken into the house of Dr. Henry Grenfell at 18, Church Street, who attended to his injuries; a nasty cut over his eye and multiple bruises. The animal was said to have only been slightly hurt, though likely incredibly frightened by the whole experience.

THEFT OF A BICYCLE AT SOUTH BRENT.

On Saturday the 20th of May 1899 at Totnes Magistrates Court, twenty-year-old Stephanas Shute of Brownston village was charged with having stolen a bicycle valued at eight pounds and ten shillings, from South Brent railway station the previous Wednesday. Mr. J.E. Philip of Brixham, the owner of the bicycle, stated that he had gone to the station at about eight p.m. and left the bicycle by some stairs whilst he went to purchase a ticket. When he returned his bicycle was missing and he informed the station master and the police of the theft. P.C. Yendell who was on duty that evening saw Stephanas Shute riding a bicycle near to the Royal Oak public house. His attention was drawn to him because he appeared to not be fully in control of the vehicle and was also carrying a walking stick. Further down the street he saw him fall off, but before he could get to him, Shute had re-mounted the bicycle and ridden off at speed. Hearing of the theft of the bicycle from Mr. Philip he made enquiries, and the following day went to Brownston where Stephanas lived with his parents. He wasn't home, but P.C. Yendell was told he could be found at Cotlass Farm [*also referred to as Cottlass/Cutlass and Cotley's over time*] where he was engaged in felling timber. When he arrived at the farm and challenged Stephanas in regards to the theft. He at first denied having taken it, but after telling him that he saw him riding it, Stephanas admitted the theft and said it was at his home hidden under his bed. They returned to Brownston, where in reply to his father asking why the police were there, Stephanas said, "I rode a bicycle away from Brent station last night. I don't know what came over me - I was drunk and didn't know what I was doing." P.C. Yendell and Stephanas then went to the bedroom, from where under the bed Stephanas pulled out the bicycle. The wheels had been taken off and packed up with the frame, whilst the chain was found under a sofa. The nuts-and-bolts Stephanas still had in his trouser pocket which he willingly handed over.

Stephanas was committed for trial the following month and given bail with two sureties of twenty-pounds, and paying five pounds himself. He was said to have never been in trouble before and came from a very respectable family and had given every assistance to the police in finding the bicycle. He was sentenced to one calendar month in prison.

MODBURY PETTY SESSIONS.

Held on Tuesday the 12th of October 1899 before Messrs. McAndrew (chairman), J, Allen, E. Allen, N. W. P. Pitts, R. Ashley, and the Reverend. W. D. Pitman, the following people were seen:

Mr. J. Yabsley of Aveton Gifford, and Mr. Luscombe of Modbury, were both exempted from having their children vaccinated.

John Pope of Aveton Gifford, was fined ten shillings plus seven shillings costs for being drunk whilst in charge of a horse and cart.

Henry Pearse of Modbury, had to pay ten shillings with eight shillings costs for using bad language in Galpin Street on August 24th. He was also fined five shillings with seven shillings costs for being drunk and disorderly at Yealmpton on September 25th. He chose to go to prison for fourteen days rather than pay the fine.

F. Graham of Ugborough, Robert Kingston, James Ellis, William Toms, and B. Woods, all of Modbury, were fined five shillings each for the non-attendance of their children at school.

Priscilla Small, a gipsy, who did not appear at the sessions, was fined thirteen shillings and six' pence or seven days in prison for drunkenness at the California Inn, Modbury.

Thomas Lyndon a gardener of Derriford, was sued by Margaret Thomas of Ugborough, in respect of her child. He was ordered to pay her three shillings and six' pence per week with an additional eighteen shillings in expenses.

SNIPPETS OF NEWS OCTOBER 1899.

Mr. John Drew aged sixty, formerly a Company Sergeant-Major of the 28th Company of Royal Engineers, and afterwards for many years a yard foreman at the local waterworks, was presented with a very handsome smoking cabinet, cap, and purse of money, by those connected with the works on the occasion of his retirement.

The death of Mr James Shepheard took place on Sunday the 8th of October after only a few weeks illness from an internal complaint. He was for many years a clerk with Mr W. L. Rogers solicitor of Modbury, and prior to that with Mr. Richard Andrews who previously carried on the business. Mr. Shepheard who was fifty-seven had acted as bandmaster of the Modbury Brass and String bands and was a member of the church choir for a great many years. His wife Sarah had died a few years previously, as had a son. Several grown up children were said to mourn his loss.

Mr Alfred Wroth of Ley Farm, Aveton Gifford passed away aged fifty-one on the 10th of October 1899. He had been in a rather delicate state of health for some time and had been ill for about ten days. His wife Annie had died tragically in 1893 after being thrown from a trap near Totnes, and earlier that year his sixteen-year-old son Arthur had been accidentally shot and lost one of his eyes. [Young *Arthur, an orphan and with only one good eye, continued to run Ley Farm with the help of his sister Beatrice who was a year older than him, along with three servants. He later went on to run Heathfield Down Farm in 1903.*]

GUY FAWKES.

Guy Fawkes day in Modbury was said to have been celebrated in greater spirit than any previous year, when in 1899 a low four-wheel trolley carrying a number of effigies was drawn through the streets, and afterwards having been set on fire they were again wheeled briskly through the town. Tar barrels were fixed on to the trolley and rapidly run into the centre of the road, leaving behind a stream of burning tar. Guys were proudly paraded and fireworks set off. The bells in the tower of St. George's Church were rung from six in the morning until well into the evening.

EXTENDED LICENCES.

In December 1899, Mrs. Chubb of the White Hart Hotel was given dispensation to have her licence extended on the 3rd of January 1900, to keep the hotel open until three o'clock in the morning for the occasion of the annual Hunt Ball. A similar application was granted Mr. Brooking of Davis's Hotel for a dance to be held on the 27th of December in aid of the of the Boer War fund. Also, for the occasion of a private function to be held on the 17th of January 1900.

1900-1950

DEATH FROM PNEUMONIA AND EXPOSURE.

In the depths of a very cold winters night in January 1900, ninety-year-old Robert Giles of Penquit Farm, Ermington, left his bedroom by the window which was ten feet from the ground. In a half-dressed state he was later met in the road by a labourer on his way to work. Mr. Giles was taken back to the house and put to bed, apparently suffering acutely from the cold. Dr. Grenfell was called and found the old man to have severe bruising to his back and shoulders, most likely caused by falling from the window. He also appeared to be suffering from delusions. Death came a short while later. At the inquest into his passing, Dr. Grenfell said that Mr. Giles had died of pneumonia, accelerated by shock and exposure.

THE BOER WAR.

Mr. William Davis, one of Modbury Rugby Club forwards, left the town in January 1900 to re-join his old regiment and to proceed to South Africa to partake in the Boer War which was then taking place in the country.

1st Bn. Devonshire Regiment during the Boer War. Picture courtesy of Wordpress.com

Mr Charles E. Green, son of the vicar of Modbury, who had also volunteered for service in South Africa was then on his way to Canada where he was to join the Canadian Police and proceed from there to the seat of war. He had previously been a member of the Canadian Police force but had resigned.

THE RETURNING SOLDIER.

Private George Edmund Wood of the 1st Devonshire Regiment arrived home to Modbury on the evening of the 11th of July 1900 to a fanfare welcome. At nine o'clock in the evening a carriage was seen at the entrance of the town. The townsfolk went to meet it, and unhitching the horse from the carriage, Private Wood on horseback was then paraded through the streets. The crowd sang patriotic songs and flags were waved. George was said to have been taken prisoner at Colenso where a bullet had passed through his boot. He then suffered an attack of enteric fever and on his recovery had been invalided home.

DIED OF PNEUMONIA.

Richard Coulton Andrews, a solicitor of Traine House, Brownston Street, died aged thirty of pneumonia on the 18th of September 1900. Even with the best help a medical man could provide in the form of his brother William, a surgeon, Richard's life could not be saved. Their father Richard Andrews Snr, also a solicitor of Modbury, had passed away on the 28th of December 1894.

MODBURY HARRIERS ANNUAL MEET.

The annual meet of the Modbury Harriers took place on Wednesday the 10th of October 1900 at the Market Cross, a day of very fine weather. Those in attendance were; Mr. W. Gage-Hodge (master- but did not hunt), Mr. F Langworthy, Mrs. Mitchell, Miss. Bartlett, Mr. P. Bartlett, Mr. S. Matthews, Colonel Bouchier, Mrs. Grenfell, Mr F. Langworthy, Mr T. Langworthy, the Reverend. A.T. Allin, Mrs. Allin, Dr. Spencer, Mrs. Spencer, Mr. J. Garland, the Reverend Honey, Mrs. Honey, Mr. Harris-Crimp, Mr. and Mrs. Baker, Miss. Jarman, Mrs. Toms of Ivybridge, Mr. C. Wyatt, Mr. H. Choake, Mr. C. Choake, J. Blight, and many others.

In the evening a dinner was held at the White Hart Hotel where Mrs. Chubb the landlady served a splendid meal to over seventy guests. Mr. Harris-Crimp who presided over the occasion remarked that he regarded the Harriers as a most interesting feature in the life of the parish and he was pleased to do all he could to support them. The Reverend Honey was described as having been like a 'second Jack Russell' during the hunt, having acted as deputy-master in the absence of Mr. Gage-Hodge, and in his speech said he was extremely glad to see a one guinea subscription from a tenant farmer over whose land they hunted that day. Some damage was unavoidable, but generally the farmers never grumbled and were always glad to see the hunt and to provide hares.

CONCERT FOR THE MODBURY HARRIERS.

On the evening of the 27th of November 1900, a concert was held at the Assembly Room in aid of the Modbury Harriers. Mrs. Matthews and Mr. Alfred Davis each played a piano solo; Miss. F. Kingwell sang 'The dear home land' and 'My love has come,' and also played two violin solos. Mr. Will Hitt of Dartmouth, sang a number of comic songs; Miss. Crabb sang 'The promise of life' and 'A May morning.' Mr. John Coleman played two flute solos, and Mr. William Gage-Hodge sang some comic songs. The assembled guests then removed themselves to the White Hart Hotel next door for a supper and smoking concert presided over by Mr. Gage-Hodge.

A TRIP TO TORQUAY.

A four-horsed brake left Davis's Hotel on Wednesday the 15th of May at quarter to seven in the morning with a party of twenty people who planned to visit an exhibition being held at St. Marychurch, Torquay. They reached the Torbay Inn at quarter past eleven and enjoyed a full afternoon at the show. The visitors then commenced their return journey back to Modbury at around seven-thirty in the evening, returning at a quarter past midnight. The trip was undertaken as an experiment to prove that the remoter parts of the beautiful South Hams district could be reached and enjoyed in one day from Torquay.

RETURNING HERO.

Thomas Pearse, the son of William Pearse of Stoliford, returned home on the evening of Tuesday the 18th of June 1901 from South Africa, after a two-year absence where he had been participating in the fighting of the Boer War with the Somerset Yeomanry. At the entrance to the town a large crowd assembled, and after taking the horse from the carriage in which he was travelling, they drew the vehicle through the town whilst singing patriotic songs.

COMPLIMENTARY DINNER.

A dinner was held in Modbury on Thursday the 25th of July 1901 for the volunteers of the town and district who had served in South Africa during the Boer War and had now safely returned home. The party included; Troopers Thomas Pearse, Harry Wroth, J. Sparrow, James Gill and George Wood of the 1st Devon Imperial Yeomanry. The men, who numbered over eighty in total were presided over by the Reverend P. Honey (Portreeve.)

WAYWARD LOCALS.

The same month (July 1901) Frederick Edgecombe of Aveton Gifford, was fined one shilling and seven' pence costs for bathing in the river Avon close to the highway without any clothes on.

For using obscene language within his own property, George Crocker of Modbury was fined two shillings and six' pence with an added six shillings in costs.

Benjamin Ryder and William Barring were both charged with stealing a cucumber, the property of Mr. Samuel Williams of Great Orcheton Farm. They had been part of a group of four men who had gone to Holbeton, and on their return called in at the farm to ask for a drink of cider to quench their thirst. A servant girl gave them both cider and milk to drink. Ryder and Barring then went into the garden of the farm, where Barring took a cucumber and handed it to Ryder who put it in his pocket. Mr. Williams told the Bench he didn't want to press charges but thought it a very mean act. Both men were fined five shillings each.

EXTRAORDINARY ESCAPADE BY TWO SERVANT GIRLS.

Bigbury was thrown into a state of great excitement on the night of the 11th of September 1901, when under mysterious circumstances many of the windows at William Wroth's Bigbury Court Farm were smashed. Alerting locals as to what had occurred and thinking there was a villain at large, a number of villagers assembled to keep guard armed with lanterns and weapons, but despite their presence windows continued to be broken. One man suggested that possibly some occult influence was at work because the stones that were breaking the panes appeared to coming out of nowhere. Four policemen were called to the scene; the farm buildings, the nearby church and churchyard were searched, and gunshots were fired into trees and shrubbery. The following night the same thing happened again and more windows at the farmhouse were broken. As no perpetrator could be found a police sergeant from Kingsbridge suggested that the mysterious culprit was possibly indoors and not out. On closer examination of the window panes, it did indeed show that the missiles had come from within the farmhouse and not from outside. Two female servants were requested to sleep away from the property the following night – and strangely the 'ghostly' happenings ceased.

The two girls; Beatrice Jarvis aged fifteen and Jane Hosking aged fourteen were brought before a very crowded and attentive Modbury Police Court the following Monday morning and charged with maliciously breaking thirty panes of glass valued at a sovereign. They both emphatically denied the offence, but the magistrates found them guilty, and expressing surprise at their delinquencies ordered them to pay for the damage at five pounds each. A further charge made against Beatrice Jarvis by Miss. Sarah Wroth that the girl had stolen a gold brooch, lace, and a ribbon, was dismissed. The items were found in her box when it was searched on a police warrant. Beatrice said she found the brooch and the Bench gave her the benefit of the doubt – a decision which was said to have been received with much applause.

BAPTIST MARRIAGE.

A wedding took place at the Modbury Baptist Chapel on Church Street on Wednesday the 2nd of October 1901, between Mr. Henry King of 16, Wellswood Place, Torquay, and Miss Margareta (Hettie) Edgcombe the eldest daughter Mr Thomas Edgcombe of Modbury. The ceremony was performed by the Reverend A. Harris, pastor of the chapel. Miss. Elsie Edgcombe, the sister of the bride, and Miss. Sissie Blight were bridesmaids, whilst Mr. John King, the brother of the bridegroom acted as best man. The bride was said to be tastefully attired and carried a beautiful bouquet, a gift of the bridegroom. The 'Wedding March' was ably played by Miss. Mitchelmore the organist. The happy pair then left at seven o'clock that evening for their honeymoon at an undisclosed location.

THE MODBURY STABBING CASE.

At the Devon Assizes held at Exeter on Saturday the 16th of November 1901, Elijah Angel a sixty-two-year-old hawker was indicted for wounding James Smith of Poundwell Street with a knife on the 8th of the month.

The Clerk of Assize: Are you guilty or not guilty? Prisoner: "I have no recollection of it. You can put me down as guilty if you like. I have been in six lunatic asylums in my time and I have not a friend in the world."

Angel then went on to state that he was a tee-totaller at the time of the alleged offence, though had no recollection at all of the action he was being charged with. Producing a blood-stained handkerchief and pointing to a scar by the side of his left eye, he alleged that he had been the one who had been wounded. The case was put back till the following Monday so that he could be mentally examined.

Monday - Mr. Bodilly who appeared for the prosecution, said that on the 8th of November Elijah Angel had knocked on the door of James Smith's house and offered rabbit skins, bottles, etc for sale. A transaction was made, but when Smith declined to buy any of the bottles saying they were not the kind he wanted, Angel, without any warning stabbed him with a knife. The knife entered his side and in trying to withdraw the weapon the blade was broken off. Angel then struck Mr. Smith in the chest with the handle of the knife before running away.

James Smith a china dealer, stated that he had had no altercation whatsoever with the accused. Mary Smith, the wife of Mr. James Smith, and a boy named Sheriff who witnessed the incident were also called to give their account of what had occurred. Dr. Spencer who examined James Smith said the stab wound was to the abdomen and about one inch in depth and half-inch long - it was a fairly serious wound. P.C. Bray, who was called to attended the scene said that as well as finding James Smith bleeding from a wound in his abdomen he noticed Elijah Angel had an injury near to his eye which was bleeding profusely. When he asked Mr. Angel how the injury had occurred, he said he didn't know, and made no suggestion that he had received it from Smith.

In summing up, the judge pointed out that if anything had been wrong with the accused's mind the prison doctors would surely have found it out. The jury therefore found Elijah Angel guilty and he was sent to prison for nine months.

BURNT TO DEATH; A MOTHER CENSURED.

The county coroner (Mr. R. R. Rodd) held an inquest on Monday the 10th of March 1902 into the death of Thomas Samuel Shute aged nine-months. Sarah Jane Shute of Back Street, the wife of Sydney Shute, a journeyman carpenter, said that the previous Friday evening she had put her three eldest children to bed in an upstairs room and left the baby in its cradle in the kitchen, close to three sheets spread over two chairs to air in front of the fire. There was a large fireguard in the room but she hadn't used it because of the sheets were drying on the chairs. There was also a curtain suspended from the ceiling to keep out the draught. She left the house for twenty minutes to go and watch a firework display that was taking place on the Green. On her return she found the kitchen to be alight. The sheets were burnt and the basket cradle in which the child had been placed was in flames. The bedclothes were destroyed and the baby severely burned. He died early the following morning. She said that before she left the house, she had placed the baby in what she believed was a safe position.

Dr. Henry Pode-Miles who carried out the post-mortem said that the child had been terribly burnt. The coroner said that the case was an incredibly sad one and he was prepared to accept the mother's statement that she placed the child in what she thought would have been a safe position, and he hoped the jury would do the same. Referring to the dangerous practice of airing clothes in front of an unprotected fire, he said in the present case it was miraculous that the whole cottage had not been destroyed and the three other children burned to death. The jury in returning a verdict of 'accidental death,' censured the mother for leaving the child in the manner in which she had done.

SEVENTY YEARS A CHORISTER.

John Cuming, who became a chorister at St. George's Church Modbury in 1832 aged eight, and had kept his voice the same ever since, passed away aged seventy-eight in April 1902. He was said to have been the oldest chorister in Devon.

MRS. DAVIS PASSES AWAY.

On May the 23rd 1902 at 12, Church Street, Elizabeth Davis, late of Davis's Hotel, died aged seventy-nine. Elizabeth was the wife of James Davis who was also the one-time landlord of the White Hart.
Was Davis's Hotel an establishment they also owned, possibly after running the White Hart? There were a number of people with the last name Davis in Modbury around this time, but it appears that only James and Elizabeth were connected to both inns. Their son Alfred who was the church organist and a regular piano player at both establishments.

AN UNDRESSED CARCASS.

This story would sound quite disturbing if you didn't comprehend that the gentleman in question was a butcher - On the 29th of May 1902 at Modbury Police Court on Monday, Charles Hurrell of Modbury was summoned for conveying an undressed carcass in a cart without sufficient covering. He was fined ten shillings with seven shillings costs.

CORONATION POSTPONED.

The Coronation of Edward VII and his wife Alexandra which was due to have taken place on the 26th of June 1902 was postponed at very short notice as the King took ill and needed surgery. The secretary of the Modbury Coronation Committee received a telegram from Sir F. Knollys, the King's private secretary stating: 'Coronation postponed, but the King wishes local celebrations to be carried out as arranged.' It was decided that the town should adhere to as near to as possible the original programme, and to turn the festivities into a peace celebration combined with a service in the parish church for the King's recovery.

The bells began to ring at six a.m., and at seven the Modbury band played 'God save the King' in the marketplace. The children, headed by the band, marched to church in the afternoon where a service was held with appropriate hymns and prayers for the King's recovery. At four o'clock the townspeople sat down to a high tea in the streets, and as soon as the tables were cleared the Reverend Honey (Portreeve) made a speech, expressing the sympathy of the parish with his Majesty's illness and their hope for his speedy recovery. After which cheers were given for the King, the Queen, and the Royal family. Elsie Edgcumbe and Miss. Blight then presented to the Vicar, on behalf of a list of subscribers with a very handsome silver bowl bearing the inscription: 'Presented to the Reverend George Clark Green by the parishioners of Modbury as a token of their esteem during the forty-three years he has been their vicar.' A cheque accompanied the gift together with an address, and a handsome book containing the names of the subscribers.

A flower show with then held and the awards were as follows:

Under 6 years old: 1st, Fred Wyatt. 2nd, Leonard Wyatt.

Under 9 years. 1st, Sidney Gillard. 2nd, Mabel Williams.
Under 12 years. 1st, May Bray. 2nd, Gertie Wyatt.
Under 15 years. 1st, Hettie Turpin. 2nd, Olive Harris.
Basket of Flowers. 1st, Hettie Turpin. 2nd, Sybil Trish.
Different kinds of wild flowers. 1st, John Ford. 2nd, Alan Andrews.
Named wild flowers. 1st, Ettie Lavers. 2nd, Emma Hingston.
Ferns. 1st, R. Rundle. 2nd, Henry Wyatt and Russell Bickford - equal.
Grasses. 1st, Ethel Cuming. 2nd, Gertrude Bickford.

A peace spoon (given by Mrs. Langworthy) was awarded Ettie Lavers for finding and naming over one-hundred different kinds of wild flowers.

CORONATION DAY.

On the 9th of August 1902, the inhabitants of Modbury finally got to celebrate the Coronation of King Edward VII and his wife Alexandra. The children, who had all gathered at the Market Cross were each presented with a commemorative medal at two o'clock in the afternoon. This was followed by a service at the church of St. George at three. Sporting events for all ages were played out in the streets accompanied by music from the Modbury town band, and in the evening a dinner was held at the White Hart Hotel over which the Reverend R.W. Honey presided.

At Aveton Gifford the Coronation celebrations were of a most enthusiastic character. Arches of flowers and foliage were erected in several parts of the village which were all splendidly decorated. A church service was followed by a procession headed by a band. A dinner was then followed with sports and dancing in the evening.

King Edward VII and Queen Alexandra in their Coronation robes.

A SAD CHRISTMAS FOR THE WOOD FAMILY.

Thirty-year-old George Edmund Wood of Galpin Street, formerly a Private in the 1st Devon Regiment, was buried on Christmas Day 1902. George had joined the army in 1889 aged eighteen and had seen considerable service in both India and South Africa. Whilst in India he was invalided home, and after being in reserve for eighteen months he was called up for service during the Boer War and sent to South Africa where he served for ten months; being present at Spion Kop during the storming of Wagon Hill, and the battle of Colenso. There he was taken prisoner along with Colonel Bullock of the Devonshire Regiment and around thirty of his men, also with several officers and men of other regiments. Wood was the only prisoner to have escaped. He made his way back to camp and arrived forty-eight hours later. He crossed the Tugela River twice and was present at the relief of Ladysmith. His health again failing, he was invalided home in July 1900 [see **THE RETURNING SOLDIER**] and since his return he had been under the treatment of the South Devon and Cornwall Hospital, Plymouth, where he died.

ABANDONMENT OF THE RIFLE CLUB.

The annual general meeting of members of Modbury Rifle Club took place at Davis's Hotel in March 1903, where it was unanimously decided that the club should be abandoned for one year as the present range was inadequate to encourage new people to join. There was said to be an ideal site for a range only two minutes' walk from the town and passed by the War Office authorities as being perfectly suitable, but the tenant absolutely refused to grant the use of the field.

RUGBY CLUB DINNER.

The annual dinner of the Modbury Rugby Club was held on Friday the 29th of April 1903 at the White Hart Hotel, where over forty members and friends sat down to an excellent spread. Mr. William Trinick, the vice president of the club presided over the proceedings. Mr Frederick Coyte, in proposing 'Success to Modbury Rugby Club,' said that the club had played twenty-three matches; won nineteen, drawn two, and lost two, scoring an amazing 1115 points for against 38.
During the evening there was a repertoire of songs sung by many of those present. Accompanied by Mr. Alfred Davis the church organist. The host, Mr. Mark Bunker, was thanked for his excellent services.

MODBURY INN UP FOR SALE.

After many decades of the Modbury Inn having been owned and run by the Wyatt family, thirty-three-year-old Charles Wyatt put it up for sale in May 1903. The inn was described as having a commercial room, two sitting rooms, bar, tap room, kitchens, dairy, cellar and offices, a large dining room, seven bedrooms, water closet, stores, a large yard, extensive stabling, cow-house, outbuildings, and a large garden at the rear. For viewing, applicants were asked to contact Mr. Wyatt at the premises, and any further particulars needed could be obtained in regards to the auction from Messrs. Andrews and Pode, Solicitors of Modbury.

COMPLAINTS ABOUT THE WATER SUPPLY.

At the fortnightly meeting of the Kingsbridge Rural District Council, held on Saturday the 8th of August 1903, the residents of Brownston Street called to attention the long distance they had go for water and asked for an additional tap to be placed mid-way along the road. Mr. T. Walter-Symons moved that the request be granted, but Mr. T. Edgecombe, councillor for the parish, described the request as the wildest he had ever heard, there being no part of the town so well provided with water in his opinion. The matter was referred to the Parish Council.

On the 5th of September at the next but one meeting of the District Council, it was reported that a new stand-pipe had been placed in Brownston Street. It was also suggested that a water tank in Church Street be connected to the main water supply to the town. This again was referred to the Parish Council.

NOT A TRAIN BUT A BUS.

As much as the residents of Modbury for a few generations had hoped for a railway station to be built in the town, in 1904 the Great Western Railway Company began a motor omnibus service between Modbury, Yealmpton, and Brixton, with intermediate stops at Flete and Dunstone. The service was inaugurated on Monday the 2nd of May, but owing to the condition of the roads and the bad weather, the going was said to be difficult. There were a good number of passengers on each of the trips and the full journey was said to take anything between fifty minutes to an hour. The trip between Modbury and Yealmpton was expected to take approximately thirty-three minutes.

SAMUEL WYATT.

Mr. Samuel Wyatt, aged sixty-three, a well-respected inhabitant of Modbury and former landlord of the Modbury Inn, was found lying unconscious in the roadway in a pool of blood. He was immediately attended to, but expired on the following day the 1st of February 1901 from a haemorrhage of the liver. He was said to have retired some years earlier due to poor health. His wife Mary Jane had passed away only a few months earlier on the 29th of June 1900.

ALLEGED POCKET PICKING AT MODBURY FAIR.

John Browning aged seventy-two, was charged in May 1904 with attempting to pick the pocket of Sarah Margaret Freeman of Brownston Street, Modbury, at the town's annual fair which had taken place on the Green. She stated that at twenty-past seven in the evening of the 4th of May, she was on the Green watching the children riding on the steam-horses on the roundabout when Browning came up and stood next to her. She felt something in her pocket, and turning round she saw her daughter-in-law accusing Browning of having dipped his hand in her pocket.

Mary Freeman, Sarah's daughter-in-law, told the hearing that she saw John Browning slide his hand under her Sarah cape, to which she exclaimed; "You blackguard, you are picking my mother's pocket!" Browning replied, "I'm sorry but you've made a mistake," and quickly disappeared off into the crowd. Mary immediately went to fetch P.C. Martin who soon after apprehended Browning for the offence.

"May I never see the light of Heaven if I did," said Browning when challenged. He then turned to Mary Freeman and said, "You will never prosper if you bring such a charge." His feeble excuse was that if he had lifted Sarah Freeman's cape, then it was simply for the purpose of seeing what was underneath. In answer to the charge against him by the Bench, he replied: "May I be as dead as my wife who died twenty-three years ago, if I had my hand in that woman's pocket." Sergeant Boughton of Avonwick interrupted at this point and said the prisoner had fifteen previous convictions recorded against him, two of them being five-year sentences. He was committed for trial at the Assizes.

At his trial held in Exeter in July 1904, it was stated that John Browning [*who also had a number of aliases*] had spent seventeen of the previous thirty-two years in prison. The judge called him an 'impudent vagabond' and that having been at this trade for the past thirty plus years he should not be at large in public. He praised the two Mrs. Freeman's for bringing the charges against him and sent Browning to prison for twelve calendar months with hard labour.

A TOURIST'S VIEW FROM A TRAIN OF THE SOUTH HAMS.

A lady traveller on a journey from London to Plymouth, described in a letter the scene as she passed through the South Hams… 'Nothing can exceed the beauty of the colouring; words fail to describe it. Every yard farther west the scenery becomes even more beautiful, and as the engine puffs its way to Ivybridge, it almost seems as though we are going too quickly through lovely Devon. Between Ivybridge and Plymouth another strange contrast is that of the sunny, luscious meadow-land, with glimpses of the rough, ragged Dartmoor, over which hang nebulous grey clouds which almost envelope and carpet the land with purple and gold. The cultivated land is dotted with flourishing farmhouses. Sheep and cattle graze merrily in the fields oblivious to the loveliness of nature surrounding their pasture.'

Postcard of the Modbury Inn, Brownston Street. Courtesy of Samuel Harrison.

POLLUTING THE WATERWAY.

At a Parish Council meeting held in July 1904, a letter was read out from the Kingsbridge Rural District Council asking what steps the Parish Council were going to do to stop residents throwing refuse into the brook in Bakehouse Lane. After some discussion it was decided that the police should be asked to warn the householders living nearby.

SAD FATALITY AT BIGBURY.

An excursion to Bigbury on the 1st of August 1904, a beautiful warm and sunny summers day, ended in tragedy with the drowning of a young man from Modbury. William Shepherd, his wife, three daughters, and a son Fred, along with two friends; John Lee a wheelwright of Roborough, and James Williams aged eighteen of Back Street, Modbury, arrived at the beach at around noon, and as the tide was out, they walked across to Burgh Island where the men decided to bathe. They chose 'Tom Crocker's Hole,' a stretch of water about ten feet deep where the fishermen stored their crab pots.

Neither John Lee nor James Williams could swim. John Lee, thinking the water too deep entered at the shallowest point, whilst Fred Shepherd at the last moment decided that it was unwise to enter. James Williams who was a strong well-developed young man, but not a swimmer, dived in and very quickly found himself in difficulty. This was noticed by Fred Shepherd, but as he was also a non-swimmer and there being no boat nearby, he could only look on in desperate panic as his friend floundered in the water and then drowned before his eyes. He quickly ran to raise the alarm, but it was fifteen to twenty minutes before the help of a fisherman called James Courtnay Boyce of Bigbury, who heard the desperate calls for help set off in his boat and rowed to the scene. Soon after Messrs. Breeze, Adlard, Tuckett, and Moreton, all of Plymouth, hastened to the spot and assisted in getting James' body out of the water, whereupon they applied artificial respiration for over an hour, assisted by ex-police sergeant Lethbridge of Devonport who was also on the beach, and a lady nurse from London. Their efforts were unsuccessful.

Old Postcard of Bigbury with Burgh Island in the distance. Courtesy of Pam Wilson.

P.C. Norris, of Aveton Gifford arrived at two-thirty p.m. along with Chief Officer Kelland of Challaborough Coastguard, and took charge of the body.

The same afternoon at Exmouth, Henry Bough, a nineteen-year-old hairdressers assistant, drowned whilst bathing in the sea. His body was carried out to sea by the tide.

MOTOR BUS FATALITY.

A very distressing fatality occurred near Flete, when between ten and eleven o'clock on Saturday the 5th of November 1904, a South Hams motorbus travelling from Modbury to Plymouth drew to a stop and the only passenger on board, James Raffill, alighted too soon.

Raffill, a twenty-year-old tailor's apprentice at Mr. Bradridge's shop in Modbury, lived with his family at the town's Gasworks where his father William was manager. He had boarded the bus at Vicarage Hill and sat next to the driver, stating that he wanted to get off at Sequer's Bridge near to Flete Lodge. The bus set off on its journey travelling at a modest eight miles an hour. Approaching the bridge, it slowed down to two miles an hour. The driver, George Miller, noticing James rising from his seat, told him to sit down until the vehicle had come to a complete stop. Then, just as he was applying the brakes, James suddenly stood up and jumped off in the opposite direction to which the bus was travelling. The young man fell and struck his head violently on the roadway. Insensible, he was with great difficulty placed back on to the bus by Mr. Miller and driven to the house of Dr. A. E. Gladstone at Yealmpton. Unfortunately help came too late as James had already passed away, the back of his skull having been smashed in. Dr. Gladstone said that death had likely been instantaneous.

Postcard of the first motor bus in Broad Street, early 20th century. Courtesy of Graham Ferguson.

At the inquest into James's death held at Yealmpton Police Station on the following Monday, Samuel Sloman, a labourer of Sequer's Bridge, stated that he watched the bus as it was going past him and that when James Raffill dismounted it was virtually at a standstill. A verdict of 'accidental death' was returned and no blame was attached to anyone.

During the intervening time between the accident and the inquest, James's body had been kept at the Yealmpton Hotel. One of the jurymen, Mr. Pode, asked whether the landlord was bound to take it in or could it have lain within one of the police cells. The coroner replied that there was no law obligating anyone to take in a dead body, there was though of course a moral obligation. The remedy was for all local authorities to have proper mortuary facilities and he did not think it was appropriate for police cells to be used for that purpose. He suggested that Plympton District Council should be approached in regards to providing Yealmpton with a mortuary.

NEW YEAR CHILDREN'S PARTY.

The children of Modbury Schools were invited to a New Year's party at Davis' Hotel on Monday the 2nd of January 1905. Buns, sweets, and oranges were distributed amongst them and a 'fairy' handed a package of gifts to each child. A giant cracker filled with treats was said to have caused great fun and laughter; the donor of which was a lady called Mrs. Peters.

DRUNKEN ANTICS IN A FIELD.

At Newton Abbot Petty Sessions in August 1905, Alfred Pedrick of Modbury was charged on the evidence of P.C. Lobb with being drunk, and assaulting him near to the town. The evidence was corroborated by P.C. Potter who said that Pedrick was found inebriated and talking to himself in a field by the side of a road. When they attempted to get him to move along he assaulted them both, striking and kicking out at them. His actions were said to like those of a madman and a conveyance had to be obtained to take him to police cells at Newton Abbot. Pedrick told the Bench that he had gone to the field for shelter and it was the two police officers who had assaulted him. He was fined five shillings.

WINTER WEATHER.

A holidaymaker visiting Modbury in the summer of 1905 asked a local what the weather was like during the winter months in the town, pointing out the fact that it was near to both the moors and the sea. The gentleman he asked responded by saying in a strong Devonshire accent, "Well, fust 'er bloars, then 'er rains, then 'er hails, then 'er freezes, then 'er snaws, then 'er rains, and then 'er bloars agin."

AN UNFORTUNATE ACCIDENT.

In February 1906, Alfred Leat, a youth, was in the process of driving a threshing machine at Ashridge farm run by Mr. Charles Pearse, when he caught a finger in a cog-wheel of the machine and the top part was sliced clean off. Alfred had been on the point of joining the Royal Navy and regrettably the accident made him no longer eligible to serve. It wasn't a happy year at Ashridge

Farm as a few months later, Charles Pearse, the much-respected farmer took ill after suffering a brain haemorrhage. He died ten days later on the 29th of July surrounded by family and friends.

AN OLD WAR HERO DIES.

There was a large gathering at the funeral of Mr John Tergiddo Mildren, a Crimean war veteran of Modbury, in May 1906. The first part of the service having took place at the Baptist Chapel with the Reverend W. Hillard (pastor) officiating, before moving to St, George's churchyard for the burial service.

Mildren, who was eighty-one and a native of Coverack St. Keverne in Cornwall had enlisted into the Royal Navy at Plymouth in 1844 aged eighteen as an able seaman and saw continuous service at sea for thirty-six years, retiring in 1880. He had spent fifteen years in the Royal Navy, three in the Merchant Navy and eighteen years with the Coastguard. His first voyage was in the 'America' a frigate which took him around Cape Horn. In 1847 he joined the 'Penguin' one of the old Falmouth packets. He afterwards served onboard the 'Britannia' and the 'Russell.' On the 'Russell' he saw extensive service and sailed to the Baltic regions. From there he was drafted to the 'Eagle' and then again served on the 'Russell' before joining the crew of the 'St. George' and the 'Revenge.' In the final few years of his service, he was appointed Chief Officer of Coastguards and stationed at the Skerries in Ireland, Salcombe, and Hope Cove near Kingsbridge.

John Mildren was said to have seen plenty of war service, being at the battles of Inkerman and Sevastopol. He had gone ashore during the Crimean war and would often relate the tale of how he served in the trenches with the late Admiral Tryon, whom he knew as a midshipman. Mr. Mildren was in possession of the Baltic, Crimea, and Turkish medals; the Crimean medal having the bars for Inkerman and Sevastopol. He and his wife Patience had come to live in Brownston Street, Modbury, in 1880 upon his retirement. His wife passed away in 1893 and the following year he married her spinster sister Ellen.

COTTAGE GARDEN SHOW AT MODBURY.

At the third annual exhibition of the Modbury Cottage Garden Society held in July 1906 at the Barracks, Modbury, there was a large attendance despite very unfavourable weather. The entries numbered nearly seven-hundred, which was three-hundred more than the previous year. This remarkable increase was chiefly due to the extra entries received for the 'cottagers' classes. The arrangements for the day were carried out in a successful manner by the honorary secretary of the Society, Mr. Alfred H. Salway. With the exception of the mile race, which was run on account of a number of competitors having to come from quite some distance away, due to the inclement weather the programmed sports events were postponed.

Mr. J. Andrews, chairman of the committee, extended the heartiest congratulations to the local M.P. Mr. Francis Mildmay and his newly-wed wife Alice, and expressed the hope that they would enjoy good health, happiness, and long life. Mr. Mildmay responded saying that it was a great pleasure that the first public function he had attended since his marriage should be at Modbury. He was exceedingly pleased to come to the town, for ties of an affectionate character had always existed between Flete and Modbury in his father's lifetime [*Henry Bingham Mildmay*] as well as his own.

Declaring the exhibition open, Mrs. Mildmay was presented with a handsome bouquet of flowers by Miss Minnie Salway and Mr. Mildmay was given a choice buttonhole by young Master Willie Salway.

The awards were as follows: Amateurs and farmers:
Round potatoes 1st, S. Pearse; 2nd, J. Coleman; 3rd, Choake.
Kidney potatoes 1st, J. Ford; 2nd, S. Pearse; 3rd, C. Wyatt.
Pods peas 1st, W. Pedrick; 2nd, Pool; 3rd, J. Coleman.
Broad beans 1st, G. Pearse; 2nd, W. Waldron; 3rd, J. Wyatt.
Scarlet rennet's 1st, W. Pedrick; 2nd, E. Meathrell; 3rd, C. Wyatt.
Carrots 1st, W. Pedrick; 2nd, J. L Walker; 3rd, J. Coleman.
Parsnips 1st, J. Hoopell; 2nd, W. Pedrick ;3rd, G. Fox.
Vegetable marrows 1st, J. C Mitchelmore; 2nd, A. H. Solway.
Tripoli onions 1st, J. C. Mitchelmore; 2nd, G. Fox; 3rd, T. Fine.
Spring onions 1st, J. Ford; 2nd, W. Pedrick; 3rd, J. L. Walker.
Eschalots 1st, J. Ford; 2nd, E. Meathrell; 3rd, Choake.
Lettuces 1st, J. Ford; 2nd, E. Meathrell
Cucumbers 1st, J. L Walker; 2nd, C. Pearse.
Leeks 1st, Bickford; 2nd, J. Coleman; 3rd, J. Hoopell.
Beetroots 1st, J. Wyatt; 2nd, J. L. Walker; 3rd, S. Pearse.
Rhubarb 1st, G, Pearse 2nd, G. Fox.
Apples 1st, G Pearse; 2nd, S. Pearse; 3rd, W. G. Luscombe.
Blackcurrants 1st, A.H. Salway 2nd, J. L. Walker.
Redcurrants 1st, Miss. Husband; 2nd, G. Fox; 3rd, J. L. Walker.
White-currants 1st, A. H. Salway; 2nd, J. L. Walker.
Raspberries 1st, A. H. Wroth; 2nd, H. W. Wyatt; 3rd, C. Wyatt.
Gooseberries 1st, J. L. Walker; 2nd, Miss H. Ford; 3rd, Mrs. Wreford.
Collection of fruit, four different kinds 1st, G. Fox; 2nd, J. L. Walker.
Collection of vegetables, eight different kinds 1st, J. L. Walker; 2nd, S. Pearse; 3rd, Davis Bros.

IRREGULAR MARRIAGES.

Great consternation arose in March 1907 when someone happened to make the shocking discovery that the eight marriages that had been solemnised in St. John's Chapel at Brownston since 1882 had been 'irregular,' the building not having been licenced for such ceremonies. The chapel which had been built in 1843 had been consecrated for the performance of divine service but not for the banns and the solemnisation of marriages. A bill was therefore presented to Parliament asking to make those marriages that had taken place valid.

SWEARING IN THE STREET.

At Yealmpton Police Court on Monday the 22nd of April 1907, Thomas Pearce, a labourer of Modbury, pleaded guilty to using bad language in the street. The arresting constable stated that Pearse behaved like a madman. The defendant then swore in court and was fined twenty shillings or take the option to serve fourteen days in prison.

KINGSBRIDGE RURAL DISTRICT COUNCIL.

The Kingsbridge Rural District Council met on Saturday the 13th of April 1907. Mr. T. Willing presided and Dr. W. H. Webb presented his annual report. He stated that new sewers had been provided at Blackawton, East Prawle and Chivelstone. At Frogmore a very important new sewer had done away with the long-standing insanitary conditions there and water supplies had been improved at West Alvington, Woodford and Modbury.

During the previous twelve months forty-three notifications of reportable illnesses had been received, against seventy-seven the previous year. Twelve cases of diphtheria had been reported; one at Aveton Gifford and three at Slapton proved to be fatal. There had been nineteen cases of scarlet fever; one at Blackawton, four at Kingsbridge, six at Modbury, three at Stokenham and five at West Alvington. Of the six reported cases of enteric fever; one each occurred at Buckland, Hallsands, Woolston and Frrogmore. Two arose at Bedlime and at Woodleigh.

There had been one-hundred and forty-eight registered deaths of all ages and causes, giving an annual death-rate of 13.02 per one-thousand of the population. For the same period two-hundred and fifty-eight births were registered, giving a birth rate of 22.6 per thousand of the population. The zymotic [*contagious diseases*] death-rate was 0.61 per thousand of the population. The previous year it had been 0.17. The birth rate had been 3.2 higher than the previous year, the highest for ten years.

Influenza accounted for five deaths; phthisis [*consumption*] fourteen deaths; cancer six deaths; violence four deaths - two said to be an accident and two to suicide. Of the total deaths over one-third exceeded the age of seventy and considerably more than half of these were over eighty.

A SHOP WITH NO NAME.

In May 1907 it was reported that in Modbury there was a butcher's shop which had no name, and it had not had one for the previous one-hundred and twenty years. When the business began, the owner for whatever reason didn't have his name inscribed on the shop front. Business thrived and in time the butcher retired leaving the nameless shop to his son. The shop then continued to be handed down again from father to son, though none of those into whose occupation it came would have his name displayed on any signage, fearing that to do so might break the run of good fortune with which the business had been favoured.

[*A little bit of detective work led me to find mystery shop – Coyte's of Church Street. William Coyte (1784 - 1855) was the founder of the business. It then passed to his son Edmund (1831 - 1915) and then on to his sons George (1864 – 1936) and Frank (1867- 1935) who were the owners of the business in 1907. In 1921 after his retirement, Frank went on to become the vice-chairman on the Modbury Parish Council and had also recently been elected onto the Kingsbridge Urban Council. Two other brothers, Percy and Charles were managers for Lloyds Bank. Charles in Plymouth and Percy in Modbury.*]

RAILWAY PROPOSAL.

The inhabitants of the South Hams put forward a proposition to the Great Western Railway Company in August 1907, suggesting that an extension to the railway line from Yealmpton to Modbury was much needed [*an earlier proposal had been made in 1845*] as the existing means of travel to the parishes of Modbury, Aveton Gifford, Kingston, Ringmore, Bigbury and Holbeton were inadequate and unreliable. It stated that with co-operation of the principal landowners a route could definitely be assured.

MODBURY COTTAGE GARDEN ANNUAL EXHIBITON.

The fourth annual exhibition of the Modbury Cottage Garden Society held on Monday the 5th of August 1907 held at the Barracks was an outstanding success, with over seven hundred entries. An added attraction that year was pony jumping competition, which was sadly marred by a regrettable accident when the pony ridden by Mr. Henry W. Allin threw him and then accidentally put its foot upon him neck, badly injuring him. He thankfully made a full recovery.

QUARELLING COUPLE

In September 1907 at the Yealmpton Petty Sessions, Richard Ford Parkhouse, a pensioner of 16, Brownston Street, was summoned for assaulting his wife Eliza, who alleged that on the 24th of August whilst she was attending to her household chores her husband beat her severely. She said he had on previous occasions thrashed her and had recently threatened to 'cleave her down like a bullock.' She absolutely denied her husband's counter accusation that he had caught her committing adultery. Dr. Andrews who examined Eliza said that she had two black eyes and had complained of broken ribs, although when examining her they were not found to be broken. A young man named George Watts was then called by Mrs. Parkhouse as a witness, who went on to create much amusement when he disputed her evidence. Mr. Parkhouse who had been in the Navy for twenty-years and in possession of a good conduct medal, said he had received much provocation from his wife and had been instructed to take divorce proceedings. The Bench said that was a case for another court and they ordered him to pay a fine of ten shillings plus costs, allowing until the date he received the next instalment of his pension to pay the fine.

THEFT FROM THE HOUSE OF GEORGE RENDLE.

John Neagle, an eighteen-year-old hawker, entered the home of George Rendle, a baker of Galpin Street, and stole some money on July the 2nd 1907.

Galpin Street, Modbury 1905. Postcard courtesy of Samuel Harrison.

At the Devon Quarter Sessions held on Tuesday the 15th of November at Exeter, Neagle, who admitted his guilt, handed over a written statement in which he attributed his downfall to gambling and asked for leniency as he promised to reform. The Court sentenced him to twelve months' imprisonment. The chairman of the jury observing that in imposing what might appear to be a heavy sentence he hoped whilst in prison Neagle would learn a useful trade.

DEATH RECORDED FORTY YEARS LATER.

On Monday the 3rd of November 1907, the Probate Court in Modbury were asked to swear to the death of Cecil Read Parminter, the son of Reverend George Parminter, the one-time curate of St. George's Church. When Cecil was seventeen-years-old in 1866, he had become apprenticed to a firm of merchant shipowners owning a vessel called the 'Strongbow.' The last sighting of the vessel was on the 1st of November 1866 when it was sighted in the Bay of Bengal whilst on its return voyage from Calcutta to England. After that day nothing more had been seen or heard of the ship or any her crew. The ship was eventually posted as missing and the insurance paid out. The present application was now being made because Cecil's mother had died, and as a direct descendant he was entitled to a share of her estate amounting about three-hundred and forty-five pounds.
Leave was granted to swear to the death of Cecil Read Parminter as of the 1st of November 1866.

A GIFT TO HIS TENANT.

Mr. John Lavers, of Penquit Farm, Ermington, on his death aged seventy-three in July 1907, left an estate of £5,489. He bequeathed to his housekeeper Elizabeth Ann Bunker, two-hundred pounds as well as his freehold cottages and blacksmith's shop at Kingston. To his tenant Samuel John Leigh, he left his orchard and cottages at Ermington. The rest of his estate he left to devolve as if had died without having left a will.

COW GIVES BIRTH TO QUADS.

In April 1908 a cow belonging to Mr. Samuel Williams of Orcheton Farm, gave birth to four calves. Three were healthy and thriving, but the fourth unfortunately survived for only a few hours.

THE UNFORTUNATE CHARLES WYATT.

In June 1908, Charles Wyatt was declared bankrupt. At his hearing at the Stonehouse Bankruptcy Court in Plymouth, he stated that he was thirty-eight-years-old and the landlord of the Exeter Inn in Modbury. He said he had been a butcher until 1896, when he gave up his trade to assist his father in the management of the Modbury Inn.

Two years later his father transferred the business to him and he agreed to pay his father ten shillings a week and thirty-pounds a year in rent for the premises. His father passed away in 1901 and subsequently the mortgagees sold the property in 1903 and he moved to the Exeter Inn, also in Modbury. He received nothing from his father's estate and started at the Exeter Inn with nothing but the trade fixtures which he brought with him from the Modbury Inn. At that time, he owed the bank one-hundred and four-pounds. That was paid back with the aid of a loan of one-hundred pounds which he obtained at Dartmouth. But by December 1903, he owed the bank one-hundred and sixty-one pounds. The Official Receiver pointed out that when his father died, he had started with a clean sheet, yet by 1903 his overdraft had grown to one-hundred and sixty-one pounds. Charles explained that he had also taken on a mixed farm of thirty acres for which he paid sixty-five pounds a year. He gave that up owing to bad luck as he had lost six horses and a number of cows from various causes.

CHURCH STREET, MODBURY.

Old postcard of Church Street. The Exeter Inn is on the right. Courtesy of Samuel Harrison.

The Bench fined Charles Wyatt fifty-shillings for a licensing offence and added to that the costs of the case which amounted to ten pounds. In his defence he stated that he had been plagued with troubles. His mother was suffering from a serious illness and his child had died from diphtheria which had left him broken and very nearly ruined his dairy and licensed business for six months. [*This was Stanley Victor Wyatt who was only a few months old when he died in late 1901*. Charles' *father, Samuel Wyatt, also passed away on 1st of February of the same year*]. He attributed his failure to keep up with his business dealings were due to sickness and to heavy bank interests, though admitted that the interest charged on the overdraft and loan was only five per cent. He also admitted to never having kept a record of money drawn from the business and had never had his books balanced. Mr. Dobell who was representing him, pointed out that during the time the overdraft was being incurred, Charles Wyatt had spent money on stocking his farm. He applied for the closing of the exanimation and the Official Receiver offered no objection, although he said he felt the losses might have been very much less if Mr. Wyatt had chosen to close down the public-house much sooner than he had rather than struggling on.

In 1911 Charles and his wife Helena were living in Redruth, Cornwall, where he worked as a coachman. Of the four children born to Charles and Helena only two were still alive; Charles Frederick [known as Fred] aged fourteen and Leonard Manning Wyatt aged thirteen. Another child having died in infancy, likely in Cornwall.

LOST AT SEA.

Mark Bunker, a fifty-two-year-old Naval pensioner, having served in the Royal Navy from 1873 until 1891 when he returned to Modbury. In 1893 aged forty and a bachelor, he married Emma Chubb a thirty-nine-year-old spinster. The following year they had a son, William. Mark's yearning to go back to sea must have got the better of him, as he is recorded as having died at sea in North Sulawesi, Indonesia on the 30th of January 1906. In 1902 Mrs. Elizabeth Chubb of the White Hart Hotel asked for a temporary licence to be handed to her son-in-law Mark Bunker. It appears that Mark may have gone back to sea around September 1905 to make some extra money, as a temporary licence was handed to George Sercombe, formerly of Exeter that same month.

MODBURY PETTY SESSIONS – AUGUST 1908.

Mary Simmons, a young woman who a police constable found lying drunk on the roadway at Modbury was fined two shillings and six' pence.

Aaron A. Tozer was fined one pound for keeping a dog without license. Edith Warren had to pay seven shillings for not having her name on the collar of her dog.

Charles Norman, for leaving his chipped potato cart at Modbury with no-one in charge of the horse was fined ten shillings plus six' shillings in costs. Aaron Andrew for a similar offence at Ugborough, was fined ten shillings and four shillings in costs.

Lewis Osborn and George Tuskerman were both fined ten shillings with four shillings in costs for driving horses dangerously and without reins at Ugborough.

William May of Shipham Farm was fined two pounds and sixteen shillings in costs for having unjust scales and weights. James Lapthorn of Ermington and Richard Hillson were both fined one pound and eight shillings for a similar offence. Agnes Reddicliffe and Peter Reddicliffe, both of Ermington, were summoned for a similar offence and fined one pound with twelve shillings costs.

James Glasson of Plymstock was fined twelve shillings including costs for driving his cart without a light in Plymstock.

Richard Jones was fined ten shillings for using foul language at Ugborough on the 29th of July.

John Lakeman and Thomas Lethbridge from Aveton Gifford were charged with being drunk and disorderly, and Charles Hurrell for using bad language. Mr. Doff a solicitor of Plymouth appeared on behalf of the defendants. He was obviously good at his job as the case against John Lakeman was dropped and Thomas Lethbridge and Charles Hurrell were both dismissed.

Postcard of Aveton Gifford, courtesy of Malcolm Henderson.

BICYCLE ACCIDENT.

Tom Reeves aged sixty-three, the steward of the Modbury Conservative Club, was riding his bicycle down the steep slope of Brownston Street in April 1908 when he lost control at the bottom and crashed into the window of Mr. Trinick's printing, stationery, and fancy goods establishment at 14, Broad Street. Four plate glass windows were smashed and the wooden frame damaged. Mr. Reeves was taken to the South Devon and East Cornwall Hospital in Plymouth where he received treatment for a broken pelvis and severe injuries to his right arm.

MODBURY HUNT, MARCH 1909.

A 1909 newspaper article covered the 'Huntsmen of Modbury' during a hunt in March of that year. The writer stated that a man had once written that it was possible to live in Modbury, and keep a hunter on one-hundred pounds a year. It was said that in 1856 Mr. William Southmead Langworthy started a pack of beagles in the town and were hunted by him for ten seasons. Mr. George May succeeded him and held the master-ship from 1866 until 1884; his huntsman being William Toms, who hunted for no less than twenty seasons. From 1884 to 1894 Mr N. W. Pitts was master, with Phil Back as his huntsman. The Harriers were next hunted by a committee with Mr. Charles Cole as huntsman, until they were taken over by Mr. William Benfield who hunted them himself. He was succeeded by Mr. William Gage-Hodge in 1899. Mr. Gerald Halifax being the next master in 1903, and in 1905 the Rev. Reginald Honey was appointed master, with Mr. Kennett as his huntsman. When Mr. Honey resigned to take up a new position within the church, the now present master Reverend Alfred T. Allin took charge, and he employed Mr. W. Goddard as his huntsman, who had got together a good working pack of hounds which he kept at kennels situated about a quarter of a mile from the town. There were presently fourteen pairs of working hounds – eight pairs of dogs and six pairs of bitches. There were also eight pairs of puppies in training.

Speaking to the hunters, the writer stated that they all appeared to know each other well, and if anyone failed to turn up for a meet or a kill they were missed, and mild chaff would greet those who parted company with their horse without adequate cause. The doctor who was mounted on his big grey was usually at hand should a more serious accident occur. He was told that the Harriers met twice weekly and usually covered around twenty square miles of ground, comprising of grass and plough in equal proportions. The field was largely made up of farmers. A mention was given to the late secretary; Major Peters, who was kindly and courteous, and liked by everyone. He was said to have died two seasons previously after a brief illness. Also, the late Mr. Pearson of Ermington who was a sportsman to the end and who, after breaking a previously injured arm in the hunting field met with his death by a fall from his dogcart while driving a young horse in July 1908. A few ladies were said to hunt with the Modbury Harriers besides the master's wife (Mrs. A. S. Allin) and their two daughters; Gladys and Evelyn, who were rarely absent from meets. Miss Eleanor Taylor, one of the younger members of the hunt aged just fourteen also rode with them on a black pony called Tommy.

Interview with the hunt members over, the writer, also on horseback, followed the pack and the riders. He watched as a hare was started at Preston and ran towards the main road near Flete, where it turned into a field and swam the river before crossing the park and heading towards Modbury where it ran through the vicarage garden, up to the back of the churchyard, and through a narrow lane into Church Street where it was killed in Mr. Coyte's butcher's shop. Afterwards the hunt master Reverend Allin commented on the fact that grey hunters were very numerous that season. Both he and the secretary Mr S. Matthews were riding horses of that colour, as was his daughter Gladys Allin, whose mount 'Grey Lad' was half-brother to 'Grey Lass,' which generally carried Mr. Goddard when her master (Mr Harold Allin) was away at university in Cambridge.

BELL INN.

At the adjourned Licencing Sessions on Monday the 8th of May 1909, Police Superintendent Jeffery objected to the renewal of the license of the Bell Inn. Stating that his objection to the house was on the ground of redundancy alone.

Postcard of the Bell Inn. Courtesy of Samuel Harrison.

Within one-hundred yards of the house there were four other licensed public houses and one wine and spirit grocer's off-license. The population of Modbury was 1,242 which worked out at one licensed house to every one-hundred and eighteen persons. The population of the town itself was eight-hundred and twenty-four, exclusive of children, which meant that there was one licensed premises per ninety-seven adults. The rateable value of the Inn was fifteen pounds gross and eleven pounds and five shillings net. The Bell Inn was the oldest of houses and the premises were dated. He did not know whether the licensee (Mr. Thomas Jones) had been requested to make any alterations, though he had nothing against the character of the house. Mr. Ward who was defending the licensee said he had occupied the premises since 1905 and there had been no complaints against the house, from which Mr. Jones had been able to make a living and there was still several years to run before his lease expired, and he was prepared to carry on. The justices decided to refer the case to the County Compensation Authority. In July of that year Mr. Maby, the owner of the Inn was compensated four-hundred and six pounds, and Mr. Jones the tenant, one hundred and seventy-five pounds.

DIED IN ST. GEORGE'S CHURCH.

Sixty-eight-year-old William Froude Langworthy, was taken suddenly ill and died during the service at St. George's Church on Wednesday the 24th of March 1909. William had been a surgeon in partnership with his brother George Vincent Langworthy, but had retired a number of years previously. He was a staunch churchman and had once held the office of churchwarden, and was also a director of the former Modbury Gas and Coke Co. (limited) and of the Modbury and Ivybridge Omnibus Company. He owned property in Modbury and was keen sportsman, and regularly hunted with the Modbury Harriers. He left behind a widow and two brothers.

THE DEATH OF FREDERICK LANGWORTHY.

Mr. Frederick Langworthy of Brooke House, died on Thursday the 30th of July 1909. He was sixty-two-years-old and the sixth son of the late Dr. William Froude Langworthy [1788 - 1851.] He had been apprenticed to the late Mr. Richard Andrews, solicitor of Modbury, and went on to become a qualified solicitor in his own right in 1874, and had practised in the town all his life. The sudden death of his brother, the late Mr. William Froude Langworthy [*see above*] in St, George's Church in March of that year had very much affected him and he was said to be already suffering from heart trouble. He was well known and much respected and had for many years served as foreman for the borough jury, and had been a prominent figure in local affairs. Frederick had never married, and lived with his brother Mr. George Vincent Langworthy, a surgeon at Brooke House. His funeral took place at St George's Church on Tuesday the 1st of August 1909, the Reverend Samuel Stidston (Modbury) and Reverend C. Green (Brixton) officiated over proceedings.

ACCIDENT ON CHURCH STREET.

A steam powered motor lorry belonging to Mr. Richard Owens, a coal merchant of Modbury was being driven up Church Street, when at around twenty to seven on the evening of Tuesday the 8th of August 1909, whilst on his way to Yealmpton Station to pick up a load of coal; half way up the hill the brakes failed and the lorry ran backwards uncontrollably and crashed into the premises of Mr. Edward Moysey, a house painter. The front part of his shop [No 6] and part of his sitting-room window were smashed in, and the front of the house cracked to the roof. Mrs. Moysey had just left the sitting room with her baby in her arms and thankfully avoided serious injury, though she was said to be suffering from shock. The house was so badly damaged that the Moysey's had to find temporary lodgings elsewhere. Mr. Owens was thankfully insured against such accidents.

DEMISE OF REVEREND GEORGE CLARK GREEN.

The Reverend George Clark Green, who for half a century had ministered the spiritual needs of the parish of Modbury, died on the 29th of August 1909 – the day after his eightieth birthday. He had lived in the reign of three Sovereigns and served under five Bishops. He was soon to have celebrated his golden jubilee. His health had been failing for some time, but he had only been seriously ill for a few days prior to his passing.

Reverend George Clark Green.

Some of the memories he recounted to his parishioners during his sermons were those of his early days living in Eton where his father the Reverend G.K. Green was a fellow. He recalled King William IV patting him on the head, and a little later when he was invited to a party at Windsor Castle, he met the then Princess Victoria. Also, in 1840, he recalled seeing some boys from Eton College leading the horses that drew the royal carriage containing the new Queen and Prince Consort through the town when they returned from their wedding.

George Clark Green was educated at Eton and King's College Cambridge. He went on the become the curate at Everdon in Northamptonshire before coming to Modbury in 1859; the post being made vacant by the death of Reverend Nutcombe Oxenham on the 13th of September of that year.

BELLS OF ST. GEORGE'S CHURCH.

The bells St. George's Church which had been out of action for some time owing to the dangerous condition of their fittings were finally rung again on Sunday the 30th of October 1909 after having been rehung on a new principle.

VILLAGE OR TOWN?

An article written in November 1909 stated that a visitor to Modbury called it a village, to which an indignant resident proclaimed that it was a town, and no ordinary one at that. The visitor was informed that according to an ancient book which was now in the possession of a lady inhabitant, it was made clear that the town was of antiquity and had once been a town of much importance. A yearly Court-Leet had been held, and at the Michaelmas Court a Portreeve was appointed, together with constables and other officers. Even in those early days Modbury had been a hive of industry and a large number of its inhabitants had been engaged in the woollen trade. There had also been a hat making factory in the town. There had been fairs and markets held twice yearly. According to Tristram Risdon in his survey of Devon in 1801, there were 1,813 people living in the town; nine-hundred of whom were employed in a trade.

FALL FROM A LADDER ON CHURCH STREET.

Mr. Cridland Choake met with a serious accident on Saturday the 16th of April 1910 when he was making some alterations to a house his father had recently bought in Church Street. As he was inspecting the work, the ladder he was on slipped and he was thrown twenty feet to the ground. Several of his ribs were broken and it was thought most probably his collar-bone. He also suffered cuts to his head.

ATTEMPTED MURDER AT COOMBE FARM.

In July 1910 at Modbury Police Court thirty-year-old Alfred Pedrick who we first met in 1905 [see: **DRUNKEN ANTICS IN A FIELD**] was charged with the attempted murder of twenty-one-year-old Ethel Mary Luscombe, the assistant housekeeper to Robert Smerdon of Coombe Farm.

On the evening of Thursday the 7th of July, Alfred, who had made an attachment in his mind to the young woman, and had previously made threats of what he would do to her if she didn't show him any encouragement, made a remark about wanting to shoot her. Not taking it seriously, Ethel still thought it best to ensure that her master's gun was well hidden. About a quarter of an hour later she made her way to nearby Bearscombe Farm to collect some eggs, and noticed Alfred following her. He began shouting at her and using bad language. Arriving at Bearscombe Farm she told Mrs. Horton the farmer's wife what had happened, and after staying for half an hour Mrs. Horton said she would escort Ethel back to Coombe Farm. Not long after she had returned home, Alfred, holding an axe, said to Mrs. Smerdon; "Where is she? I'm going to chop her head off and do for her.' ['*to do for' was a phrase often used meaning to do time in prison for murdering someone.*] Hearing this, Ethel rushed upstairs to her room where she locked the door behind her. Moments later Alfred began to knock through one of the panels of the door with the axe, kicking the lower portion violently and smashing it off its hinges. He rushed towards her just as she was about to jump from the window, but instead of jumping she tried to fight him off. The first strike he made towards her hit the bed, but the second strike caught her on the side of her head, just above her right eye. Mrs. Smerdon had by now ascended the stairs after hearing the commotion and was able to wrestle the axe from Alfred's hands. Seeing the blood pouring from Ethel's head, Alfred appeared to calm down a little and asked her to come downstairs so he could 'tie it up.' She refused and told him to go downstairs alone and she would follow on, which he did. Ethel then made her escape by running from the house and back to Bearscombe Farm about quarter of a mile away, where Mrs. Horton cleaned the wound before escorting her back to Coombe Farm once more. They found Alfred sitting in a chair looking quite remorseful. Mrs. Horton told him to go and fetch the doctor and she would stay there with Ethel and Mrs. Smerdon, who were both in a state of shock.

At ten-thirty that evening, Alfred knocked on the door of Dr. William Henry Andrews and asked him to come to Coombe Farm, admitting that he had attacked Ethel with an axe and adding that he wished he had chopped her head off. He said that if he didn't come right away then he would have to give himself up to the police. On his way to the farm, Dr. Andrews stopped off at the police house to inform the officer on duty that he would likely be needed and to follow him to Coombe Farm. When Dr. Andrews arrived, he found Ethel with a one-inch wound above her right eye. He dressed it and put in a stitch. P.C. George Lendon arrived soon after and arrested Alfred, not without a struggle. The following morning Sergeant Beer of South Brent visited the prisoner in the cell. After being cautioned Pedrick said; "She should not have run upstairs and locked herself in. It was her own fault. It was a good job she spoke, as the second time I should have finished her which I intended on doing. I will kill her the very first time I get at her, and him as well. It's all his fault." He then broke down in tears saying; "If I'd have known they were going to put me in here I would have kept the axe and chopped the heads off the lot of them. I wish I had killed them all now."

Twenty-one-year-old Ethel Luscombe, whose parents lived at Dunscombe near Kingsbridge, had only come to work at the farm in May of that year. Alfred had been in the employment of Mr. Smerdon for about two years. The couple had got on fairly amicably, though Ethel it was noted had not wanted to get too friendly with him. In October 1910 Alfred Pedrick was found guilty of intent to cause grievous bodily harm and was sentenced to eighteen months imprisonment with hard labour.

But that wasn't the end of the story... At one o'clock in the morning of the 25th of January 1912, Alfred Pedrick was charged with assaulting Police Constable Walter Perry Blee of Ugborough, with intent to do him grievous bodily harm at Coombe Farm. Late the previous evening, having only been released from Exeter prison hours earlier, a drunken Alfred made his way to the farmhouse. He knocked on the door, and when it was answered by Mr. Smerdon he said he wished him no harm and would he be prepared to take him back into his employment? To which of course Mr. Smerdon refused and asked him to leave immediately. Shutting the door on him Mr. and Mrs. Smerdon then barred the entrance, which angered the intoxicated and uninvited Alfred who began to shout and made threats to kill them both. Robert Smerdon quietly left the property by another exit, ensuring that his poor terrified wife and other servants were safely barred it behind him and set off in search of P.C. Blee, who accompanied him back to the farm. Searching the exterior of the property they found Alfred lying on the backdoor step as if asleep, his head covered with his coat. P.C. Blee roused him and told him to get up, asking what he was doing there. Aware that Alfred was in a very agitated state he handed his lamp to Mr. Smerdon, telling him to keep the light on the prisoner at all times. Alfred slowly got up and began putting on his coat. When P.C. Blee explained that he was a policeman, he suddenly felt a sharp blow to the cheek. Alfred Pedrick had hit him with a heavy stick which caused him to receive a black eye and a wound to his cheek as well as a cut to his ear. Although stunned and wounded, with the assistance of Mr. Smerdon he threw Alfred to the ground and handcuffed him. He became aggressive and started shouting; "Let me up. I'll murder the lot of you. I have been waiting for you!" At this point P.C. Blee tied Alfred's legs together to stop him trying to escape and attacking either of them any further. Whilst being conveyed to the police station, Alfred again said "I'll murder the lot of you when I come out."

At his trial, Alfred Pedrick was found guilty of common assault and sentenced to nine months imprisonment with hard labour. He also had to pay a recognisance of five pounds to keep the peace for twelve months after he came out of prison towards Mr. Smerdon and his household.

TEACHER RETIRES.

Miss. Sarah Husband, who had been mistress in the Brownston and Modbury Schools for thirty-seven years, resigned at the end of school summer term in July 1910 on account of her on-going ill health. She was presented by the managers, teachers, scholars, and others involved with the school, with an armchair as a token of gratitude and recognition of her valuable services to the cause of education in the parish. Despite her ill-health, Sarah lived to the grand old age of ninety-three, dying in Kingsbridge in 1943.

MODBURY LAD'S DEATH.

Richard Broad aged fifteen was killed on Saturday the 3rd of June 1911 when working for Mr. Arthur Wroth of Heathfield Down Farm, Averton Gifford, alongside his father. At the inquest into his untimely death, his father described his son as a strong and active lad who was able to manage a horse and cart, and had appeared to be happy in his employment with Mr. Wroth.

Servington Hodder who farmed at Harraton Farm, Averton Gifford, noticed a cart turned upside down in a field at Heathfield Down. Going to investigate he found Richard Broad trapped under the cart with just his head projecting from the front. The full weight of the cart being on his neck. With assistance he was able to extricate the lad, who unfortunately was quite dead. Examining the cart, he found the harness to be sound and nothing had given way. It was his opinion that the wheels of the cart had gone over a heap of wood on the ground, and there being a slight dip in the field the turning over of the cart could be accounted for if the lad had pulled quickly on the left rein.

Arthur Harris Wroth who had been his employer for the past eight months, said that the horse Richard had been driving that day was about fifteen-years-old and very quiet. He agreed with Mr. Hodder as to the likely cause of the accident. Another witness Nellie [Ellen] Hurrell aged fourteen who was also employed by Mr. Wroth, said she had seen Richard drive out of the farmyard about a quarter of an hour before the cart was found overturned in the field. Dr. Henry Pode Miles, also of Modbury who later carried out a post-mortem, said Richard Broad's neck had been broken, causing instantaneous death. The jury returned a verdict of 'accidental death' and they and the coroner expressed their utmost sympathy to his family.

THE LANGWORTHY WINDOW.

Surgeon George Vincent Langworthy of Brooke House, commissioned a stained-glass window to be placed in the 12th century church of St. George in 1911, in memory of his many relations who had died during the previous two-hundred-years who had resided in the town and were now resting in the old churchyard.

The window, which is on the south side and nearest the porch, was designed to correspond with the fifteenth century tracery, in the style of that period in regards to colour massing and borders. Beneath the window is placed memorial tablet in latten brass containing the names of his many departed relations, along with the Langworthy coat of arms and the motto 'Vestute Digne.' St. Luke, the patron saint of doctors, was chosen for this window as a great many of the Langworthy family had been in the medical profession. The window contains four lights, the two central lights encompass the subject of Christ healing the sick at Capernaum and illustrating the text of St. Luke chapter 4.4. 'Now when the sun was setting, all they that had any sick with divers diseases brought them unto him; and he laid his hands on every one of them, and healed them.' The glass work was made by Messrs. Wippell and Co. of Exeter and London, and the tracery and mullions were prepared by Mr. William Ash, monumental mason of Modbury.

IMPRISONED FOR HOUSEBREAKING.

Stephanas Shute, a thirty-four-year-old carpenter, pleaded guilty to breaking into the home of William Edgcumbe at Blackawton on the 20th of December 1912, and stealing four pounds seven shillings and six' pence. When arrested he immediately admitted to the offence and told the police where the money was hidden. Brought before the Bench they were told that he had a previous conviction against him in 1899 when he was charged with stealing a bicycle at South Brent and was given a one-month prison sentence, but apart from that one misdemeanour he had borne a good character. [see **STEALING A BICYCLE**.] He was sentenced to four months' imprisonment with hard labour.

MEMORIAL TO REVEREND GREEN.

Miss. Emma Martin Green, daughter of the late Vicar Modbury, applied at a Consistory Court, held at the Chapter House in Exeter Cathedral on the 3rd of January 1913, for a faculty to erect a baptistry font, and a window in the tower of the parish church in memory of her father. The Chancellor (Sir C. E. H. Chadwyck-Healey) said the present Vicar (the Rev. J. E. Champernowne) did not oppose the faculty, but was afraid that the provision of a window in the tower would endanger the structure, whilst an architect thought it would strengthen it. In face of these contrary opinions, he had to decide which was right, because he could not pass anything which might be a danger to the structure of the church. Then again, he understood that the memorial would involve considerable reduction in the seating accommodation of the church. He said he was unable to conclude the matter that day, but only wanted to obtain all the information he could to enable him to come to the right conclusion.

Miss E. M. Green said the seats which would be removed had always been a difficulty because of the bad behaviour of the boys there. On special occasions she had known one-thousand people in the church. The proposed memorial had been approved at the Vestry meeting at Easter 1911, and she wished to know whether that had been rescinded at a later meeting. The Chancellor said at meeting held in 1912 it was agreed that the proposed memorial should be carried out. Miss. Green also stated that the memorial was to be in accordance with the architecture of the church. One of the churchwardens, who was a builder, had stated his opinion that the window would not injure the safety the church. The Chancellor responded saying that the churchwarden would have to give his own evidence. The architect was asked whether the window would imperil the structure, and whether the tower would seriously oscillate when the bells were rung. The reply was in favour of the faculty. Miss Green was informed by the Chancellor that would go into the matter a soon as possible.

HAY RICK FIRE.

During a spell of very warm weather in August 1913, a rick of hay belonging to Mr. James May of Knighton Coombe was seen to be on fire. The Modbury fire engine was quickly on the scene. Nearly all the hay in the field, amounting to sixteen tons was destroyed. Spontaneous combustion was thought to the cause of the outbreak.

FARMER'S DEATH ON EVE OF EMIGRATING.

Richard (Dick) Pearse, aged thirty-six, who managed Ashridge Farm alongside his mother, was found dead in a field on the morning of Saturday the 14th of March 1914. Dick had already sold most of the farm implements and had arranged a sale of what was left for the following week, as it was his intention on emigrating soon after. He and his mother planned to leave the farm on Lady Day [25th of March.]

On the Friday morning he went out at about eight o'clock to turn the sheep out of the meadow into a grass field. His dog returned to the farm alone at around lunchtime, but there was no sign of Dick. This wasn't too unusual as he often went off to meet friends and wouldn't return till late in the evening. At seven o'clock the following morning as he was making his way to work, Nicholas Furzeland, a labourer who was employed on the farm, noticed something unusual in a field. When he arrived at the farmhouse Mrs. Ellen Pearse, Dick's mother, told him that her son had not been home since the previous day and asked him to go and look for him. Recalling that he had seen something in the field, he immediately made his way there and found the body of Dick Pearse lying face downward in the grass.

At the inquest into Dick's death on the Monday morning, the coroner asked if it was usual for him to just go off and no-one raise concerns. Samuel George Pearse, a cousin of the deceased and who lived at Oldaport Farm, said that as most of the stuff belonging to the farm had been sold there was little to keep Dick there. He had personally visited the farm twice on the Friday; in the morning he had been told Dick had gone to turn the sheep out into the field, and when he called again in the evening it was mentioned to him that his cousin had still not been back. He replied saying "Oh, I expect he's gone to Modbury," assuming his cousin had simply gone to see some friends, stayed for a drink, and then possibly having had too many stopped over. He said Dick had done that once before and stopped out all night. His cousin was a popular man and had many friends. The reason no-one had gone out looking for him was because he was often in the habit of going out and returning late without informing other members the family of his intentions.

Dr. W. H. Andrews who carried out the post-mortem said that death had been due to suffocation. There was very marked cirrhosis of the liver due to alcohol, and the heart was fatty.

From the manner in which the deceased was found he assumed that Dick Pearse had probably had an attack of syncope, causing him to fall - hence the suffocation. The jury returned a verdict in accordance with the medical evidence. The foreman then remarked that he supposed the deceased never had an enemy in the world. The coroner concurred saying that he had been told Dick Pearse was a very popular man.

Richard Pearce's funeral took place that afternoon at St. George's Church, officiated over by the Revered J.E. Champernowne, and as had been mentioned at the inquest, Dick Pearse certainly was a very popular young man. The mourners included; Mrs. Hoppin (sister), Messrs. J. Pearse (uncle), S. J. Pearse (cousin), S. Hoppin (brother-in-law), P. Wyatt. J. Wyatt J. Boon, H. Manning, and S. Manning (cousins). Also present were; Messrs. J. Andrews, A. C. Pode,. F. Coyte, H Choake, S. J. Williams, R. Smerdon, T. Witchcombe, J. Hooppell, S. Wilcocks, W. Latimer, T. Tribble, A. Davis, W. Wyatt, R. nod J. Sherrell, J. Blight, W. H. Trinick, Dr. Andrews, Messrs. N. Gilroy, J. S. Coleman, H Peedle, N. P. Lakeman, T. Irish, H. Dennis, S. and J. Cockram, S. Mayes, E. Gee, A. Pox, J. Warne, S. Warren, Police Constable Lendon and many others. Wreaths were sent by his mother, Nellie and Sidney, 'All at Oldaport.' Dorothy, and Miss. Ashley of old Traine.

THE GREAT WAR.

The Great War saw thousands of men from various backgrounds, drawn together to fight in what at the time was assumed to be the war to end all wars. When the call for mobilization was made on 5th August 1914, Territorial Army reservists gathered at various drill halls across the country. Many men chose to enlist at the first opportunity, whilst others held off and awaited their call up.

Heavy losses on the various battlefronts meant that although conscripts were coming through, more men were needed. The Government introduced the 'Military Service Act' in January 1916, which specified that men from the ages of 18 to 41 were liable to be called-up for service unless they were married (or widowed with children), or else served in one of a number of reserved professions (usually industrial but also included clergy). Within four months a revised version of the Act was passed. All men - regardless of marital status, from the ages of 18 to 41 were liable to be called up to serve their country. The government also gained the right to re-examine men previously declared medically unfit for service. The act was modified again a number of times during the war, finally extending the age of eligibility to all men aged 17 to 51 and applied to men in Ireland, the Channel Islands and the Isle of Man. Between August 1914 and the introduction of the first Military Service Act as many as three million men volunteered for military service. From January 1916 until the close of the war a further 2.3 million men were formally conscripted.

Below is a list of the names of men listed on the Modbury War Memorial that died fighting for Great Britain. Many other men served and fought, but were lucky enough to return home to the families once the war was over. Some with physical injuries, some without, but all with mental scars that would last a lifetime.

Private Harry Blight Service No: 435434, 31st Battalion, Canadian Infantry (Alberta Regiment). Died 6th November 1917. Aged 23. He is commemorated on YPRES (MENIN GATE) MEMORIAL, Ypres.

Petty Officer Stoker John Borne, Service No: 288252, H.M.S. Dolphin, Royal Navy. Died 24th January 1919. Aged 42. He is buried on the south boundary of ST. GEORGE'S CHURCHYARD, MODBURY, Devon.

Chief Petty officer John Bunker, Service No: 143536, H.M.S. Goliath. Lost at sea on the 13th May 1915. Aged 47. He is commemorated on the PLYMOUTH NAVAL MEMORIAL, Devon. Panel 5.

Sergeant Walter Coyte, Service no: 416157, 60th Company, Chinese Labour Corps, formerly SS/16818, Depot, Royal Army Service Corps. Died of wounds 19th March 1918. He is buried in DOZINGHEM MILITARY CEMETERY, Poperinge, West-Vlaanderen, Belgium. Plot IV. Row I. Grave 11.

Private Maurice Davis, Service No:203373, 2nd Battalion, Devonshire Regiment. Killed in action 16th August 1917 Aged 25. He is commemorated on TYNE COT MEMORIAL, Zonnebeke, West-Vlaanderen, Belgium. Panel 38 to 40.

Sergeant William Dillon, Service No: 9687, 8th Battalion, King's Own (Royal Lancaster Regiment). Killed in action 26th September 1917, aged 27. He is commemorated on TYNE COT MEMORIAL, Zonnebeke, West-Vlaanderen, Belgium. Panel 18 to 19. William was the step-son of Henry Holden, and son of his wife Sarah Holden. Also, the husband of Hilda (née Hurrell) of Modbury. Born in Bolton in 1890 but lived in Manchester.

Lieutenant John Dobell (Royal Navy) of South Gifford House, Aveton Gifford, whose father originated from Modbury is buried in St. George's Churchyard. Formerly of H.M.S. President, He died on the 1st of March 1919 in Cambridge from meningitis. He was twenty-two.

Gunner Wallace Hannaford, Service No: 59123, "D" Battalion, the 82nd Brigade, the Royal Field Artillery. Died 4 July 1916 aged 28.

Private Arthur John Haskell, Service No: 26123, 8th Battalion, Prince Albert's Somerset Light Infantry. Killed in action 28th April 1917. He is commemorated on the ARRAS MEMORIAL, Pas de Calais, France. Bay 4.

Leading Stoker Charles Robert Hill, Service No: 311712, H.M.S. Indefatigable. Lost with his ship on the 31st May 1916. Aged 29. He is commemorated on the PLYMOUTH NAVAL MEMORIAL, Devon. Panel 15.

Leading Stoker Sidney Herbert Hill, Service No: K/14449, H.M.S. Indefatigable Lost with his ship on the 31st May 1916. Aged 24. He is commemorated on PLYMOUTH NAVAL MEMORIAL, Devon. Panel 15.

Private Edward Benjamin Hoskin, Service No: M2/203888, Base M.T. Depot, Royal Army Service Corps. Died in Mesopotamia 17th May 1917. Aged 25. Buried in BAGHDAD (NORTH GATE) WAR CEMETERY, Iraq. Plot XV. Row K. Grave 1.

Private James Howard, Service No: PLY/10759, H.M.S. Monmouth, Royal Marine Light Infantry. Died 1st November 1914. He is commemorated on the PLYMOUTH NAVAL MEMORIAL, Devon. Panel 5.

Private Alfred Hurrell, Service No: 11327, 11th Battalion, Devonshire Regiment. Died 16th February 1915. Aged 29. Buried in PAIGNTON CEMETERY, Devon. Grave 2771.

Chief Petty Officer, Blacksmith James B. T. Kennard, Service No: 342680, H.M.S. Monmouth, Royal Navy. Died 1st November 1914. Aged 42. He is commemorated on PLYMOUTH NAVAL MEMORIAL, Devon. Panel 4.

Private Sidney George Kennard, Service No: 5061, 1st/4th Battalion (Territorial), Devonshire Regiment. Killed in action in Mesopotamia 3rd February 1917. Aged 19. Buried in AMARA WAR CEMETERY, Iraq. Plot XVIII. Row F. Grave 2.

Second Lieutenant John Pearse Lakeman, 20th (Tyneside Scottish) Battalion, Northumberland Fusiliers. Died of wounds 20th April 1917. Aged 19. Buried in ETAPLES MILITARY CEMETERY, Pas de Calais, France. Plot XVII. Row C. Grave 7.

Private Sidney Thomas Luscombe, Service No: 2172, Lewis Gun Section, 19th Battalion, Australian Infantry, A.I.F. Killed in action at Bullecourt 3rd May 1917. Aged 25. He is commemorated on VILLERS-BRETONNEUX MEMORIAL, Somme, France.

Private William R. D. Luscombe, Service No: 78253 who served with the 6th Bn. Devonshire Regiment, died on the 19th of August 1920 and is buried in MODBURY (ST. GEORGE'S) CHURCHYARD, Devon.

Chief Petty Officer Charles Frederick Martin, Service No: 172603, H.M.S. Defence. Lost with his ship on the 31st May 1916, aged 40. He is commemorated on the PLYMOUTH NAVAL MEMORIAL, Devon. Panel 11.

Private Horace John Mitchelmore, Service No: 10043, 2nd Battalion, Duke of Edinburgh's (Wiltshire Regiment). Killed in action 28th July 1915. Buried in ST. VAAST POST MILITARY CEMETERY, RICHEBOURG-L'AVOUE, Pas de Calais, France. Plot I. Row H. Grave 4.

Private Harry Elford Mortimore, Service No: 290424, 2nd Battalion, Devonshire Regiment. Killed in action 25th November 1917. Aged 23. Buried in TYNE COT CEMETERY, Zonnebeke, West-Vlaanderen, Belgium. Plot LVII. Row C. Grave 43.

Private John Olver is mentioned on the Modbury War Memorial and is buried in ST. GEORGE'S CHURCHYARD, but does not have a Commonwealth headstone and his death is not recognised by the military as being associated with the war. He died aged twenty on the 13th of February 1921 at Lower Modbury Farm.

Corporal Allen Rendle, Service No: 10665, 8th (Service) battalion, Devonshire Regiment. Died 14th February 1916. Buried in VILLE-SUR-ANCRE COMMUNAL CEMETERY, Somme, France. plot/Row/Section C. Row 8.

Gunner Warwick Rendle, Service No: 330211, 234th Siege Battery, Royal Garrison Artillery. Killed in action 18th July 1917. Aged 26. Buried in VLAMERTINGHE NEW MILITARY CEMETERY, Ieper, West-Vlaanderen, Belgium. Plot IV. Row E. Grave 13.

Private Samuel Rogers, Service No: 10563, 8th (Service) Battalion, Devonshire Regiment. Died of wounds 19th June 1917. Aged 23. Buried in ACHIET-LE-GRAND COMMUNAL CEMETERY EXTENSION, Pas de Calais, France. Plot I. Row L. Grave 25.

Lance Corporal Stephanus Shute, Service No: 100872, 134th Army Troop Company, Royal Engineers. Killed in action 2nd August 1916. Aged 36. Buried in DARTMOOR CEMETERY, BECORDEL-BECOURT, Somme, France. Plot I. Row F. Grave 67. [*The spelling of his first name is incorrect, although it does vary on the census and in newspaper articles. On the 1911 census in his own handwriting and on his headstone, his name is spelt Stephanas.*]

Second Lieutenant Reginald Penkwill Oliver Weekes, 10th Squadron, Royal Flying Corps and General List. Killed in action 7th May 1917. Aged 19. Buried in CHOCQUES MILITARY CEMETERY, Pas de Calais, France. Plot I. Row F. Grave 30.

Able Seaman Ernest Wood, Service No: 193330 (RFR/DEV/B/3034), H.M.S. Defence, Royal Navy. Lost with his ship 31st May 1916. Aged 39. He is commemorated on PLYMOUTH NAVAL MEMORIAL, Devon Panel 12.

Private William Henry Wood, 1st Battalion, Devon and Cornwall Light Infantry. Died 13th of April 1918, aged 30. He is commemorated on the PLOEGSTEERT MEMORIAL, Belgium, panel 6.

Henry William Wyatt, Service No: S4/217642, 8th Lines of Communication Supply Company, Royal Army Service Corps. Died 20th February 1918. Aged 27. Buried in BLARGIES COMMUNAL CEMETERY EXTENSION, Oise, France. Plot I. Row B. Grave 2.

Private Norman Edward Tall of C Coy, 8th Bn. Devonshire Regiment died on the 25th of September 1915 and is remembered on the LOOS MEMORIAL and the Bigbury War Memorial. He was eighteen-years-old. His parents then lived at 1, Institution Place, Brownston Street.

Other men not mentioned on the Memorial, but originally from Modbury or connected to the town include:

Egbert Henry Oldrey, a fireman onboard H.M.S Laurentic. He died on the 25th of January 1917 aged fifty-two. He was born in Modbury but moved to Plymouth when he joined the Navy in 1885. When he and his parents were still living in the town. He is remembered on the PLYMOUTH WAR MEMORIAL, panel 26.

Rifleman William John Smith of the 1st Bn. Kings Royal Rifle Corps was killed on the 14th of September 1914 aged nineteen. He was one of the first British soldiers to be killed in the war. He is commemorated on the Le FERTE-SOUS-JOUARRE MEMORIAL in France. His parents lived at Heathfield Cottage, Modbury.

Private John W.M. Millard of the 1st Bn. Honourable Artillery Company died on the 26th of April 1917 aged thirty-four. His parents were at the time living on Church Street. He is buried at DUISLAND BRITISH CEMETERY, Etrun, France. Plot IV. E. 38.

A GERMAN SPY IN MODBURY?

In the opening days of August 1914, a German subject, Herbert Wilhelm Blumenthal of Modbury, was brought before Stonehouse magistrates in Plymouth. Although he claimed to be British, during a search of his papers he was found to be in possession of a German passport

issued on the 22nd of April 1914, and it was therefore suspected that information he was gathering was being passed on to foreign intelligence, but after a thorough search of the room he was occupying, nothing incriminating was found. It was therefore decided that Blumenthal was to report to the constable on duty in Modbury at eight a.m. and eight p.m. every day, and if he wished to leave the town, he was to inform the constable and of the whereabouts of his destination. Herbert Blumenthal accepted these conditions and was discharged by the magistrates. Speaking in very good English he expressed his thanks.

Across the country people suspected of being spies were arrested, especially German citizens or those suspected of being German. The public were asked to give the police the names and addresses of foreigners living in their locality.

H.M.S. MONMOUTH.

On the 14th of November 1914, the North Devon Journal stated that news of the fate of the crew of H.M.S. Monmouth, which was reported to have been destroyed in a naval battle off the Chilian coast, was being anxiously awaited by Mrs. Tom Harris, of Atherington, whose brother named James Kennard was on board.

H.M.S. MONMOUTH.

Kennard, who was native of Modbury, had only been on the Monmouth since the outbreak of war, having recently arrived back to England from the China Station. He had a wife and three children. No official news at that time had been received as to his fate. The family were later to learn that Chief Petty Officer James had died on the 1st of November 1914, along with the entire ships company of seven-hundred and thirty-five men.

MODBURY HARRIERS GETS A LADY MASTER.

At the annual meeting of the Modbury Harriers at the Great Western Hotel in March 1915, Mr. John Andrews who presided, stated that at the last meeting of the committee a resolution was passed that Miss Elfrida Allin of Woolston, Loddiswell, should be asked to accept the Mastership for 1915-16. The previous year Mr. Harold Allin undertook the duties of Master, but when war broke out, he joined the King's Shropshire Light Infantry, and his sister (Miss E. Allin) was good enough to carry through the season his behalf. The Hunt he said owed her a deep debt of gratitude. With regard to the financial position, Mr. Allin Snr, said the effect of the war had been distinctly felt. The Hunt had eighty-nine pounds and three shillings in subscriptions, either received or promised, and there was a balance of twenty-two pounds and eleven shillings from the previous year. It was said that a pack of hounds could not run for less than one hundred and fifty pounds a year. The shortfall he said he was having to make up himself. That year would be an exceptional one as there was no sale of hounds and no income from entertainments.

Harold Wyse Allin of the 6th Battalion Shropshire Light Infantry died on the 13th of December 1917 aged twenty-eight at No. 43 Stationary Hospital, Sinai Peninsula, having been wounded whilst on active service.

Harold Wyse Allin, courtesy of Ancestry.co.uk.

HORACE MITCHELMORE.

In early August 1915 news reached Warminster informing Mr. and Mrs. Cruse of Silver Street, that their son-in law, thirty-two-year-old Horace John Mitchelmore, a native of Modbury had been killed. Mitchelmore was a schoolmaster and had a promising career ahead of him. He had previously been an English master at a school in Ghent, Belgium. Being in Warminster visiting his in-laws at the outbreak of war, he heard the call of his country and told friends "I am wanted and will go and enlist." He did so on the 2nd of September 1914, where he joined the 1st Wiltshire Regiment, being afterwards drafted into the 2nd Wiltshire's.

After leaving Kingsbridge Grammar School, Horace went to Edinburgh where he worked for the Civil Service for two years. He then went to London where he worked in the Registry Office, but due to poor health he resigned this position and after spending several months recovering chose to go in to teaching. When war broke out, he was living in Bangor, Wales, and teaching in Tregarth, but being on holiday in Warminster at that time he decided he needed to join the men at the fighting front. After basic training in Weymouth, he was sent to France just before Christmas 1914. His son being born after he had left England. Days before his death, his name had been put forward recommending him as a recipient of the Distinguished Conduct Medal for action he had been involved in on the 15th of July 1915.

EXEMPTIONS.

At the Kingsbridge Rural Tribunal held in March 1916, seventy-nine cases were heard of men appealing their call up to serve overseas. These included a number of sons running farms on behalf of aged or ill parents. There were also appeals from farmers asking for their sons to be kept home to help run their farms, the farmhands already having been called up. One gentleman, a fisherman, asked that his son be released from having to serve as he already had three sons serving on minesweepers and thought that was enough for one family. His application was refused.

A Sherford farmer appealed on behalf of a young farmhand. He said he had two old men and the lad. His sister had been canvassing the village for women workers to help out. He had managed to get some women to help with milking, sorting potatoes, and other farm work, but they were unable to do the ploughing. He was given an exemption for six months.

A Primitive Methodist preacher had his application refused even though he stated he was a conscientious objector and that he could not kill another man. A draper from Modbury said that one of his brothers had already been killed in the war, another was in training, and a third was awaiting his call up. He said he was running the business on behalf of his widowed mother and if he were to be called up the business would have to close. He was given three months to find a manager to run the shop.

Postcard of Church Street, Modbury 1916. Courtesy of Samuel Harrison.

LANDLORD'S TEMPERAMENT.

Eli Owens, the landlord of the Modbury Inn, was summoned before the Plympton Petty Sessions on the 10th of March 1916 for being drunk on licensed premises – he pleaded guilty. P.C. Watts said that he visited the Modbury Inn on market day and found the defendant in a drunken condition and rambling about. Mr. Spear acting on behalf of Mr. Owens said that the defendant had been suffering from 'temperamentality' for some months, and practically one drink now upset him. The police agreed to the proposal to grant a temporary transfer of the license to his wife while Mr. Owens who had decided to abandon all intoxicating liquor until his health was restored. Eli Owens was fined ten shillings.

BROTHERS DIED TOGETHER.

Charles Hill aged twenty-nine and his brother Sidney aged twenty-four were both serving aboard H.M.S. Indefatigable as leading stokers and were killed when the ship was sunk on the 31st of May 1916 at the Battle of Jutland. Only three of the one-thousand and nineteen crew survived. They were the sons of Bessie and Samuel Hill of Galpin Street.

REST AND RECOUPERATION.

The Plymouth Co-operative Society who then leased Whympston House, and also Stoke House at Membland, in the summer of 1916 offered the accommodation to society members for rest and recouperation. For adults it was one pound a week, and for children prices ranged from two shillings and six' pence to twelve shillings and six' pence depending on their age. Conveyance from Plymouth was provided at one shilling and six' pence per single journey. Children half price.

KILLED ON THE SOMME.

Lance Corporal Stephanas Shute, a carpenter by trade, was killed in action on the 2nd of August 1916 aged thirty-six. He is buried at Dartmoor Cemetery, Becordel-Becourt, Somme, France. Although his name is spelt Stephanus on the Modbury War Memorial and on some other records, it is spelt 'Stephanas' on his headstone and on all of his military records as well as a number of other documents. Unfortunately, his service records no longer survive. They were destroyed along with thousands of others during a WWII bombing raid on London. We do though know he enlisted at Exeter and was a member of one of the Royal Engineer Signal Companies of the Territorial Force (Army Troops.) Presumably he joined up mid to late 1915 or early 1916, as he didn't serve overseas until 1916 as he was awarded the British Service and the Victory medal, but not the 1914/15 medal.

We previously met Stephanas in 1899 when he was living in Brownston village with his parents, and again in 1912 when living in Loddiswell when he got himself into some trouble with the law. In 1905 he married Lily Maud Triggs of Modbury at Kingsbridge, and by 1911 they were living in Loddiswell with their five children; Wallace, Samuel, Lilian and Silvanus and Vera. They then went on to have another two children; Harold who was born in 1912 and a daughter Stella in 1915, who died at just a few months old. Sadly, Vera also died in 1919 aged just eight-years-old. After Stephanas died, Lily and her children moved to Lynmouth in North Devon.

STANLEY MORTIMORE.

The funeral of twenty-three-year-old Stanley (Stan) Russell Mortimore, a former sick bay steward onboard H.M.S. Tiger, and fifth son of P.C. William Mortimore, took place on the 12th of November 1917 at St. Peter and St. Paul's Church, Ermington. Stanley had participated in the Dogger Bank and Jutland battles, and was mentioned in despatches for outstanding bravery in the latter. He was invalided out of the Navy having been gassed at Jutland, and died after a long and painful illness caused as a result, at parents' home on the 7th of November. His coffin was carried by P.C.'s Pike of Ivybridge, Watts of Modbury, Toder of Lee Mill, Cawse of Yealmpton,

Hutchings of Cornwood, and Pearse of Holbeton. All members of the Devon Constabulary, in the charge of Sergeant Endicott of Yealmpton.

UNPOPULARITY OF THE TRACTOR.

At a meeting of the South Devon War Agricultural Committee held at Totnes in November 1917 it was said that there had been a ploughing failure in the district due to the machines not being powerful enough. One gentleman stated that he had six or eight tractors rusting in his yard for two months, they were of no use and should be removed. Mr. Coyte of Modbury said that within the last month a ploughman had been sent to his district who had never seen a steam plough before. It then took the man seventeen days to plough less than nine acres of land. With a shortage of food in the country it was vital that crops were gathered and planted within the required amount of time.

COLONEL BIRDWOOD.

Colonel William Spiller Birdwood, formerly of the Indian Army along with his second wife Altha whom he married in Plymouth in 1917 settled at Colmer House, Modbury in 1918.

Colonel Birdwood's first wife Ellen [Nellie] Turner, died on the 14th of December 1910. His son, Second Lieutenant Gordon Alick Brodrick Birdwood of the 2nd Bn. South Lancashire Regiment, lost his life on the 20th of September 1914 aged just eighteen.
To serve overseas at that time troops had to be nineteen-years-old. It wasn't until April 1918 that men aged eighteen years and six months were officially sent overseas. Of course, many young men lied about their age and as many as two-hundred and fifty-thousand boys under the age of eighteen served in the British Army during the First World War. Many young men, mainly officers, got written consent from their parents as presumably Gordon had. He is remembered on a special memorial at Vailly British Cemetery in France. Less than a year later, on the 7th of June 1915 Colonel Birdwood lost a second son. Thirty-three-year-old Captain Charles W.B. Birdwood of the 1/6th Gurkha Rifles was killed in Gallipoli. He is buried at Pink Wood Cemetery, Helles. Turkey.

Colonel William Birdwood died on the 26th of December 1930 aged seventy-six. His wife Altha had passed away just weeks previously on the 11th of November.

SHOT IN THE FOOT.

In October 1917 Private William John Winsor of the 3rd Reserve Battery of the Royal Garrison Artillery, previously a Police Constable living at 7, Poundwell Street, was shot in the left foot whilst on active service. After initial treatment in France, he was sent to the Red Cross hospital at Sherborne in Dorset before being sent home to recuperate. William had joined the Army at Bristol in 1915 and was posted overseas on the 27th of March 1916. He was discharged from the service on the 28th of November 1918. He re-joined the Police Service, and in 1939 was stationed at Kingsbridge.

William's younger brother Harold George Winsor attested to the Training Reserve Battalion at Exeter in 1917, aged seventeen, and was later attached to the Worcester Regiment. Unbelievably, he also received a gunshot wound to the left foot two years to the day that his brother was posted overseas – the 27th of March 1918. Harold completed his home service and was discharged from the army on the 6th of November 1919 due to the disability he was left with.

D.S.O. FOR MODBURY OFFICER.

In 1918 thirty-six-year-old Captain Reginald Guy Pearse who had joined the Public Schools Battalion shortly after the outbreak of war and received his commission in 1915, was awarded the Distinguished Service Order. The son of William Pearse; farmer, auctioneer and surveyor, Reginald had already been awarded the Military Cross whilst serving with the 3rd Bn. Sherwood Foresters (Notts and Derby Regiment). Prior to the outbreak of war, he too worked as an auctioneer and surveyor in partnership with his brother Thomas, and at the time of his marriage to Constance Evelyn Steels at St. George's, Hanover Square in London in January 1914, he was living at Albemarle Street in London.

Modbury War memorial. Postcard courtesy of Samuel Harrison.

THE LANGWORTHY CURSE?

Mr. George Vincent Langworthy, surgeon of Brooke House, Modbury, died aged eighty-two on the 3rd of January 1919. He had practised in partnership with his brother William Froude Langworthy in the town for many years, but had also enjoyed a happy twenty-five-year retirement. George was the last surviving son of William Froude Landworthy Snr, also a surgeon. His funeral took place at St. George's Church on the 8th of January 1919.

By a strange coincidence, another of the Langworthy's extended family died the same day - Colonel Vincent Upton Langworthy, a well-known sportsman and chairman of Ilminster magistrates, who died aged eighty as the result of a motoring accident in Somerset. His funeral also took place on the 8th of January. During the service, his sister Miss. Ellen Langworthy aged seventy-five, sank down on to her knees in the pew and was carried out of the church lifeless. She had been in apparent good health. You may recall in an earlier story I stated that William Froude Langworthy, the brother of George Vincent Langworthy, also died during a church service in March of 1909.

THE DEVON COUNTY SHOW.

Held at Exeter in May 1920, the Devon County show was the first to be held since 1914 due to the outbreak of war. The show featured a great display featuring machinery representing every aspect of agriculture, for the farmyard, the dairy, and the land. At various stands the experts explained the mechanisms of the machinery with all their modern features. The time and labour-saving features were said to be what all enterprising farmers were now looking for as a solution to the industrial problems affecting farming.

Higher wages and shorter working hours now being worked by agricultural labourers which increased the demand for such machines. The tractor, which had been severely tested during the war years, was said to be now here to stay. There were many other mechanical farm machinery items on display such as self-lift tractor ploughs, cultivators, electric lighting plant, grinding mills, cream separators hay tedders, potato lifters etc.

ROAD CONDITIONS.

In June 1920, the Royal Automobile Association published road conditions for drivers in the South Western counties. The Plymouth to Modbury road was described as in fair condition but rough in places. The Bigbury to Modbury road was said to be in a fair condition, but rough and pot-holey in places.

MENTIONED IN DESPATCHES.

In April 1921, Gunner Ernest J. Luscombe of the Royal Field Artillery and Little Orcheton Farm, was informed by the War Office that he had received a mention in Despatches from General S.G.F. Milne dated March 1919, for gallantry and distinguished services in the field whilst in Salonika.

REVEREND LEADBITTER.

The Revered M. G. Leadbitter was appointed the Vicar of Modbury in March 1921. Originally from Warden in Northumberland, he married Miss. Eirene Swete, a descendant of the Swete family formerly of Old Traine, Modbury.

WHITE HART HOTEL FOR SALE.

The White Hart Hotel on Church Street, was put up for auction in Plymouth in August 1921. Described as being twelve miles from Plymouth, seven and a half miles from Kingsbridge, and five miles from Ivybridge Station. Callaway and Co auctioneers had been instructed to offer it for sale. There was a good attendance and bidding rose to £1,750, at which point the property was withdrawn from the sale. A private buyer later came forward and the sale was completed. The hotel which was well built of stone, faced with cement and with a slate roof, contained an entrance hall, small sitting-room, bar, bar parlour, billiard-room, tap-room, store-room, cellar, larder, kitchen, scullery, water closet, assembly room which measured sixty-six feet by twenty-one, dressing-room, sitting-room measuring twenty-seven feet by thirteen feet, five bedrooms, bathroom with hot and cold running water, and lavatory. Outside there was a coal house, four-stall stable with loft above, two loose boxes and a carriage house. The new owner would take possession in January 1922. The hotel was said to be very popular amongst charabanc parties, and an excellent trade was carried on.

A buyer having come forward for the property, the furniture and effects therein were put up for auction on the 27th of October 1921. These included; a large dining table, oak sideboard, mahogany chiffonier, sofa, two ebonised over-mantles, glass corner cupboards, sitting-room suite in leather, full compass piano in walnut case, butler's trays and stands, large kitchen chairs, eighty chairs, carpets, combined press and chest of drawers, iron and brass bedsteads, Singer sewing machine, six circular bar tables, culinary requisites, forms, casks etc.

RESTORING MODBURY CHURCH.

A well-attended public meeting was held on the evening of Saturday the 24th of September 1921 in the Assembly Rooms of the White Hart Hotel, Modbury, with the vicar (Rev. M. G. Leadbitter) presiding, to consider the question of restoration of the parish church the spire which required immediate attention. It was hoped that the townsfolk could raise the sum of five hundred pounds towards it. Many promises were made and therefore a committee was appointed, including Mr. I. Andrews (chairman), Mr. W. F. Treneer (honorary treasurer) and Mr. F. Coyte (honorary secretary).

By December 1925, the Reverend. M. G. Leadbitter and the Parochial Church Council along with the Restoration Committee had carried out some very necessary repairs to the tower and spire. The repairs consisted of renewing the perished portions of the large west window. At the east end and beyond at the war memorial clergy desk, the sanctuary had been adorned by a carved oak altar piece with a beautiful painting of the Crucifixion The richness of the colouring was said to give a brightness to the former rather dull sanctuary.

AN AGEING BIRD.

Evidence of how long a pheasant could survive season after season was proved on the 3rd of October 1921 when Mr. J.J. Berry of Exeter, shot dead a cock pheasant wearing a ring dated 1909. [*How many more years would it have lived if it hadn't been shot one wonders?*]

HUNT BALL AT THE GREAT WESTERN HOTEL.

Modbury Harriers held their annual Hunt Ball on the 15th of February 1922 at the Great Western Hotel, Modbury. Dancing from eight p.m. till two a.m. Tickets costing seven shillings and sixpence were available from Mr. Alfred Wroth, Honorary Secretary of Heathfield Down Farm.

MODBURY MOTOR ACCIDENT.

William John Moriarty, of Redland, Bristol, was driving a two-seater car through the Devonshire countryside in June 1922 when it overturned whilst negotiating a bend in the road just outside of Modbury. The car then ran into a hedge with such force that the vehicle toppled over and threw the occupants out. The passenger, Mr. Samuel Beal of Leicester died at the scene. Mr. Moriarty who was badly injured, in one of his conscious moments before being removed to hospital where he unfortunately succumbed two days later, said that the brakes on the vehicle had failed.

Another theory was that Mr. Moriarty, who wore glasses, was blinded by the sun in attempting to negotiate the right-angled bend in the road, as a few yards from where the car had overturned, an examination of the tyre tracks showed that after it had rounded the corner it went a distance of some ninety feet before striking the hedge. It then appeared to have travelled another sixty feet with its left side wheels banked up in the hedge before overturning.

GAS PLANT AND HOUSE DESTROYED, TOWN IN DARKNESS.

On the evening of the 2nd of January 1923 damage to the value of one thousand pounds was caused by a fire which broke out at Modbury Petrol Gas Works. Shortly after eight o'clock William Coker who was in charge of the works and lived on the site, locked up the power house. A few seconds later there was a loud explosion and the generating plant burst into flames. Two men; Mr. Bunker and Mr. Mear, who were passing at the time, quickly spread the news of the incident which occurred about a quarter mile from the town, and in a short space of time the fire brigade arrived on the scene. Fortunately, the wind blew the fire away from the direction of the gasholder, and after half an hour the fire brigade along with many helpers had the fire extinguished, but not before the plant and Mr. Coker's house had been destroyed. Meanwhile, the whole town was left in darkness overnight.

MIDNIGHT MYSTERY.

A steeplejack solved the mystery of gunshots heard late one night in October 1922. A rigorous investigation followed, but no information could be obtained as to the origin of the shots and the affair was half forgotten. However, in May 1923 a London steeplejack, Mr. G.L. Alger came to examine the spire of the church and found that the weathercock at the top to be riddled with bullets. He said that he often found weathercocks in country districts potted with bullets.

THE PRINCE OF WALES VISITS MODBURY.

On Whit Monday 1923, the Prince of Wales arrived in Devon for a few days tour of the county, and included in his trip he made visits to some of his farms in the South Hams, including those at Stoke Climsland and Modbury. One of the farms he visited was Sheepham Farm run by Mr. and Mrs. Jenkins along with their daughter. The Jenkins were known for their prizewinning bulls; one of which was 'Sentinel' who the prince met on his visit.

His Royal Highness started his trip in Exeter before finally rounding off the first day with a game of golf at Budleigh Salterton, where he spent the night as a guest of Lord Clinton. Apart from the unveiling of the Devon War Memorial near Exeter Cathedral, the prince's chief objective was to meet with as many Devonians as possible including school children who sang for him and bands that entertained him. His trip also included visits to Hayes Barton, the birth place of Sir Walter Raleigh, Exeter, Exmouth, Axminister, Kenton, Starcross, Dawlish Brixham, Torquay, Paignton, Dartmouth, Modbury and Princetown. At Dartmouth he addressed the Royal Naval cadets at H.M.N.B. Britannia.

ANOTHER MOTORING TRAGEDY.

A serious accident occurred on the afternoon of the 30th June 1923 at Hellier's Corner, on the road between Modbury and Aveton Gifford. Mr. Williams-Lyouns of The Knowle, Kingsbridge, was driving a five-seater motor car, and when negotiating the corner was struck by a cyclist riding on the wrong side of the road; twenty-one-year-old Sydney Lethbridge, a slaughterman, employed by Messrs. Charles Choake and Sons of Modbury, who was returning to his home in Aveton Gifford. The bicycle was smashed to pieces and the car badly damaged, though Mr. Williams-Lyouns escaped injury. Sydney unfortunately fared much worse, and prior to an ambulance arriving on the scene he was attended to by Mr. A. Luscombe along with the district nurse. He was then taken by St. John ambulance to the South Devon and East Cornwall Hospital in Plymouth. He had suffered two broken wrists and a compound fracture of the right thigh. He was said to have been convalescing well in hospital, but in mid-August he slipped and fell in his hospital ward and broke his thigh again in the same place. Doctors attempted to fix the break, which unfortunately proved impossible to do and Sydney died of blood poisoning, the result of the compound fracture to this thigh, accelerated by the second fracture.

WIDOWERS WORST FEARS LED TO SUICIDE.

A sad tragedy occurred in July 1923 when widowed boot-maker Richard John Gilley, aged sixty of Back Street, decided to end his life, rather than he said risk dying from a seizure.

A neighbour, thirty-three-year-old Edwin Watts was walking down the street on the evening of Sunday the 15th, when he heard a scream and saw twelve-year-old Ivy Gilley standing at her front door crying hysterically saying that her father had cut his throat. Entering the house and lighting a match as the room was in darkness, Edwin was able to see Richard Gilley sitting on a stool with his head leaning over onto the window sill. He was able to knock the razor from Mr. Gilley's hand and immediately laid him down on the floor. At the same time telling Ivy to go and get help. In the meantime, he administered what little first aid he could to stem the flow of blood. Dr. W.H. Andrews arrived within a few minutes and found Richard Gilley to be still alive - just, with two wounds across his throat. One was superficial but the other had penetrated his jugular vein. There was no hope of survival and poor Richard died two hours later.

At the inquest into Mr. Gilley's death, his brother said that Richard had recently said he feared he would 'go the same way' as his father had, and that he worried about the future of his children. He had also recently visited Dr. Andrews when feeling faint, saying he feared that he might be heading for a seizure, but the attack soon passed.

Richard had already suffered much tragedy in his life and his fears were likely a culmination of things; two of his children had died in infancy and his wife Florence had died two years previously aged forty-five. He left behind three children, the youngest just seven-years-old. A verdict of 'suicide whilst temporarily insane' was returned.

HOUSEKEEPER WANTED.

Mr. Luscombe of Yarnacombe Farm, was looking for a housekeeper in October 1923. The requirements were simply to be a good cook and butter-maker.

DEATH OF A NOVELIST.

Emma Martha Green was the eldest daughter of Reverend George Clark Green, who had been the vicar of the parish for almost fifty years. Although born in Everdon, Northamptonshire, Emma had lived in Modbury since she was just over a year-old. She had never married, and after her parents' death she moved in with her widowed sister Mary Augusta Langworthy on Church Street. Emma died on the 23rd of August 1924 aged sixty-six after a short illness.

Educated at home, she was said to have had a wonderful gift for teaching, and spent some years in her early life coaching at a well-known preparatory school. She was particularly gifted in the instruction of music and voice production. She was also well-known as E. M. Green in the writing world and her children's books had a peculiar charm. She wrote for a great many magazines and newspapers. All of her writings were said to have had a distinctly religious tone, which came as no surprise both her father and brother being vicar's and she herself having been brought up in the vicarage and attending regular church services. During the Great War she wrote a pamphlet entitled 'Christmas Eve' of which the Young Men's Christian Association bought thirty-thousand copies and sent them in their Christmas letters to the men at the front. Miss. Green was also interested in missionary work and would often speak at public meetings for missions or religious work. She worked for a number of years for the 'Young Women's Christian Association' and for 'Waifs and Strays.' She was also for many years a member of the Kingsbridge Guardians representing the town of Modbury.

"WHERE YOU BE GOING TO JARGE?"

This is an abridged reminiscence of a football match at Modbury, by Mr. A. Scholes, printed in the Burnley Advertiser, Saturday the 11th of April 1925.

Sometimes things that have happened many years ago pass out of one's mind altogether until one day something occurs which brings back memories with a rush. Whilst reading the other day, I came across a sentence which brought back memories of a little place near Plymouth. The events of the afternoon had almost disappeared from memory until I came across a Devonshire story, where one of the characters asked another a question, and in my mind I heard one of the Modbury natives say, "Where you be going to Jarge?" For almost ten years I had forgotten that there was a place called Modbury, and our reason for going there – to play a football match with the locals. I recall that it was a nice afternoon when we set off. The first part of the journey was by train and then by wagonette to an old-world village down a steep hill where we stopped at an inn. Going to the field where the match was to be played, we noticed that amongst our opponents some well-built lads - the kind who when they run up against you make their presence felt. For some reason I have the idea that all the members of the Modbury team were relatives; six of them I believe they were brothers. Some of our side came along with a bit of the 'heavy stuff' - in a legitimate manner of course, but our Modbury hosts were no match for their guests. I use the words, 'hosts' and 'guests' intentionally, for rumour had it that we were to have a fine spread after the match. After we had scored a few goals, some of the members of our team seemed more concerned about that rumoured feed after the match. After we had scored seven or eight goals, a command was surreptitiously passed from player to player, like orders were at times conveyed from soldier to soldier, that the forwards were to refrain from scoring any more goals or we would spoil our chance of receiving the good feed. By what powers of reasoning or what method of deduction our defenders had reaped that conclusion, we at the front knew not or cared not; we just obeyed the instruction, for we seldom had 'enough and to spare' in the eating department. When those days came – if ever they did, they were red letter days and were entered in our diary. So, after these seven or eight goals, we went on merrily and whenever we got near the Modbury goal we 'dispossessed.' Sometimes we were glad to get out of the way as the Modbury men and their flying feet had a habit of following the ball and the man in possession, and if we tried any fancy footwork, we were generally surrounded by the Modbury hosts, and if we dodged the flying feet, we were lucky. However, it was an enjoyable afternoon, especially in the early part when the enthusiasm of our hosts was at its height.

When the match was over and the home team had had quite enough running about for one afternoon, we returned to the inn and satisfied the inner man, thus proving that sometimes there is a good deal of truth in rumour. Of course, if during the game we had disobeyed the 'cease fire' orders, I don't know whether would have been so fortunate. After tea an impromptu concert filled the evening until the time came for us to depart. After many handshakes, the afore-mentioned wagonette took us from that inn, up that hill, the remembrance of which is so vivid now, back to some station and we returned from whence we came. They were happy days!

[*Little did the Modbury boys know, but some of the visiting army side had been professional footballers prior to the outbreak of war. The team referred to were members of the Lancashire Fusiliers and played sixteen matches, scoring 127 goals against their opponents 16. One of the visiting players, Jonathan 'Johnny' Brown who played for Burnley, was killed in France on the 6th of November 1918.*]

A TALK ON TALK.

Modbury's Women's Institute was given a lecture by Miss. Raymond in October 1925 on 'Our mother tongue' where she described how the English language as we know it today was the result of centuries of sifting and gradual absorption of many languages; Celtic, Saxons, Danes, Romans, and Normans – all having left their traces in it. She referred 'Americanisms' and slang phrases, which she said spoilt the beauty of our pure English language. "Our mother tongue is an heirloom which we only have the guardianship of, and it is our duty to see that we handed it down intact."

MODBURY FOLK-DANCERS.

A social evening held on the 13th of January 1926 saw the children of the Council Schools present a varied programme, including country, Morris, and sword dancing, as well as a play; 'The Toy Shop.' A string orchestra, under leadership Mrs. W. F. Treneer, accompanied the dancing, and refreshments were served by a committee of ladies who were all members of the Adult Folk Dance Class. All the proceeds of the evening were to go towards the expenses of the children attending a folk-dance festival in Plymouth that June.

GIFT TO MODBURY POSTMASTER.

Mr. J. Burring, on behalf of the staff at Modbury Post Office presented Mr. William Trinick, postmaster, who retired in July 1926 with a silver-mounted walking stick. Mr. Trinick said he had seen many changes during his sixteen years of office and would always value the token, and he would never forget the happy days he spent at the Post Office. His position was taken over by Mr. C.H. Cawsey.

Trinick's Post Office, printing, stationery, and fancy goods establishment at 14, Broad Street. Postcard courtesy of Susanna Miles.

MODBURY AMBULANCE BRIGADE FORMED.

A meeting under the auspices of St. John Ambulance Association was held in Modbury in March 1927. Mr. Miller and Mr. Perkins of Plymouth spoke of the great need for ambulance work in every town and village. Certificates were then presented to those who had been successful in the recent First Aid examination. Mr. F. Coyle presided over the formalities.

A concert had been held at the White Hart Assembly Rooms on New Year's Eve 1926 to raise funds for the setting up of the Ambulance Brigade. It had featured community singing conducted by the Reverend A. Calder and various local entertainers contributed to the show. A sketch was given by young members of the ambulance classes to show their work and the Ambulance Cadets of Modbury School performed sword and Morris dancing. This presentation was followed by a dance, with music supplied by an orchestra consisting of Mrs. Treneer, Miss. Hannaford, and Miss Walker.

OLD MODBURY

'Old Modbury, the house and its early owners,' was the subject of a talk given at Exmouth in July 1927 by the Reverend John L. E. Hooppell, who stated that the earliest records gave Traine the name 'De Arboribus and later 'Trewyn' and then 'Treyne.' By a deed dated May the 10th 1489, the property was in the ownership of John Scoos of Milton near Thurlestone, and of Brownston. It appeared to have been in his family since 1435. One of the principal monuments in Modbury Church he said, was of Adrian Swete, a descendant of John Scoos who died in 1647, having lived during the long struggle between the King and the Commons. The records left behind he said went to show to what extent landed proprietors were compelled to supply King Charles with the means to continue his struggle against Parliament. One of these records which was dated October the 16th 1630, referred to what was called the history of England 'Coronation Knighthoods,' and where Swete had written; 'I paid to Sir James Bagger, to the use of the King's Majesty thirty shillings in discharge of my pretended contempt's for not receiving the Order of Knighthood at His Highness Coronation (on Feb. 2nd, 1626), for which I have acquaintance. Here Mr. Hooppell added that a contemporary record of how knighthood was brought so low in public estimations, as to be referred to in one ballad as; "Knighthood in old times was accounted an honour, which the noblest did not disdain; but now it is used in so base a manner, that it's no credit, but rather a stain."

ALARMING MISHAP AT MODBURY, SIX PEOPLE THROWN FROM MOTOR LORRY.

An alarming road accident occurred on the 20th of July 1927, when six people were injured in a motoring mishap at Modbury, when the front axle of a lorry broke and the occupants were thrown out. The lorry belonged to Messrs E. Marquand and Co., fruit merchants of Devonport market. Those injured, fortunately not seriously, were Mr. Marquand's son and daughter - Mr. Fred and Miss. Elsie Marquand, Messrs. E. Bamfield, W. Cook, Mr. Higgings, and W. Gunn, the last named being the driver of the lorry.

Shortly after midday the lorry had left Modbury and was returning to Plymouth. It had just passed the school when the front axle snapped and the lorry swerved into a hedge. A woman motorist who was passing at the time, took the injured to Modbury where they were given medical treatment by Dr. Murphy and Mr. Cole of the ambulance brigade. Fred Marquand was said to have suffered from a cut to his head and sprained wrists; Elsie Marquand suffered a cut to her head, and Mr. E. Bamfield, a severely cut head. Mr. W. Gunn injured his elbow; and Messrs. Cook and Higgins also suffered cuts to their heads.

MODBURY WATER, NEW SCHEME APPROVED.

A heated discussion took place at the Modbury parish meeting on the 1st of September 1927, when the question of whether the town should adopt the scheme (an ongoing debate) for an additional water supply from Buckland, and on a vote being taken sixty members were in favour of it and thirty-four against. Mr. F. Coyte (chairman) who presided, said the time had arrived when Modbury should determine one way or the other. The present system was said to be in a very defective state. The numbers of pipes that had to be mended and leakages were very serious. For years this question had been more or less the paramount topic of the Parish Council. Dr. Miles said if they did not pass the scheme that evening a petition would be sent to the Ministry of Health, and that would mean that their water supply would cost double.

In October a petition was sent to the Minister of Health calling attention to and requesting an inquiry into what it described as the utterly insanitary condition of the town through the absence of a sufficient supply of water. Adequate flushing of the drains or lavatories (where such exist) was not always possible, and nearly all the houses including the Council schools, were without any proper and constant supply of drinking water. Should a fire take place said the petitioners, it could not be extinguished, and there was also the possibility of an epidemic breaking in the town. The petition was signed by Dr's W. H. Andrews, Henry Pode Miles, and Thomas Terence P. Murphy. Also Messrs. E. Coulton Rogers, George Swinterton, and Rev. J. Nelson.

PLOUGHING COMPETITION.

In late October 1927 a ploughing competition was arranged by the Modbury and District Agricultural Discussion Society, and was held at Yarnacombe Farm. Mr. W. Honey of Plympton made the following awards:

Class 1 (21 years and over): 1st G. Spurrel of Brownston. 2nd T. Burt of Ley Coombe. 3rd W. Jackman, Whympston; 4th C. Rogers, Whympston. 5th S. Hannaford, Whympston.

Class 2 (under 21 years of age): 1st J. Ryder, Widland, Modbury. 2nd W. Luscombe, Lupridge, North Huish. 3rd R. Brimacombe, Coombe, Aveton Gifford. 4th F. Ashridge, Modbury. 5th A. King. Kingston, Kingsbridge.

Mrs. W. Luscombe distributed the prizes.

CHRISTMAS CAVES.

Mr. C. H. Cawsey, who had recently been appointed sub-postmaster of Modbury, added a unique attraction to the delight of the local children at the Broad Street Tradesman's Christmas Show in 1927, by adding a 'cave' at his recently extended premises at 14 Broad Street. The cave, which was near to four-hundred feet in length, had surprises for visitors at every turn, from the painted lions and tigers, to the moving teddy bears. A snow scene in the largest cavern won the greatest admiration from the adults, but Cinderella and Dick Whittington were the favourite with the children. Electric lighting was cleverly arranged, and with its glistening gave the caves a very real effect. A fairy and Cinderella were also there to give out presents to the children who visited Father Christmas in the final grotto.

A FESTIVE SNOW FALL.

A heavy fall of snow in late December 1927 left Modbury looking very festive and was a delight to the children, but left the inhabitants of Bigbury totally cut off by road. On the 30th of the month the inhabitants were supplied with food from Modbury, which volunteers carried strapped to their backs through the snowdrifts. Heavy falls were also reported on Dartmoor and in Torquay. Thirteen men had been busy at work in the preceding days clearing the road between Flete and Modbury. In other parts of the South Hams, drifts were said to be up to fourteen feet deep and working parties were busy clearing roads so that traffic could pass through. Between Totnes and Marley Head, sixteen men were busy clearing the road, but said it would take them at least another four days before it would be open to traffic.

AGED COUPLE'S FUNERAL.

Little groups of villagers stood in respectful silence on the pathways as a hearse containing the remains of two Modbury octogenarians; William Hooper and his wife Annie, who had met their deaths in tragic circumstances at their cottage on the morning of Saturday the 3rd of March

1928. A candle having set fire to the blankets of the bed in which Annie Hooper had been sleeping.

Mr. and Mrs. Hooper lived alone in a cottage in Galpin Lane, just off Galpin Street on the outskirts of the town. Jane Furzeland, a neighbour on Galpin Street noticing the blinds had not been drawn the following morning, and that neither Mr. nor Mrs. Hooper was out and about as was their custom, she informed the police. Having forced an entrance, they found the house filled with smoke and Annie Hooper lying dead in bed with her husband beside her with one arm around his wife. The bedclothes having smouldered to ashes without bursting into flames. William Hooper was said to have been in the habit of sleeping downstairs, and suspecting something was wrong, either by a cry for help from his wife or smelling the burning bedclothes, it was assumed he had gone upstairs to investigate but had been overcome by the poisonous fumes whilst trying to drag his wife from the smouldering bed. Both bodies were said to have been extensively burned. The couple were said to have been dearly loved by everyone who knew them, and despite the cold and persistent drizzle, many of the townsfolk came out to pay tributes to their memory at the parish church of St. George. The service was conducted the Vicar Rev. A. Calvert. The twin coffins of oak bore wreaths of daffodils.

A FALL OF EARTH NEAR.

Prompt action by a passing Automobile Association [A.A.] patrol man in early April 1928 on the road near Modbury, prevented what might have led to a serious accident. A large quantity of earth and bushes had fallen during the night, blocking over half the roadway. The patrolman placed red flags and lamps at the spot, and gave information immediately to the responsible authorities, with the result that the obstruction was promptly cleared.

THE DEATH OF CHARLES CHOAKE.

The death eighty-four-year-old Charles Choake took place on Monday the 7th of January 1928. Charles had carried on an extensive business in both Modbury and Plymouth as a wholesale butcher and fellmonger [a dealer in hides or skins, particularly sheepskins] for more than fifty years, and was the owner of a considerable amount of land in the parish. He was at one time a prominent figure in the Plymouth market but had not taken any active part in business for many years. He was also at one time a director of the Modbury Gas Company, and a member of the Parish Council.

Postcard of a horse drawn cart Modbury. Courtesy of Samuel Harrison.

MEMORIAL TABLET DEDICATION IN ERMINGTON CHURCH

In December 1928, at Ermington Church, a memorial tablet carved by Miss. Violet Pinwill, the daughter of the late Reverend Edmund Pinwill, vicar of Ermington and Kingston for forty-four years, from 1880- 1924, was erected in his memory. Reverend H. J. Chaytor, senior tutor at St. Catherine's College, Cambridge, and son-in-law of the late vicar dedicated the tablet and preached the sermon.

[*Violet, along with two of her sisters Mary and Ethel were ecclesiastical carvers. They had been taught the skills by workmen who had come to St. Peter and St. Paul, Ermington Church in the mid 1890's to restore the church. Violet's first piece of work was unveiled at the church in 1889 when she was just seventeen-years-old. The sister's work was of such a high standard that the sisters set up their own company and many churches across Devon and Cornwall, as well as beyond to this day have specimens of their artistry and fine craftsmanship.*]

ARCTIC BRITAIN.

Northern Europe was blasted with cold winds and heavy snow in February 1929. In many parts of Europe, including Czechoslovakia and Poland, it was said to be the severest weather they had experienced since 1729. In Devon the snows began to fall on Wednesday the 13th of February and continued for several days. In many parts of the West Country, it was said to be the coldest it had been for thirty years. By Saturday the 16th Modbury had six to eight inches of snow. Roads were described as treacherous and the R.A.C advised that drivers used chains on their tyres when driving in the extreme conditions.

THE ANGELL MILLIONS.

Henry Sidney Bowhay aged sixty, a Naval pensioner, passed away unexpectedly at his sister's residence, Ruggadon Farm, Chudleigh, on the 8th of May 1929. Henry was the son Angell Bowhay, a blacksmith of Modbury, and had emigrated to Australia with his wife, daughter and two sons in 1912 to start a new life in farming. His wife Harriet unfortunately died in 1923 aged forty-nine. Hearing of the 'Angell millions' controversy he though the family's luck may be about to change and he returned to England in November 1928 and went stay with his sister Eliza Kerswell and her husband Robert. Whilst staying with them he was able to find the necessary birth and marriage certificates which established him as one of the rightful heirs to the some of the money as his grandfather had married Mr. Angell's sister in 1830. But just as Henry was preparing to travel to London with the papers, he died. He was buried at Chudleigh on the 11th of May 1929 - Was it the stress of the realisation that he was possibly a very rich man that killed Sidney Bowhay?

[*The Angell Millions - John Angell who died a bachelor, made a will in 1774, bequeathing his estates in Surrey, Kent and Sussex, to the male heirs of his father and grandfather. Part of which consist of over forty acres in greater London, Stockwell, Brixton, Kennington, Streatham, Balham, and Clapham. The estate covered and area of about sixty square miles.*]

THE GHOST OF ROY REEVES - SPEEDWAY RIDER.

This event didn't occur in Modbury, and I'm not sure of Roy's exact connection to the town, but his mother Louisa 'Mabel' Reeves (formerly Metherell/ Meathrell) was related to the many people of the same name living in Modbury, so it's very likely that Roy spent much of his childhood in the town. Today his name is likely unknown, but in the late 1920's when speedway was a fledgling sport, Roy Reeves was a well-known if not a slightly 'famous' sporting character in Devon. Roy Sims Reeves was born in Plymouth in 1907. He was a daredevil, and passionate about motorcycles. In June 1928 he had been fined one pound at Torquay Magistrates Court for performing stunts for onlookers on the Promenade. Motorcycle speedway came to the County Ground in Exeter on the 9th March 1929 and Roy made his debut a week later on the 16th. Six months later on Saturday the 21st September, whilst riding at the 'Super Speedway' Melton Road in Leicester, Roy lost his balance and was thrown from his machine and unintentionally ran into by another rider. It was obvious that the accident was bad and women allegedly fainted at the sight. The crowd of thirty-thousand spectators were advised to quietly leave the stadium; the meeting being abandoned - Roy had suffered a fatal head injury.

On the following Monday night, forty-eight hours after Roy's death and the evening before the inquest, Dorothy his wife, along with three of her husband's friends visited the track where the accident had occurred. They walked around the course in darkness; presumably someone had a torch, because as they approached the spot where Roy had met his untimely passing, his spirit appeared to them. Mrs. Reeves told the inquest in to Roy's death held on the 24th of September; "Last night, mysteriously something compelled me to go to the track. I was with a chum of Roy's; Cyril Hefford, and two mechanics. We were walking around the track in the dark when we came to the spot where poor Roy was killed, when suddenly he appeared. He smiled at me." Cyril Hefford confirmed the story and said that when they got to the spot where Roy had crashed, Mrs. Reeves had stood still and said Roy's vision was with her.
"We were so startled," said Dorothy. "We couldn't move. I heard a cry from one of the mechanics who was just behind me. My husband spoke to me and said that he wished me to wear one of his medals and his mother to wear another, and his favourite to be buried with him. There was good a deal more in the conversation, but it is far too sacred to reveal."

Cyril Hefford, said he had previously been inclined to be amused at the keen interest Roy had taken in spiritualism and the afterlife. He then went on to described how when standing near to Mrs. Reeves he too saw the apparition of his dear departed friend. He also heard the mechanic cry out, "My God, I have seen him!" He looked around and saw the mechanic leaning against the safety fence sobbing. Roy's vision he said, appeared before them dressed in his racing attire and wearing a crash helmet. He then saw Roy's mouth moving, but he didn't hear what he said – possibly he thought from the shock of the occurrence. The two mechanics who also saw the vision were said to have still not recovered from the shock the following day. One of them being too ill to attend the inquest; the shock and upset of it all keeping him to his bed. The other mechanic told the inquest, "Everybody was greatly upset. I broke down, I couldn't help it. We were walking around the track and when we reached the bend, we all suddenly stiffened. It was an eerie strange feeling. I can't really describe it. I'd been thinking about my visit to see his body at the mortuary at that very moment, I looked up and saw Roy, he was just as he was when we had seen him in the mortuary."

Roy was buried in the graveyard at St. George's Church on the 27th September 1929. His coffin was carried into the church by a number of his fellow speedway riders. Many floral tributes were sent from clubs across the country, and from individuals. The collection for his widow at Exeter Speedway amounted to eighty-four pounds seventeen shillings and sixteen' pence.

Roy's grave is now long overgrown, he shares it with his devoted mother Mabel who died 14th November 1942 aged fifty-eight. Did the grief-stricken quartet really see the ghost of Roy Reeves. Was it simply a trick chance of shadows and light that deceived them all into believing what they wanted to accept as true what they thought they were seeing. Did the spirit of Roy

Reeves who through his belief in spiritualism (which increased hugely during the First World War and post war years) communicate with his loved ones one final time?

The final resting place of Roy Reeves and his mother Mabel in St. George's Churchyard.

DEATH OF A VETERINARIAN.

Mr. John Blight, a veterinary surgeon of Palm Cross Green, Modbury, died on October 1929 aged seventy-three. He had practised in the town for over forty years and had only retired eighteen months previously. He had been a popular figure in the hunting field, being a supporter of the Dartmoor Foxhounds and the Modbury Harriers. He had also at one time been a member of the Modbury Parish Council. His youngest son Harry who served with the 31st Battalion, Canadian Infantry was killed aged twenty-three in Belgium during the Great War.

HOLBETON FARM TRAGEDY.

A verdict of 'accidental death' was returned on the death of William John Andrews, aged seventy-seven, of Vicarage Hill, Holbeton, in March 1930. Mr. Andrews had been a farm labourer for the previous twenty-five years in the employment of Robert Sherrell of Brownswell Farm. Because of his age, Sherrell's son had in recent years accompanied Andrews in his work. On the day of the accident, Robert Sherrell had requested Mr. Andrews to cut some wood from a hedge, telling him not to climb on the hedge as his son William would do that a little later, but when William Sherrell arrived, he found William Andrews on his hands and knees in the middle of the road with blood coming from his nose and a wound to the back of his head. Not getting any sense from the man, he moved him nearer to the hedge and out of danger of any passing traffic before going for assistance from his father, who conveyed Mr. Andrews to his home, while the son went to summon Dr. Andrews of Modbury to come as soon as possible.

Dr. Andrews told the inquest that he had known the deceased for forty-years and generally he had been in good health; strong, and not unsteady his feet. Death was due to a haemorrhage of the brain, due to a fractured skull, likely from falling from a height.

MODBURY WATER SUPPLY.

A meeting was held by Kingsbridge Rural District Council at the White Hart Hotel in April 1930, in relation to the application for a loan to bring a suitable water supply to the town. Mr. E. Butler, an inspector to the Ministry of Health expressed surprise when he heard that a considerable proportion of the population of the town still collected their water from standpipes. These residents pointed out to him that they could not afford to pay to have a system installed to bring the water directly to their houses. Mr. William Beer, clerk to the Rural District Council, said the matter had been under discussion for a considerable period. At times the water supply was very short and an engineer had recently inspected the site of a proposed water treatment plant, and the reports and analysis had been sent to the Ministry of Health who apparently considered the matter satisfactory.

The Council proposed that they would draw water from springs at Butland Farm. Standpipes would then be provided at various points in the town from which people who did not take the water into their houses could draw their supply. This would be ample for the town's population which was said to rise to around nine-hundred people during the summer months, and the quantity of water gauged at the new site was 16,312 gallons per day. Even that minimum would supply the population with eighteen gallons a head per day, whereas at present they only got seven gallons a day at times. A question was then tendered as to whether the supply would prove sufficient for the future needs of a possibly enlarged population. Mr. Butler said that examination of the records of Modbury showed that such enlargement was unlikely, and at any rate remote. The inspector added that it would cost the residents of Modbury three hundred and seventy pounds for the next thirty years to clear the loan and meet the interest on it. The charge for standpipes on people who did not install a water supply to their property would be nine' pence, and would decrease the three-hundred and seventy-pounds loan amount annually. By paying an additional three' pence however, and bringing in a water connection to their houses, those residents would have the supply ready at hand.

MODBURY FAIR AN OLD-FASHIONED CUSTOM.

The St. George's Fair, Modbury, was opened with time-honoured ceremony Saturday the 3rd of May 1930. At the market cross the town crier made his proclamation, announcing to all and sundry that according to the old statute, the fair would continue for nine days. Interest in the ceremony was said not so great as it had been in previous years, but the ringing of the town crier's bell did bring people into the street to watch the proceedings, in which the principal character was Mr. Fred Wood. For five minutes he patiently tolled the bell, and then proceeding to the town's cross crying out the familiar 'Oyez, oyez, oyez! ' He then requested silence for the reading of the proclamation. Mr. Wood had been town crier for the past seventeen years, and with the exception of the war period when he was on active service, had opened the fair according to custom by the hoisting of the 'glove,' a silver-coloured hand set amid a garland of flowers and placing it on top of the town bell.

MODBURY FAIR A RELIC OF THE PAST.

From the Western Morning News, 7th of May 1930…

Modbury Fair, in common with many other equally ancient institutions, seems in a mechanical age to be reaching the end of its tether, for yesterday practically all the business was completed in the morning. Time was when the business, as well as the merry-making, lasted over three or four days, but yesterday, although there was a fair dealing in cattle which fetched good prices, little other business was conducted. A few sheep and pigs only being penned in the streets, and by the end of the afternoon the quaint little street was almost emptied. Under the town crier's staff, erected on high over a house, a few pens were being taken down by labourers and the streets were being disinfected with lime. A small group of farmers and dealers stood waiting and chatting, their business for the day finished. A little bent old man, surprisingly agile for his evident years, was driving a few pigs through the street making vicious cuts with a stick at an old sheepdog which evidently wished to help in the herding of the pigs. A horse and its rider cantered down the road with a hardy collie making way in front. A few motor cars were standing stationary with the motor bus to Ivybridge, which has superseded the old horse-bus, but there was little else, and the scene was as it might have been on any ordinary market-day.

During the evening villagers went to a tiny fair on the Green above the hill, carrying bags of highly-coloured sweetmeats obtained from a couple of specially-erected stalls in the main street. There seemed little enough sale for these too, although it was quite usual in the past to have the street crowded with such vendors. Out on the roads leading away from the village, drovers were taking their cattle away after a fair which must have been only a miniature of those held in former times.

HORRIBLE CASE AT MODBURY.

Thomas Hingston, a fifty-year-old farm labourer of Modbury, appeared at Devon Assizes on the 3rd of July 1931 charged with 'grave offences' committed at Modbury and Ugborough. It was stated that he had left school at the age of nine and gone to work on a farm. He had been convicted on ten occasions for obscene language and fifteen times for drunkenness between and for stealing a dog at Yealmpton in 1927 he had been was bound over for a year. In 1916 he had been found not guilty of arson by setting fire to a shed on a farm. "This is a horrible case and the least said about it the better" remarked the Commissioner Sir. Lancelot Sanderson when passing a sentence of five years' penal servitude.

[*What Thomas Hingston's crimes were, I do not know, but they were of the severest category and we can only make assumptions. I can't even find a record on ancestry's court, government and criminal records of this sentencing.*]

A TRIP TO BIGBURY.

On Sunday the 23rd of August 1931, Plymouth Speedway Supporters' Club arranged a trip to Bigbury-on-Sea, something that turned into an annual event throughout the 1930's. An entourage of thirty motor cycles, private cars, and three charabancs filled with riders and supporters journeyed to the seaside for a day of fun, games and a cricket match. On their way they stopped off at Modbury to top up on refreshments. The following year, forty-motorcars and motorcycles along with four coaches made the trip. Hearing of the event, other supporters made their way to Bigbury and by mid-afternoon there were over one-thousand enthusiastic Plymouth Speedway supporters on the beach.

Hearing of the fun the speedway supporters had at the beach, Plymouth Argyle Supporter's Club in 1936 decided to make Bigbury their annual outing destination. Two hundred members of the supporters club along with Argyle players under the direction of Mr. T. Nicholls, the chairman of the club, enjoyed a day of sea, sand, cricket and other amusements. Prizes of chocolates, confectionery and cigarettes were handed out to the winners of the sporting events. The shop-keeper's and publicans of Modbury, although overwhelmed, made very good profits from such day trips.

HAPPY 90th BIRTHDAY!

On Saturday the 26th of March 1932, early in the morning and again in the evening, the bells of St. George's Church rang out in celebration of the occasion of the 90th birthday of Mr. William Pearse, of the Green, the oldest resident in the town. Mr. Pearse who was born in Stoliford in 1842 and succeeded his father in the business of farmer, auctioneer, and surveyor. The family business having been establish in 1837. In the 1870's and 80's he had farmed in a large way, and besides Stoliford, he also oversaw Stubson and Shipham farms. He sold the latter to the Prince of Wales in 1919, who was still running the farm in 1932.

Mr. Pearse was also on the board of the Kingsbridge Guardians, and had been Portreeve of the town in 1907. He has not taken any active part in business for a number of years; that role having been passed on to his son, Mr. Thomas W. Pearse. Considering his age, Mr. Pearse still enjoyed very good health, and took in a daily walk. William Pearse passed away in April of the following year, aged ninety-one.

ANOTHER UNFORTUNATE SHOOTING ACCIDENT.

Phillip Henry Steer, the eighteen-year-old son of Mr. P. Steer, a farmer, met with an accident while out shooting on the 20th of July 1932. Having shot a rabbit, he was picking up his gun when it accidentally discharged and he received a gunshot wound to the arm. He was removed to the South Devon Hospital, where an operation was performed to remove the charge.

A VISIT HOME.

Charles Cornish, now aged eighty-five and living in Bathurst, Australia, returned to England in the summer of 1932 for a visit after having left fifty-nine-years previously. Taking a motor trip to Brownston, Modbury, and Higher Lutton in South Brent where his father had been born. He recalled the days of his youth living in Brownston Street. His father William Cornish was a medical practitioner in Modbury, and for a number of years his brother followed the same profession in Ivybridge. Another brother, an assistant pay-master in the Royal Navy, lost his life when H.M.S. Captain was sunk in the Bay of Biscay in 1871. On the death of his mother, Charles left for London where he joined the full-rigged ship 'City' and travelled to Dunedin, New Zealand, where he landed on New Year's Day 1872, and subsequently proceeded to Australia.

He said that although he had been away from Modbury for many years, he still had two copies sent to him weekly of the Western Morning News.

ST. GEORGE'S FAIR 1933, REMINISCING THE PAST.

Mr. Fred Wood, the town crier, opened the annual fair on the 3rd of May 1933, attired in his three-cornered hat and braided costume as he fastened a pole carrying a stuffed glove to a wall in the main street, and afterwards read the proclamation. The gloved hand was said to be regarded as a symbol of a Royal Command for peace, and had been used annually at the fair for over one hundred and twenty years. The glove, made of real doeskin had now been painted silver to preserve it and make it more conspicuous. The clapper bell which Fred used to call for silence was of a similar age. The modern-day fair he said now continued in the form of a cattle market, and as an added attraction roundabouts and swings were provided for the entertainment of the townsfolk. The fair he said was now poor in comparison to the event of fifty years earlier. Apart from the opening ceremony, the cattle market, and the travelling fair which paid a brief visit to the town, there was nothing to make the event resemble the hilarious nine-days celebration that it used to be.

Mr. William Martin, who at the age of eighty-two and one of Modbury's oldest inhabitants was interviewed by a reporter from the Western Morning News. A former farm labourer, Mr. Martin said he had only retired three years previously. He went on to say that he deplored the gradual decline in the popularity of the fair. "When I used to take part in the fair fifty years ago," he said, "the streets used to be filled with people. We had beefeaters and ale-tasters who paraded through the town, and then carried out their own particular ceremonies for the amusement of the crowd. Forty years ago, the fair used to be spread over nine days, but now it lasts barely a day. Then there used be ten inns here which used to keep open all day during the fair. The Exeter Inn, which is about the oldest house in the place, and the Bell Inn were popular meeting places. In the cattle sale, farmers made more money than today and there were more cattle available. Seven men were stationed on all the approach roads to charge two' pence per head of cattle at the toll. They would hold a chain across the road to stop anyone pass until the tariff had been paid. I used to be toll collector. We were paid two shillings and nine' pence a day. In those days they used to have a fresh Mayor every year. He received the money from the cattle tolls, and if it was insufficient to meet his collectors' wages, he had to pay the difference from his own pocket. During the whole of the fair, skittle playing was a popular pastime in the streets which were always lined with cheap-jacks. After six o'clock everybody joined in dancing at the inns. St George's Fair gave us a nine-days holiday. The only one in the year for many of us."

Fred Wood the town crier, who had fulfilled this duty for many years explained that the place of the Mayor of Modbury had long since been taken by a Portreeve, a position at present occupied Mr. Arthur Crawley Pode, of The Barracks, Modbury.

RICK FIRE.

A rick of straw and bags of corn were destroyed by fire at Edmeston Farm, Modbury, occupied by Mr. John Irish, on Tuesday the 22nd of August 1933. It was thought that a cigarette thrown from a passing charabanc had most likely started fire; the rick being near a road. The fire brigade had to carry their hose-pipe across the main road where there was heavy vehicular traffic. They were able to save another rick of straw nearby, and also extinguished the hedge at the edge of the field which also caught fire.

MODBURY HARRIERS DANCE AT IVYBRIDGE.

The Modbury Harriers held their annual dance at the London Hotel, Ivybridge, on Wednesday the 17th of January 1934. The ballroom had been tastefully decorated with an abundance of red, blue, green, and yellow balloons. A myriad of coloured paper streamers formed a curtain overhead of the dancers, and coloured paper arranged to resemble the rays of the setting sun formed a stunning backdrop for the musicians. The stage on which they played was outlined with green and gold lattice interlaced with prettily coloured fairy lights. Supper was served in an adjoining room. The popular event was organized by a committee, of which Mr. W. M. Smith was the secretary. Dancing continued from nine p.m. until two o'clock in the morning to the strains Mr. Grant Arnold's Band, from Plymouth.

RIOTOUS SCENES AT A PARTY.

A Christmas party was held on Boxing Day 1934 in aid of the Church Choir Fund. Everything was going swimmingly until two men, likely having a tipple too many, began to argue and throwing punches at each other. Within minutes a number of the other partygoers who tried to intervene, became involved in the free for all fracas. Blood flowed freely from some of the faces of the men engaged in the fight, and the music which continued to play was drowned out by the sounds of women screaming. The local constable could not be found, and so the struggle continued for about half hour before order was finally restored and the rowdy element ejected. When the police eventually arrived, the dance was again in full swing. In spite of this incident, the dance was said to have been a great success and a significant sum was raised for the fund.

ANTHRAX OUTBREAK IN MODBURY.

In late July 1935 there was an outbreak of anthrax in cattle at a number of farms in and around Modbury. Under the supervision of the police, farmers had to destroy and then burn the carcasses of five animals. One infected carcass was traced to the kennels of the Modbury Harriers, where a number healthy young dogs being trained for coming season. As a consequence, a quantity of feed had to be destroyed and the kennels thoroughly disinfected. The outbreak affected two farms and a suspected case occurred at a third. All were mixed farms and practically adjacent to one another. The most serious losses were at Widland Farm, where Mr. Bertram Camp had to destroy one bullock, one cow, and one horse. At Trehele, Mr. Herbert Luscombe lost one cow, and a suspected case occurred at West Leigh, a farm occupied Mr. George Blackler. The police were forced to limited the movement of other animals which had been exposed to the possibility infection on the affected farms. All farms were visited by an official from the Ministry of Health. Modbury was said to have experienced a particularly severe outbreak of the disease in 1921 when a number of farms within the parish were affected and numerous animals had to be destroyed.

THE WIRELESS RADIO.

Harold Baker writing in the 'Daily Mirror' in 1935 on the topic of radios, said that it was now generally accepted as a medium of entertainment, though it was not worth the ten shillings licence fee. On the other hand, there were a great deal of people who viewed the wireless as one of the wonders of the world - particularly those who lived in the countryside. He mentioned a recent holiday he had spent in Modbury and a visit to one of his favourite haunts; the six-hundred-year-old Exeter Inn. Among the towns inhabitants was a gentleman called Harry. The writer would meet Harry on each of his visits – no doubt Harry being a regular at the Exeter Inn. Harry, he described as being a 'philosopher' and on a recent visit he asked him what he thought of "this 'ere wireless."
"O, woireless be all right - it be wunnerful. But, dang me, wi' all this 'ere 'lectricity in the air and in the ground, summit's bound to 'appen sooner or later, ain't it?"
Whilst chatting about the 'modern' radio, the writer noticed in a corner of the room a baby grand piano, which he was informed had previously been used in a BBC radio studio broadcast from that very inn.

CAT ADOPTS A PUPPY.

In January 1936 a grey and white cat belonging to Mr. Alfred Davis of Modbury, gave birth to a litter of five kittens, but when a smooth-haired terrier died after giving birth to a pup, the cat killed the last of her kittens [*presumably very weak and unlikely to survive?*] and adopted the orphaned pup. At six weeks old the little fellow was said to be healthy and strong, thanks to the vigilant eye of his foster-mother who looked after him with lavish maternal care.

MODBURY HOUNDS RESCUED FROM THE SEA.

Whilst being pursued by the Modbury Harriers after the meet at Lolesbury Cross in March 1936, a fox took to the cliffs at Stoke Fleming, and turning down on to the rocks jutting out into the sea he found himself cut off by the pack just a few yards behind him. Thereupon he made an amazing leap over a crevice. The hounds tried to follow, but the jump proved to be too wide for them and three fell into the sea below and had to be rescued by the huntsman. After having been taken around by a safer path the hounds got the scent of the fox again, and caught up with him and killed him near Revelstoke Point.

BAKEHOUSE FIRE.

The bakehouse of Mr. H. J. Cawsey at 45, Galpin Street, was gutted by fire in the early hours of the 1st of April 1936. Just after half-past midnight a fire was discovered on the premises and the

alarm was put through to the telephone exchange. Shortly afterwards the Modbury Fire Brigade under the instruction of Mr. W. Williams were on the scene and tackled the outbreak which had by then become much bigger. Kingsbridge brigade were also sent for and arrived at a quarter past one, by which time the Modbury brigade had gotten the blaze under control and in another quarter of an hour the fire was completely extinguished, but by this time the bakehouse had been entirely gutted.

A GIFT OF EGGS.

The children of Modbury Church Sunday-school, with the co-operation of the town's Baptist Church and other friends in the parish, in August 1936 sent over one thousand eggs to the Plymouth hospitals for the benefit of the patients there.

A view of Modbury taken in 1928, courtesy of britiainfromabove.org.uk

MODBURY SCHOOL RE-CONSTRUCTION.

Modbury schools closed in December 1935 as they were in much need of modernisation. They opened again the following year on September the 29th 1936. During the intervening months the children had been taught at various buildings across the town, and also at Brownston some three miles distant. This together with paying for the conveyance of children from Ringmore, Bigbury and Kingston, had for the school been very costly. The children were glad to now be back with their friends in a modern, well-lit airy building, with central heating and proper dining facilities, along with science and domestic rooms. At the opening, the chairman of the school managers, Mr. W.G. Luscombe, said the children now had a school which was second to none in the county. All that was now needed was a playing field to complete the work.

THREE ARRESTED.

Three men were remanded at Totnes in October 1936, having been discovered by P.C. Hawkins in possession of items stolen from Corner Croft, North Huish, the property of Mr. F.H. Kingdom-Fox of 4, Church Street Modbury. Corner Croft was a small-holding where he occasionally slept when working there. Mr. Kingdom-Fox discovered the break in on the morning of the 9th of October and immediately informed the police. The men had entered through the scullery window and stole food and other articles including knives, forks, spoons and a clock. James Rigby, Robert McEwan, and Peter MacDonald, all of no fixed abode, were discovered later the same day and charged with breaking and entering. All pleaded guilty. James Rigby was sentenced to one month imprisonment, Robert McEwan to six weeks, and Peter MacDonald to two months – all with hard labour.

EX-SERVICEMEN'S PARADE

A church parade of ex-servicemen was held at Modbury on Sunday the 22nd of November 1936. The proud veterans assembled at Traine Terrace under the charge of Major Ratcliffe of Comer, and led by the Bluejacket band of the Royal Naval Barracks, Devonport. The parade included contingents from the Holbeton, Kingsbridge, and Plympton branches of the British Legion, all carrying their standards. At the War Memorial a wreath of poppies was laid at its base by the president; Admiral L. C. S. Woollcombe, in memory of those who fell in the Great War. This was followed by a service in St. George's Church conducted by the Vicar, Reverend. A. Calder. The Bluejacket band played the accompaniment for the hymns. Afterwards Admiral Woollcombe inspected the men in Broad Street. The parade was held with a view to reviving the Modbury branch of the British Legion.

WELL-KNOWN FARMER DIES.

Mr. Langley Thomas Luscombe of 15, Church Street, died on the 23rd of April 1937 at the age of eighty-one. He had been well-known in local agricultural circles until his retirement ten years previously. He had farmed at Little Orcheton, and prior to that Leycombe Farm. He left behind a widow, three sons, and one daughter. His second born son Ernest Luscombe was then running Little Orcheton Farm. Another son was in the Merchant Navy, and the third in Canada. His daughter, Miss. Ida Luscombe, was living with an aunt at Hartley, Plymouth. His eldest son Sidney Thomas Luscombe had been killed in the Great War whilst serving with the Australian Forces in France.

CARNIVAL QUEEN.

Fifteen-year-old Mary Hine was proclaimed Modbury Carnival Queen on the 12th of May 1937, the day of King George VI's Coronation. A party atmosphere was present in the town, and after the townsfolk had listened to the Coronation service broadcast live on the wireless from Westminster Abbey, the celebrations continued with games, sports and dancing. Mary and her attendants Leonora Ash, aged seven, and Peggy Stevens aged six years were paraded through the town in a car decorated with red, white, and blue streamers. She was dressed in a flowing golden gown topped with a midnight blue velvet cloak lined with gold. She also wore a golden crown studded with brilliantly-hued gems. "It's such a thrill to think on the day of the Coronation I am wearing a crown too, even though it may only be a cardboard one," said Mary. Mugs and medals commemorating the event were also given out to all the children.

BRAVE MRS. TRINICK.

When one of the worst fires for many years broke out in a sixteenth century three-storey house on Church Street in the early hours of the 3rd of August 1937, sixty-year-old Mrs. Elizabeth Trinick, made a rope by knotting bedclothes together and lowered her sixty-eight-year-old husband, former post-master William Trinick to safety from the bathroom window, and then clambered down herself. Within a matter of minutes of them making their brave escape the house was enveloped in flames. It was all but destroyed and all they had left were the night-clothes they were wearing.

The fire was first noticed by Mr. Thorn who was passing at around midnight when he saw smoke issuing from the property and he rang the street alarm – which woke Mrs. Trinick. When she opened her bedroom door to see what the fuss was about, she noticed the old oak staircase, said to be one of the best in the whole of Devon to be on fire. The fire brigade arrived soon after but the blaze was so fierce they knew that saving the building would be impossible and so they concentrated on saving the two adjoining properties, the homes of Mr. P. Steer and Mr. T. Davis.

Some townsfolk said the house was reputed to be haunted and strangers to the town as well as residents had previously described seeing a 'dear old lady' in the building. Mrs. Trinick said she had seen the old woman herself, describing her as looking like an 'old English' gentlewoman.

TRAGIC DEATH OF THOMAS WILLIAMS.

A tragedy occurred at Great Orcheton Farm in August 1937, when fifteen-year-old Thomas Blatchford Williams, the youngest of the six sons of Mr. and Mrs. Samuel J. Williams was found shot dead in a field near to his home with a gun lying near his body. A short while earlier Thomas and his father had quarrelled whilst working in the field in regards to the sheaves of corn not being stacked properly. Thomas said he was leaving the field and headed back towards the farmhouse. Back home he asked his mother where the gun was as his brother wanted it. Not realising his intention, his mother told him where it was kept. When his elder brother Stanley, who was a police officer in Surrey but home on leave at the time, heard that Thomas had taken the gun, he immediately went in search of him. Sadly, it was too late. He found him slumped over some railings - shot through the head. His poor parents were said to be in a state of collapse when being told the dreadful news.

Thomas was described by his father as an impulsive lad and highly strung. He had recently sat an examination to join the Royal Airforce and had been unhappy with the result. The coroner, Mr. A.K.G. Johnstone, said that he regretted to hear that the gun which was kept in the kitchen was in such easy reach. He thought that if the lad had spent more time looking for it, he would likely have had time to change his mind. A verdict that he had 'caused the wound upon himself whilst of unsound mind' was recorded. At Thomas's funeral, many mourners including mothers with perambulators or small children in their arms attended the service. Thomas had been a pupil of Hoe Grammar School in Plymouth, and six of his close school friends acted as pall-bearers. The funeral arrangements were carried out by Messrs. G. Steer and Sons of Modbury.

YOUNG AND OLD FOLLOW THE HOUNDS.

Mr. William Elliott, who was eighty-one-years-old and mounted on a twenty-six-year-old pony which he had been riding for the past twenty-four-years, was among the followers at an opening meet of Modbury Harriers on the 12th of October 1937. Mr. Elliott, who has been riding with the Harriers since he was seven-years-old, proudly claimed to be the oldest member of the Hunt. Another rider of considerable age was Mr. William H. Fairweather of Shilston Barton, who was eighty-five. He was not an old follower of the hunt as he has only recently moved to the district, but had the reputation of having ridden with all the foxhound and harrier hunts in Devon.

Modbury Harriers 1937. Picture courtesy of Samuel Harris.

Amongst the riders, who numbered around fifty, only twelve were women. One of them was the Honourable Helen Mildmay of Flete, who was the only one to ride side saddle. Maj. H. Fox, the field-master led the pack with the huntsman Mr. J. Farley. Another member of the field was Mr. Arthur Wroth, who had been huntsman for many years prior to the First World War. Also present at the meet was little Miss. Helen Wroth, aged one-year and eleven months, who was securely strapped in a basket in the form of a saddle on a small pony. She was said to have taken a delighted interest in all that was going on and displaying no fear, even when her mount was disturbed by the traffic and crowds surging around her.

CELEBRATORY SUPPER.

Modbury Rovers Football Club held a supper to celebrate their winning the Eastern Section of the Plymouth and District United Churches League in1939. The players and officials were entertained to supper by their president Mr. H. J. Cawsey, on Tuesday the 16th of May, who expressed his pride at the team's success, and paid tribute to the way in which the United Churches League was run.

A DEVON SUPERSTITION – OR NOT?

On Monday the 14th of August 1939 at between two and two-thirty in the afternoon, Edward Horton of Grove Park, Modbury, noticed three white owls feeding in the garden amongst his potato plants. Thinking it very unusual he asked his mother who was then in her ninetieth year to come and look - but she refused, saying that when white owls feed by day it foretells the coming of a national catastrophe. He wrote to the Western Morning News saying he wondered

if this was just an old Devon superstition...Britain declared war on Germany just over two weeks later.

WORLD WAR II

Britain declared itself to be at war with Germany on Sunday the 3rd of September 1939, and the war in Europe continued until the 8th of May 1945, although the war in the East continued until August of that year. Modbury, as with the Great War that lasted from 1914 to 1918 lost many of its menfolk. Below are the names of those who sacrificed their lives and are remembered today on the towns' War Memorial:

Private **WILLIAM FREDERICK DARE**, Service No: 5617238. 2nd Bn. Devonshire Regiment. Died on 17th September 1944, aged 38. William is buried at VALKENSWAARD CEMETERY, Netherlands. The son of William and Susan Dare and the husband of Norah Evelyn Dare of Loddiswell.

Private **VICTOR CHARLES DEVILLE**, Service No: 5625156. 2nd Bn. Devonshire Regiment. Died 19th June 1944, aged 28. Victor is buried at HOTTOT-LES-BAGUES WAR CEMETERY, France. The son of Thomas and Mary Deville, Modbury.

Chief Mechanic **WILLIAM GEORGE HENRY FOX**, Service No: D/K 61141. HMS Samphire. Died on 30th January 1943. The son of Richard and Hannah Fox and husband of Emily Hannah Fox of Modbury. William is remembered on the PLYMOUTH NAVAL MEMORIAL, Devon, Panel 81, Column 2.

Sergeant **GEORGE JOHN ARSCOTT MILES**, Service No: 900970. 49th Squadron Royal Airforce Volunteer Reserve. Died 2nd June 1942. Buried at HEVERLEE WAR CEMETERY, Belgium. The son of Henry Pode Miles and Marjorie Helen Miles of Modbury.

Petty Officer Stoker **HARRY PEARCE LOWRY**, Service No: D/K 60918, H.M.S. Basilisk. Died 1st June 1940, aged 36. Husband of Bertha Edith Lowry, of Elburton, Devon. He is commemorated on PLYMOUTH NAVAL MEMORIAL, Devon. Panel 40, Column 2.

Chief Petty Officer **EDGAR GEORGE WATTS**. Service No: Cook (S) D/MX 47250, H.M.S. Repulse. Died 10th December 1941, aged 34. Son of George and Amy Watts; husband of Olive Susan Watts, of Camel's Head, Plymouth. He is commemorated on the PLYMOUTH NAVAL MEMORIAL, Devon. Panel 55, Column 2.

Petty Officer Stoker **FRED TOMS**. Service No: D/K 32894, H.M.S. Itchen. Died 23rd September 1943. He is commemorated on the PLYMOUTH NAVAL MEMORIAL, Devon. Panel 81, Column 3.

Able Seaman **JAMES ANDREW YOUNG**. Service No: D/J 11882, H.M.S. Rawalpindi. Died 23rd November 1939, aged 45. Son of James and Mary Ann Young of Modbury. Husband of Olive Young, of Dorking, Surrey. He is commemorated on the PLYMOUTH NAVAL MEMORIAL, Devon. Panel 33, Column 3.

Not mentioned on the War Memorial is Private Dorothy Eileen George of the Auxiliary Territorial Service (ATS). Service No: W/192325 who died on the 18th of December 1946 aged 23. She is buried in Illogan Churchyard, St. Illogan, Cornwall. Dorothy was the daughter of Alfred and Eliza Jane George of Little Modbury. Also, Lieutenant Commander Percy Mark Cox, of H.M.S. Calliope who died on the 26th of February 1945, aged 55 and is commemorated at West Road Crematorium, Newcastle upon Tyne. He was the son of Joseph and Caroline Cox and husband of Lylie Amy Cox, of Modbury, Devon.

MODBURY NEWSAGENT.

A member of what was believed to be one of the oldest newsagent's businesses in the Westcountry and of a family associated with 'The Western Morning News' since its foundation in 1860; Mr. Clarence Short Ellory, of Brownston Street, died at the age of sixty-seven in March 1940.

Mr. Ellory had taken over the business from his father, the late Mr. Thomas Short Ellory, twenty-three-years previously.

The father and son had an unbroken record of sixty-years as newsagents for 'The Western Morning News.' Clarence had started delivering papers as an eleven-year-old. One of his proudest memories was of the time of the great blizzard towards the end of the nineteenth century [1891] when he started out from Modbury at four o'clock in the morning to deliver his papers on foot, and completed the round which included visits to Yealmpton and Ermington, at one thirty in the afternoon. A feat which earned the name of 'The boy who defied the blizzard.'

A FIGHT OVER WASHING.

Neighbours living in Poundwell Street found themselves brought before the Plympton Police Court on the 29th of April 1940. Garland John Hodge Rogers an old-age pensioner, summoned Laura Humphreys for assault. He was then cross-summoned for assault by Mrs. Humphreys and her husband Morris. Mr. Rogers lived on the ground floor of the property and the Humphreys resided above him. There was passage at the side of the property to which they both had access.

This was his story of the washing-day episode: "I looked out through my door and saw the passage full of washing. I said to Mrs. Humphreys, "Do you pay all the rent for this place?" She said, "Yes, and you have no business out here." She then jumped in my face, caught hold my cheeks and pulled them. I had to shove her to get her off. Then she shoved me into the doorway and kicked me. I closed the door and left her." He added that Mr. Humphreys only came out when Mrs. Humphreys was pushing him into the doorway.

Facing him across the courtroom, Mrs. Humphreys said: "Mr. Rogers, didn't you strike me first?" Rogers: "No; I can swear my life away in this place."

"So can I," retorted Mrs. Humphreys. As a prelude to her side of the story, she said she had gone to the outside tap for water and was joking with her neighbours. "I was singing when I was doing my washing." She said Mr. Rogers swore at her. "He smacked my face across the right eye. Of course, I hit him back in self-defence, and he gave me another hit across the right arm. Then I gave him another hit back naturally, and he caught me by the throat."

Morris Humphreys, who said he was nearly blind, deposed: "I heard a call for help, and I said to myself, my God, that's Laura! I went down and felt someone's hand on my wife's throat. I pushed him away and he struck me across the ear."

Each side denied the allegations of the other, and Mrs. Humphreys said in reply to the chairman (Lieut.-Col. J. C. Hoyle): "We have been having these quarrels about the washing for ten years." The chairman (to Rogers) "Who does your washing?" Rogers: "My daughter does it on Sunday afternoons, but we put it on the line outside to dry."

All three parties were bound over for twelve months and fined five pounds each.

OLD CUSTOM KEPT UP.

Owing to the war, the Modbury Fair was celebrated rather differently on the 3rd of May 1940. Mr. Fred Wood, the town crier, was not allowed to ring his bell under the 'Noise Restrictions Act,' but he otherwise carried out his duties as normal and read out the proclamation which dated back to Edward III. Fred had carried out this role since 1914, other than for the war years when he was on Military service. A few weeks previously the Lord of the manor and Portreeve, Mr. Arthur Pode had died, and without having anyone to give the glove and have the fair proclaimed open, Miss. B.C. Pode, the sister of the deceased, allowed her name to be used instead. The market rather than being held in the street, was moved to Poundwell Meadow on the request of the military.

MODBURY BOY MAKES GERMAN MODEL PLANES FOR THE ARMY.

This is a rather unusual but wonderful story: Fourteen-year-old Stanley John Clapham, the son of Mr. A. J. Clapham, of Church Street, Modbury, was sent an official requisition order from the military authorities in August 1940, asking him to make model aeroplanes for army instructional purposes. For several years, Stanley, who was very adept at making models of all kind, had followed his craft with great enthusiasm, and when the war started, he turned his attention to aeroplanes. Studying the charts, particularly those of German planes, his nimble fingers set to work and it was by a chance visit to his father's shop by an officer that led to him receiving an order for the Army. He had so far made models of twenty-two German machines. Explaining how he did it, he said he first off drew the design on paper to scale, and from this with a penknife he shaped the various parts. These he then glued together to complete the model. The complete pieces of work with their accurate colouring and distinguishing marks were said to have attracted a lot of admiration. He told 'The Western Morning News' reporter that he was very proud at having been able to make models for army instruction and was now going to make some models for sale. With the money from the Army, he intended buying more materials. "I love making these models, although I have no great desire to take up flying when I grow up" he said. "I have been making models ever since I was old enough to use a knife, and I have made all sorts of things, including cranes, a miniature writing-desk with reading lamp, and other articles of furniture for dolls houses."

'The great beauty of the work of this boy is the accuracy of detail and the miniature character of each piece,' wrote the reporter. 'For instance, the aeroplanes have a span of only about three inches, but the officer who saw the first models realized that they were all made so true to type that they would be invaluable for military instruction.'
"Now and again, I have had one sent back for repair." Stanley said. "In addition to the twenty-two varieties of German machines, I have also made models of eight British fighters and a Wellington bomber." Two years previously, Stanley was said to have won a scholarship enabling him to attend Kingsbridge Grammar School.

In 1943, Stanley held an exhibition at the Red Devon Hotel, Modbury, where he displayed one hundred and thirty models of aeroplanes as well as a model airfield. A small charge was made for entry to the exhibition which raised six pounds two shillings and six' pence, which he donated to the Modbury branch of the Red Cross.

Stanley Clapham went on to become an architect and artist, and exhibited his work at the Royal Academy. Much of the work which he did in pencil and in watercolours, is still available to buy.

MINISTRY OF INFORMATION FILMS.

A travelling show put on by the 'Ministry of Information' visited Modbury on Saturday the 2nd of November 1940, to show a number of short films to the townsfolk, who now included many evacuees from London. The show was put on in the school gymnasium. The 'cinema' operator Mr. C. R. Bond, showed several films including one on careless talking, entitled 'Now You're Talking.' A tragedy in which the worst actually did happen. Instead of turning up smiling on the last few feet of the reel the hero is blown to bits as the result of a careless word dropped by a lorry driver at an inn. There was another on the manufacture of aircraft propellers, a film about military recruitment, and one about the Canadian Navy in which the big guns, torpedoes, and depth charges were seen in action. The girls particularly liked a film about a village school and another explaining how to grow vegetables for victory. One little girl, an evacuee from London, particularly liked the film about 'The Big City' hoping that she might see her house.

THEYRE DROPPING BOMBS!

In November 1940 three high-explosive bombs caused the electricity supply to be cut off in the Bigbury-on-Sea, Ringmore, Aveton Gifford and Kingston districts. The only casualty was a bullock, killed at Modbury. Forty-five incendiary bombs dropped in a circle around farm buildings at Bearscombe Farm, Kingsbridge, owned by Mr. George Kerswell, but thankfully did no damage.

WHEN BOMBS BEGAN DROPPING.

Although Modbury was a fairly safe place to live during the war, being far enough away from Plymouth as to avoid the destruction played out upon the people there, they were still affected by the conflict. Many of course had family in Plymouth, and their plight during the heavy bombing raids of 1941 would certainly have concerned them. Evacuees from London and Bristol were sent to Modbury, and also of course bombed out family members from Plymouth and beyond came to stay with relatives or friends until alternative accommodation could be found. In February 1941, one-hundred and seventy-five children arrived in Kingsbridge from Bristol and were from there dispersed to billets within the area.

BRISTOL EVACUEES ARRIVE.

In February 1941, the first evacuees arrived at Kingsbridge Station from heavily bombed Bristol. Members of the Civil Defence Committee along with doctors and nurses boarded a train at South Brent where the children changed trains, and during the forty-minute journey to Kingsbridge every one of the one-hundred and seventy-five children were inspected by the doctors, and the Civil Defence members worked out how the children were to be distributed among the various parishes.

When the train arrived at Kingsbridge, buses and cars were waiting to take them to their destinations, where a tea of drinks and sandwiches was made avaiable. There were six groups of children, consisting of junior and senior boys and girls. The hope was to billet the children from the same schools within the same parish, or at least in adjoining parish so as they would still be with their friends. One group totalling twenty-eight children were sent to Modbury, a group of twenty-nine went to Malborough, and a group of thirty-one children were split between Aveton Gifford, Loddiswell and Churchstow. Another group was billeted between South Huish, South Milton, and Bigbury-on- Sea, and a group totalling twenty-six children went to Kingston. The remaining group after being accommodated overnight at a communal house at Thurlestone were sent to Lower Coombe Royal. Teachers and voluntary helpers who accompanied the children were also directed to the parishes where their help would be needed. Each child was given a postcard to write home and inform their parents of their safe arrival.

The first batch of evacuees had arrived in Kingsbridge the previous June from London, and the District Council now had two and a half thousand mothers and children in their care, though unofficial evacuees brought the total up to nearer three thousand. The authorities requisitioned a number of empty houses; one or two families were able to live on their own in the smaller properties, but in the larger houses up to five families were accommodated together and shared amenities. There was also work underway to cultivate the gardens surrounding many of these houses, the produce was to be used communally to help feed the extra mouths that needed feeding.

Postcard of Broad Street, Modbury. Courtesy of Samuel Harrison.

JOB VACANCIES.

The Kingsbridge Rural District Council invited applications for staff to work at the Infectious Disease Hospital 'Treveor,' Modbury, namely: A cook, who would receive fifty-pounds per annum, plus full board and laundry. A kitchen-maid and general help who would receive thirty-five pounds per annum, plus full board and laundry. Two ward-maids who would each receive a salary of fifty-five pounds per annum, plus full board and laundry. Applications with full particulars and a copy of testimonials was asked to be sent to the Medical Officer of Health, Council Offices, Plympton. To reach him not later than 17th March 1941.

WELFARE CENTRE NEEDED.

At the Kingsbridge Rural Civil Defence Committee meeting on the 3rd of June 1941, it was decided there was a need for a building in Modbury that would serve jointly as a communal feeding centre, nursery, and child welfare centre. The chairman (Mr. Harold Helby) said the only possible building was the former tannery in Brownston Street, which was now used for housing an A.R.P. ambulance lorry. Miss Hope Bonsall the assistant chief billeting officer, asked if it would be possible to find a room in the vicarage which was rather large. She suggested that the dining-room there was a good place to house a welfare centre. The committee decided to request the Ministry of Health and the assistant sanitary surveyor to report on the position.

MODBURY FAMILY'S ACHIEVEMENTS.

Joan Clapham aged ten, became the third child of Mr. and Mrs. Arthur Clapham of Church Street to win a scholarship from Modbury Council School, in the summer of 1941. The following term she was to attend Crediton High School where she would join her twelve-year-old sister Gwendoline. Their brother, Stanley Clapham who was then at Kingsbridge Grammar School, had recently received an official requisition order from the military authorities to make and supply model aeroplanes for the Army for instructional purposes. [see: **MODBURY BOY MAKES GERMAN MODEL PLANES FOR THE ARMY**.] Stanley had recently given a radio broadcast during 'Children's Hour' and was hoping to soon hold an exhibition of his seventy or eighty model planes in Plymouth.

As well as Joan Clapham, two other children from Modbury School had been successful in the county school examination and gained a scholarship. Philip Hodder aged eleven, a farmer's son, and Peggy Stevens aged ten.

The Claphams 'triple' achievement had been equalled some years earlier at the school by a family called Roper. Harry, who was now in the R.A.F; Kathleen now a nurse; and Mary who was now the school's secretary, had all gained scholarships.

LOST RESPIRATOR.

On the 18th of October 1941, a service respirator No: 1,036,395 was lost somewhere between Elburton and Modbury Cross. Whoever found it was kindly asked to return it to Mr. Small of Galpin Street.

FARM BOY.

In October 1941, it was reported that Philip Hoskin aged four had been milking cows for the past six months at Croppins Coombe Farm, so as to release his elder brother Roger aged seven, to carry out other work on the farm.

VICAR LEAVES.

Reverend Archibald Calder, who had been the vicar of Modbury for sixteen years, left in the summer of 1943 to take up an appointment at St. Mark's Church in Exeter. He was presented with an inscribed silver salver and a cheque for twenty-five pounds by his parishioners. Mrs. Calder was presented with a pouchette by members of the Housewives Service whom she had trained, and who had won many competitions in the district.

LLOYDS BANK MANAGER RETIRES.

Mr. Philip Senders took up the appointment as manager of the Modbury branch of Lloyds Bank on Broad Street in March 1945, upon the retirement Mr. William Francis Treneer, who had entered service with the bank in February 1913. During the Great War he had served with the Tank Corps and was wounded. After his discharge from the army in early 1919 he returned to work for the bank working in various branches across Devon and Cornwall.

GYMKHANA AT MODBURY IN AID OF THE HARRIERS

A gymkhana event in aid of Modbury Harriers was held on the 6th of August 1945 at Mary Cross, Modbury. It included competitions such as; best pony under sixteen hands which was won by Miss P. Blackhurst on Miss Roberts-Brown's pony. First prize in the best child rider went to Miss P. Jarvis on Hunter.

The handy pony for children under 16 was won by Miss J. Anstice. Miss. P. Harris took first prize for the best working carthorse, and the egg and spoon race was won by C. Manning. The open jumping first prize went to R. Hard.

The walk, trot and gallop open first prize went to Mr. Spry. J. French claimed first prize in the novelty race, and Dr. Goss was awarded first place in the novice jumping open. J. Manning and J. Distin took first prize in the wheelbarrow race, and in the egg and spoon race for children sixteen years and under, Miss J. Hawes came in first.

H.M.A.S. AUSTRALIA.

Members Of the ships' crew of H.M.A.S. Australia were invited in August 1945 to visit farms associated with the Plymouth Co-operative Society in Modbury and surrounding district. They were taken in special buses from St. Levans Gate, Devonport Dockyard, to Modbury accompanied by Mr. C. J. Harris, the chief administrative clerk, along with members of the Farmers Committee and the Management Committee, who acted as their hosts. The Australian seamen were shown round Whympston, Membland, Lambside and Caulston Farms. They were said to be greatly interested in the very modern and up-to-date farming methods. The party were then entertained to tea at Stoke House where the captain of H.M.A.S. Australia thanked the society for their hospitality and expressed the pleasure he and his men had at being able to visit the farms.

VICTORY WEDDING.

At eight o'clock in the morning of Wednesday the 15th of August 1945, Miss. Barbara Elizabeth Cawsey, the youngest daughter of Mr. and Mrs. H. Cawsey of the Exeter Inn, married Corporal Harold Brown of the 10th Squadron, Royal Australian Airforce (R.A.A.F.) of Sydney, Australia, who was then based at Mount Batten just outside of Plymouth.
The bride wore a gown of turquoise blue trimmed with orchids. Officers and N.C.O.s from the Australian base at Mount Batten formed a guard of honour. A reception was afterwards held at the Exeter Inn. The bride and groom planned to leave for Australia within the next few months and make their home in Sydney, New South Wales.

FILM SHOW.

At the October meeting of the Modbury Women's Institute in 1945, held in the Poundwell Room. Dr. Ronald Davis of Torquay gave an interesting film show of the towns, cities, and cultural life in Europe, America, New Zealand, and Australia. There was then an interlude for the children [*who likely had by now become very bored*] with cartoons, after which scenes of the Derbyshire Peak District were shown as well as some local views.
A competition called 'Autumn Flowers' was then judged by Dr. Davis, who awarded eight prizes; Mrs. Irish, Mrs. Stribling, Mrs. Ford, Mrs. W. Crocker. Mrs. Axon, Mrs. Bickford, Mrs. Davis and Mrs. Cawsey all being winners.
Bundles of clothes for the 'Help Holland' effort were also brought in by the members, many of whom had been busy making baby's nightgowns to be sent to the needy children of Europe.

SUPERIOR MAN WANTED.

Mr. Sidney Harris of Spriddlescombe Manor Farm, Modbury, advertised in March 1946 for a 'superior young man with a general knowledge of farm work' who was to live as a member of the family. Suitable applicants were asked to telephone Modbury 227.

LOTS FOR SALE.

In September 1945 R.H. Luscombe and Sons of Kingsbridge, in conjunction with John Pearse and Sons of Plympton, were instructed to sell on behalf of the trustees of the late Charles Choake, Cridland Choake, and Mr. Francis H. Choake of 18, Brownston Street, a commodious and well-built freehold residence and garden. The building solidly constructed of stone covered stucco and with upright slating. On the ground floor there was said to be a spacious entrance passage, three convenient sized reception rooms, a strong-room kitchen and larder, washhouse and water closet. On the first floor were four good sized bedrooms, a bathroom with airing cupboard, and also a water closet. The basement it was said could be approached directly from the street, and communicated with the kitchen. At the rear was a conservatory and veranda adjoining the lounge which overlooked a pleasant small grassed lawn, and on a lower level was a productive vegetable garden which was partly walled. Electricity and public water supply had been installed.

In February 1946, R.H. Luscombe and Sons of Kingsbridge, again in conjunction with John Pearse and Sons of Plympton, were instructed to sell another twenty lots of land, farms, small holdings, properties, cottages and residences in and around the town of Modbury, all having been properties owned by the late Charles Choake, Cridland Choake, and Mr. Francis H. Choake. They were as follows:

LOT 1 - With vacant possession; valuable enclosures of rich pasture land adjoining Galpin St, known as Fridays Hills, and having a frontage of approximated four-hundred and thirty feet. Well supplied with water and containing an area of seven acres, three roods and twelve perches. Main water adjoining. [*A rood is a measure of land area equal to a quarter of an acre.*]

LOT 2 - With vacant possession; valuable grazing farm known as Avlestone, containing an area of sixty-two acres, one rood and fifteen poles at Avleston Cross near the main Wrangaton and Kingsbridge roads. Excellent residence and superior outbuildings. Mains water.

LOT 3 - With vacant possession. a charming and well-situated residential property close to the town, known as 'Madeira Vale' containing an area of thirty acres, one rood and three poles. Excellent residence, good yard and buildings and situated on the main Plymouth to Kingsbridge road. Frontages of approximately five-thousand-two-hundred feet.

Lot 4 – Adjoining lot 3, containing an area of eighteen acres, two roods, and thirty-eight poles, together with the buildings erected thereon and known Higher and Lower Langworthys,

205

Sedgewells, Ashley, Davis, and Playstone. With road frontages of approximately two-thousand-six-hundred and fifty feet.

LOT 5 - A small residence and garden known as 'Toll House Cottage' on the main Plymouth to Kingsbridge road. Supplied with water by gravitation and having frontage of approximately one-hundred and fifty feet on the main road. Presently in the occupation of Mr. W J. Beddoes at a rental of thirty pound per annum. Tenant paying the rates.

LOT 6 - With vacant possession. A productive well-sheltered orchard, with two buildings therein known as 'Stoliford Orchard,' and containing an area of one acre one rood and eleven poles.

LOT 7 - With vacant possession. A very valuable enclosure of exceptionally good land, supplied with water. Known as 'West Whetlands,' it adjoins Lots 3 and 9, and is close to Lots 8 and 10. It contained an area of seven acres, two roods and eight poles, with its frontage of approximately seven-hundred and seventy feet on the Bigbury road.

Lot 8 - With vacant possession, enclosure and excellent grazing land supplied with water, called 'East, or Second Whetlands.' The area comprised of three acres, three roods, and fifteen poles. Frontage again on the Bigbury road of approximately three hundred and eighty feet.

LOT 9 - With vacant possession of the yard and buildings therein. The dwelling-house, orchard, garden, yard, and buildings, all known as 'Gas House.' This contained an area of one acre and twenty-six poles. With the exception of the yard and buildings, it was in the occupation of Mr. E. C. Groves paying a rental of ten shillings and six' pence per week. The tenant paying the rates.

LOT 10 - With vacant possession, with the exception of the two cottages and mill. A desirable holding adjoining the town, known as 'Swanbridge Mill,' containing twenty-nine acres, two roods, and twenty-nine poles. Exceptionally good and well-watered land. One cottage and mill let to Mr. C. Watts at ten shillings per week. The other cottage is let to Mr F. Marks at five shillings per week, both tenants paying the rates.

LOT 11 - Valuable plot pasture land with the buildings thereon at present used for holding Modbury Cattle Markets and Fair, containing an area approximately three roods and fourteen poles, with road frontage of approximately three-hundred feet on the road.

LOT 12 - With vacant possession, except 'The Kennels.' A compact holding of pasture, meadow, orchard, and arable land known as 'Cotlass' or Cotleys,' with a small dwelling-house and buildings, containing an area of forty-seven acres and two poles. The Kennels being rented to the Committee of the Modbury Harriers at a rental of ten shillings per annum.

LOT 13 - With vacant possession. A block of seven enclosures of productive Land. Copse, and buildings, adjoining the road from Modbury to Bigbury, known as 'Prigdon,' containing an area of thirty-four acres, three roods, and fifteen perches.

LOT 14 - With vacant possession. A valuable enclosure of meadow land known as 'Kennel Meadow,' containing an area of two acres, thirteen roods, and thirty-seven perches of rich land, adjoining the road leading to Modbury Kennels and fronting on Cotlass Lane.

LOT 15 - With vacant possession. A block of eight enclosures of productive pasture and arable land, together with coppice, barn cattle lin-hay, and a yard known as 'Westerns.' containing an area of twenty-nine acres, three roods, thirty-one perches. Close to Copythorn Cross, on the main road from Plymouth, having a long road frontage from Copythorn Cross to Aylestone Cross.

LOT 16 - With vacant possession, a very valuable enclosure of productive land known 'Whympstone Cross Field,' containing an area of seven acres, one rood, and eleven perches. Supplied with water and having its frontage of approximately one-thousand feet on the Bigbury road.

LOT 17 - The dwelling-houses and cottage, being No's 19, 19a, and 20, Brownston Street, Modbury. With lawn, gardens, paddock, courtyard, and buildings, containing an estimated area of one acre, and one rood and abutting on Back Street.

LOT 18 - 2 Stone and asbestos-slated cottages and garden on Galpin Street, Modbury. Presently in the occupation of Messrs J. Hurrell and A. J Stevens.

LOT 19 - With vacant possession. An excellent garden on Galpin Street, and abutting on the road on the south, with an estimated area of twenty perches. Occupied by Mr. W. Treneer.

LOT 20 - Cottage and buildings in Poundwell Street with garden in Church Lane. Estimated to be about twelve perches. Presently in the occupation Mr P. H. Maunder.

For viewing, interested parties were asked to apply on Tuesdays and Thursdays, from ten a.m. to three p.m. As to the residences, cottages, and Madeira Vale; to the occupiers. For the farms and accommodation lands, apply to 'Hillside' No. 19. Brownston Street. Modbury.

It was later reported that every single Lot sold, the total amount raised from the sale was £36,115 – which in today's money would be around £1,200,000.

MODBURY WOMEN'S INSTITUTE.

The Hon. Mrs. Peek described the work of the W.V.S. in London at the Modbury Women's Institute February 1946 meeting. She said how the ladies carried out the work of packing, stringing, and checking the parcels for the prisoners of war. Tea was then served by Mrs. Moysey and Mrs. Mugridge. Arrangements were made for a visit on the 26th of the month to the Theatre Royal, Exeter, on the occasion of the Devon Women's Institute 25th birthday pageant in which the Modbury W.I. drama group were to take part.

MIRACULOUS ESCAPE.

Three occupants of a car driven by Mr. Harry Coyte of Butland Farm had a remarkable escape in September 1947, when their vehicle skidded on the Modbury Road and crashed through a fence before hurtling forty feet into a field. Mr. Coyte, his wife, and a friend who was in the vehicle with them were all allowed home after medical attention. The car was surprisingly only superficially damaged.

WAR MEMORIAL HALL.

In 1947 Modbury locals set themselves a task of six-thousand pounds for the provision of a parish hall, with all the amenities of a social centre. This was to be Modbury's War Memorial. For a town with a population of less than one-thousand people, this was a huge sum to raise, but the residents set themselves the task with great enthusiasm. They had already raised, by subscriptions and public efforts, over two-thousand pounds. That entitled them to a grant of one-thousand pounds from the National Council of Social Service.

YOUNG FARMERS LIKE TRACTORS.

It was stated at the South West Devon Group of Young Farmers' Club annual field day in October 1947, by Captain A. Rodd who president over the event, that the obvious reason for the decline in an interest in horse-ploughing among the younger generation was because of the tractor.

Although the tractor could cover the ground quickly, it could not provide the quality of finished workmanship that was associated with the horse. Another of the horse ploughmen spoke in sorrow at the present-day conversion to the tractor. He said, "Nearly all the horse ploughmen in ploughing competitions in this part of the country are in mid-life."

CRIPPS UPSETS THREE OLD MEN.

Sir. Stafford Cripps, the Chancellor of the Exchequer gave his first budget speech in April 1948 and it didn't go down well with three of Modbury's older residents. A reporter came to visit on Wednesday the 7th of April, early closing day and the day following the budget. Walking around the town looking for people to interview he called in at four inns where there was not a single customer. "The shock," said one of the landlords, "seems to have been too much for them." But then, from the cosy back room of the White Hart came a call; "Three more pints of Budget and show a leg there," called out Billy aged sixty-nine.

Three old Naval men, two of them pensioners, drank to the doom of the Government. For Billy Hill the Budget was "proper abominable." Charlie Wood another of the pensioners said, "We are greatly upset. We thought that beer and baccy would go down. This will cause strikes for more wages." Sam Williams aged sixty-five added, "The only people to benefit are teetotallers and non-smokers."

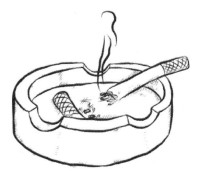

The three old men of the sea then took a pencil and paper and after frank admissions, decided that their combined daily consumption of drink totalled sixteen pints of beer and four tots of rum. "So, we reckon that's an extra fourteen shillings a week for our daily talk of old times. On top of that Charlie and I both smoke three ounces more than our pensioner's tobacco allowance," said Billy Hill. "That's nothing," said Sam Williams. "I smoke sixty Woodbines a day."

In the school hall, the Reverend Hugh Read was putting the final touches together for that evening's presentation by the Modbury Youth Club of the play 'The passing of the third floor back.' He said that the budget's remission of the tax on entertainment in towns of less than two thousand people was a God send and it meant that home entertainment could proceed without a crippling burden. "I can see the day when people won't have to make the twelve-mile trip to Plymouth for practically all their relaxation. Sir. Stafford is helping community life." Seats at the Modbury travelling cinema were also said to now be cheaper.

MODBURY HARRIERS LOSE HUNTSMAN.

At a meeting of the Modbury Harriers in June 1948, their huntsman Mr. L. Farleigh gave his resignation, having carried out the role for the past fourteen seasons. Mr. R. H. Rickman's offer to hunt in his place during the coming season was unanimously accepted.

A DILAPIDATED HOUSE.

Mr. J. G. Sloman, his wife, and two children, were living in a house in September 1948, that was in such a bad state of repair that it was said would probably collapse in bad weather, and that repairing it would be a waste of time and money. The case was brought before the Kingsbridge Rural Council meeting by the Modbury Parish Council, who, along with the recommendation of the Sanitary Inspector and the Medical Officer recommended that the family should be re-housed immediately - the Rural Council Housing Committee disagreed stating that they were bound to accept the views of the Parish Council. Thankfully the following month common sense prevailed and the family were offered and accepted the tenancy of another property in the town.

AN INTERESTING VISIT.

Members of the Plymouth and District Devonshire Association visited Modbury on Saturday the 23rd of October 1948 and were given a tour of St George's Church by the Reverend H. Read, who showed the party some valuable items including an Elizabethan chalice and a fine silver gilt 18th century flagon, said to have been a gift from a member of the Champernowne family. The earliest part of the church he told them dated back to the late 13th or early 14th century.

OLD TRAINE.   Photo: A. S. Roopell, A.M.I.E.E.
THE DWELLING—ON THE LEFT, THE EARLIEST REMAINING WORK; ON THE RIGHT, THE LATER HOUSE.

The party then visited 'Old Traine,' where they were welcomed by Mrs. H. Mitchell and Mrs. Gosling, who told them about a member of the Swete family who once lived there. Adrian Swete had kept a journal in which he recorded that in 1625 six soldiers were billeted on him at Traine, and for whom he received four' pence for every week day and six' pence on Sunday.

Adrian Swete was no Royalist, and had to pay thirty-shillings for refusing a knighthood at the Coronation of Charles I. In 1636 he was recorded as paying the constable of Modbury fifteen shillings and nine' pence towards providing a ship of war for the Kings service, and a similar sum to the constable of Ugborough for another ship of war. In 1642 he paid the constable of Modbury five pounds towards soldiers' pay, for defence against the Cavaliers of Cornwall. His beliefs and activities apparently led him into a lot of trouble, as he wrote in his journal in 1644 stating he was sent to the Marshalsea [court] at Dartmouth and fined ten pounds.

Postcard of St George's Church, courtesy of Samuel Harrison.

ALLEGED ATTACK BY THE TOWN CRIER.

In September 1949 Fred Wood of Galpin Street, the sixty-eight-year-old town crier of Modbury, was alleged to have knocked out the two front teeth of a local road sweeper on May the 21st of that year. Charged with assault and battery at Plympton Magistrates' Court, Fred Wood was fined two pounds. His cross-summons against the sweeper, Edwin Watts of Back Street, was dismissed. Watts, who was represented by Mr. W. E. J. Major, said the assault occurred while he was out 'brooming'. Having lost his two teeth in the assault, he raised his broom in self-defence but did not strike out.

"He ran against my fist," said Wood. "If I had intended to fight, I should have first disposed of my basket of groceries, taken off my glasses and taken out my false teeth."

Fred Wood had been town-crier since 1914 – a total of thirty-five years.

BANTAM SHOW.

 The British Bantam's Association annual show was held in King's Lynn, Norfolk in February 1950. Known to be the largest all-bantam show in the country, if not the world. In the sixty-nine classes there were over one-thousand-six hundred birds on show. The show was held with special authorisation from the Ministry of Agriculture and Fisheries. In the 'Modern Game' class Mr. Charles Watts of Modbury, was one of the prize winners. During the late 1940's and 1950's Charles Watts entered his bantams in numerous competitions across Devon winning a number of prizes.

NINE-DAY FAIR AT MODBURY.

The opening of the popular St. George's Fair at Modbury, one of the oldest in the Westcountry, was performed by the new Town Crier Mr. John Rogers on Wednesday the 3rd of May 1950. [*Possibly Fred Wood was asked to stand down after his scuffle with Mr. Watts the previous May?*] Villagers and visitors crowded the road at the Market Cross to see Mr. Rogers hoist the glove, garlanded with flowers, on to the old market bell in the centre of the main street. Here it was to remain for the nine days of the fair as a sign of goodwill.

BOUND FOR AUSTRALIA.

'Burlew of Glyncoombe' an eight-month-old Pembroke Welsh Corgi, bred by Mr. R. J. Ellis of Coombe Farm, bade farewell to Modbury on the 5th of December 1950 and started on the first leg of his long journey to Australia. He first travelled by car to Liverpool where he was kennelled aboard the S.S. Trewiddau ready for his passage to Australia where he was to join his new owner Mrs. Jessie M. Campbell of Castle Hill, New South Wales. Mrs. Campbell had recently been in Engand on holiday, and as an exhibitor and breeder herself, had been anxious to obtain a good Pembroke Corgi. Having heard of Mr. Ellis and his breeding acumen, she agreed to purchase the pup and have him brought over to her in Australia.

INNS AND ALE HOUSES IN MODBURY.

Before we leave our trip through time, let us take a look at what would have often been the main meeting places in the town – the local pub. You will have read numerous stories in this book of the landlords/landladies and events that took place within the public houses of Modbury. There have been numerous inns and licenced victuallers in the town over the years, though only a few have survived into the twenty-first century. The local hostelry was in centuries past an ordinary dwelling house where the householder served home-brewed ale and beer. If lodging for travellers was  offered, this might be no more than bedding on the floor, and shared accommodation was not unusual. You could find yourself sharing a bed with at least one other person. Inns were generally larger and purpose-built to accommodate travellers. They were more spacious and would have stabling.

Taverns often catered for the more affluent patrons as they sold wine which was more expensive than beer or ale. Inns, taverns and alehouses advertised their business with a pictorial sign hanging outside so that it could be identified in what was then a mostly illiterate age. Advertisements would usually describe an inn such as the Bell public house as 'at the sign of the Bell.' With the coaching era of the 17th century came larger premises such as the White Hart Hotel with its adjoining Assembly Rooms which held many a grand function.

Records of licensed premises in the town are as follows. Many would have simply been a front room in someone's house, others a larger premises with a number of separate rooms such as the bar, saloon, and sitting rooms. Others with accommodation, the supply of food and stabling for the travellers' horses. Landlords and landladies of the inn's would have been very familiar faces around the town, known for their welcoming hospitality and for entertaining guests.

The earliest mention of the Exeter Inn was in 1773 when George Brutton the landlord died aged fifty-three. In 1787 Mr. and Mrs. Winsor were the licensees of the inn. They were still in residence in 1897. In 1806 Mr. Brooking was landlord of the London Inn on Church Street. Here are some of the names of some of the inns, inn-keepers, and licensed victuallers that have served Modbury over the years. This list is of course not exhaustive and there were likely many other inn-keepers and publicans in Modbury over the years, I have just not come across them.

The 1822/23 Pigot's directory listed the following inn-keepers:

John King: The Bell, 3, Broad Street
Robert Lyndon: Dartmouth Inn, Church Street
Robert Webber: Exeter Inn, Church Street

John Boon: Maltman's Arms, Brownston Street
Richard Boon: Plymouth Arms, Poundwell Street
Nicholas Cove: Rose & Crown, Church Street
G. Lakeman: Union Inn, Poundwell Street

Kelly's directory of 1830 lists the following inn-keepers:
John King, The Bell, Broad Street.
Robert Lyndon, Dartmouth Inn, Broad Street.
Thomas Prout, Devonport Inn, Church Street.
Edward Stidworthy, Exeter Inn, Church Street.
Edward Mitchell, London Inn, Church Street.
John Boon, Maltman's Arms, Brownston Street.
John Boon, jun, Plymouth Inn, Poundwell Street.
Francis Steer, Union Inn, Poundwell Street.
Roger Tarring, White Hart, Church Street.

The 1840's give mention to the following inns:
1841 Maltman's Arms.
1841 Roger Tarring ran the White Hart Hotel.
1842 Harraton Inn, near Modbury
Exeter Inn.

The 1850's lists the following inn-keepers:
1850 Mr. Pitts, Exeter Inn (owner).
1851 Philip Brown, 4 Church Street.
1851 Grace Taylor, 3 Broad Street
1851 Henry Huxham 49 Galpin Street.
1851 John Lakeman, 1 Church Street.
1851 Robert and Mary Lyndon, 7 Broad Street (Dartmouth Inn.)
1851 Henry Nicholas 19 Church Street.
1851 John Aldrey, 48 Brownston Street.
1851 John and Elizabeth Boon, 1 Poundwell Street.
1851 Edward Stidworthy, Exeter Inn.
1852 Robert Lyndon, Dartmouth Inn.
1852 Samuel Elliott, Modbury Inn.
1858 James Davis bought the White Hart and let it out to Richard Carlisle.

The 1860's had the following inn-keepers in Modbury:
1860 Thomas Luckraft, Kingsbridge Road Inn (California Inn.)

214

1861 James Davis, White Hart Hotel.

1861 James Webber of 60, Brownston Street was a spirit dealer and maltster.

1861 James Boon, Union Inn, Poundwell Street.

1863 Mr. Matthews, Exeter Inn.

1866 Maltman's or Malster's Arms.

1868 Henry Meathrell Dartmouth Inn, Broad Street.

In the 1870's the following get a mention:

1870 Mr. Tiddy, Exeter Inn.

1871 Samuel Wyatt, Modbury Inn.

1871-1877 Henry Meathrell, Darmouth Inn, 9 Broad Street.

1871 Mr. Gard, White Hart Inn.

1871 Globe Inn.

On 1881 census the following licensed victuallers are listed:

Samuel Wyatt, Modbury Inn, 27 Brownston Street.

Elizabeth Davis Broad Street.

Frank Bourne, White Hart Hotel.

James Beard Broad, Street.

Georgina Matthews, Broad Street.

George Tiddy, Exeter Inn.

1886 Mr. Mortimore was running the Exeter Inn.

1887 Mr. G. Matthews was at the Exeter Inn.

1887 Mr. S. and Mrs. E. Chubb ran the White Hart Hotel.

James Davis, landlord of the White Hart died in 1880.

Records from 1890's name the following landlords:

1891, Harry Pearce, Church Street.

1891 Elizabeth Davis, Broad Street.

1891 Richard Jackson, California Inn.

1893 George Treeby, Bell Inn.

1897 Elias John Miller, California Inn.

1899 Elizabeth Chubb, White Hart.

Moving into the 20th century, we find the following:

1903 Licence transferred from Mrs. Emma Chubb to Mark Bunk, White Hart Hotel.

1905 Licence transferred from Alfred Hill to Thomas Fice, Modbury Inn.

1905 Licence transferred from George Mabey to Thomas Jones, Bell Inn.

1906 Charles Haskell, California Inn.

1908 Thomas Stephen Warren, Modbury Inn.

1909 Mr. Jones, Bell Inn.

1910 Joseph Tregaskis, White Hart Hotel.

1910 Herbert Steer, Modbury Inn.

The 1911 shows the following licensees:

1911 Harry Dennis, Great Western Hotel.

1911 Mr. John Martin, White Hart Hotel.

William Haskell, California Inn.

Emily Mortimore, Exeter Inn.

Eli Owens, Modbury Inn.

1922 Licence transferred from Mrs. Owen to Alfred Jago, Modbury Inn. Mr. Jago was in residence until 1925.

1923 Mrs. Ellen Owen, Exeter Inn.

1923 Albert Hocking, Great Western Hotel.

1930 Mr. Inall, Modbury inn.

1930 David Main, Exeter inn.

1932 Mr. Wade, Modbury Inn until 1939.

1935 Bruce Rowland, Modbury Inn.

1935 Bert Cawsey, Exeter Inn.

1939 Licence transferred from Cecil Wade to Louisa Willmott, Modbury Inn.

1941 Mrs. Willmott, Modbury Inn.

1945 Mr. H. Cawsey was landlord of the Exeter Inn.

In 1949 if you wanted to make a reservation at the Exeter Inn, you were to call the operator and ask for Modbury 239. [*I recall my own mother when phoning my granny in the early 1970's calling the operator and asking for Scots Gap 272*].

The Harradon Inn, said to be near Modbury (mentioned 1873) but which I have been unable to find an address for. The following licenced houses are also said to have been in Modbury, but of which I can find no record.

New Inn

Tanners Arms.

Rose and Crown, Church Street.

The Red Devon Hotel, Broad Street (most likely the former Great Western Hotel) was still operating up until the 1970's.

Printed in Great Britain
by Amazon

33624344R00123